P9-DMY-478

PRAISE FOR *EMBODIED LEADERSHIP*

'Through this book Pete Hamill offers leaders something we really need – a practical and progressive take on leadership that is highly relevant to how we work today and the daily issues we face. By introducing the ideas and techniques of Embodied Leadership he brings together modern thinking from neuroscience as well as ancient philosophies that have stood the test of time, and does so in a way that is accessible, provocative and importantly, motivating. Having read many a book on leadership, my experience is that this is a field awash with admittedly interesting theories and concepts, but the practical application when in the thick of it is often overlooked. However, this book is all about understanding and improving how we operate within the messy world of work, and offers practical solutions for thriving and being the best version of ourselves we can. It's a must read.' **Karen Callaghan, People Director, innocent drinks**

'A thought-provoking book that rattles through the physical and the metaphysical and provides a radical blueprint to reconnect us with our bodies, enablingus to become more effective in our everyday lives. If you've struggled with business school leadership models and the endless leadership "how to" books then this will provide a refreshing alternative.' **Professor Chris Bones, Professor of Creativity & Leadership Manchester Business School, Dean Emeritus of the Henley Business School & winner of the UK's Management Book of the Year 2012**

'A thought provoking, practical, accessible guide on how to use your body to develop authority, presence and impact as a leader.'
John Leary-Joyce, CEO of the Academy of Executive Coaching

'This book offers refreshingly practical ideas for everyone wanting to develop their leadership skills. It takes deliberate practice – we are what we practice, in the author's words, but building on the principles of embodied leadership it opens our eyes to how much choice we actually have when we don't let our past determine our behaviour, and hence our potential at work.'
Eeva Sipila, Chief Financial Officer, Cargotec Corporation

'What makes this leadership book unique, powerful and necessary is the voice of practical, deeply educated and compassionate wisdom that Pete Hamill brings to it. He cuts through the fluff and nonsense bandied about in pop culture and grounds what he says in real science, the practical know-how of experienced practitioners, and in the human body itself, which is, in every case, the sole instrument of leadership. Mr Hamill evokes real trust in the reader as he maintains his clear-sighted optimism and warm humanity, while never shirking from the real difficulties facing leaders today. He lays out a powerful methodology for developing leaders that it is compelling, realistic and inspiring. Full of intriguing references and examples, the book is a marvellous resource for anyone involved in leadership and its cultivation.' **James Flaherty, Founder, New Ventures West Integral Coaching**

'If it's true that practice makes perfect, we might as well understand more about which particular practice actually works and why. Pete Hamill's book guides the reader in this discovery, venturing into a field that constitutes a significant advancement in leadership studies, and in the process accomplishing a rare balance of engaging style and richness of references and argumentations. Heoffers a journey that is populated by the likes of Descartes, Ekman and Chomsky, through stimulating concepts such as the rational mind, somatic markers, embodiment and deliberate practice.' **Alessandro Paparelli, Regional Executive Director, Human Resources & Organization, Asia Pacific, Salvatore Ferragamo**

'I really enjoyed this book. Pete Hamill offers a very fresh and momentous perspective on leadership as an embodied practice, rather than an innate capability. His work is grounded on some great research and weaves in some of the latest thinking around leadership, neuroscience and somatics in a very practical and engaging way.' **Paulo Pisano, EVP and Global People Director, Pearson International**

'The challenges and demands on leaders and collective leadership are increasing at an exciting and yet frightening rate. Yet the world of leadership development is failing to evolve at the same rate. The gap is growing ever larger between what is required to support next generation leadership and what leadership development is currently providing. Pete Hamill's book provides clear guidance on some of the areas that need to radically change in the field of leadership development, supported by both the latest research in neuroscience, EQ and mindfulness, as well as stories and examples of new practice. These include: the move from cognitive learning to embodied learning; from over-focusing on the left-brain neo-cortex as the main vehicle for learning to using all four parts of the brain and the wider knowing that resides in the whole body; and from learning through reflection on the past, to learning from experimenting with future challenges right now in real-time.

My hope is that this book will stimulate every reader to go out and learn differently and to tryout some of the new practices of developing others that Pete provides.' **Peter Hawkins, Author and Professor of Leadership, Henley Business School, Emeritus Chairman at Bath Consultancy Group**

'This is a book of and about balance. East with West, philosophy with psychology, empiricism with practical reasoning. Pete Hamill explores a multitude of philosophical approaches to leadership that are grounded in well-being, and goes on to develop a practical supporting toolkit. This book will help you become a balanced, mindful, healthy and resilient Leader.' **Keith Wilson, Global HR Director, Change & Talent Management, AstraZeneca**

'A thoroughly insightful and fresh perspective on leadership which makes a compelling case for a different approach.' **Melanie Richards Partner, KPMG**

Embodied
Leadership

Embodied Leadership
The somatic approach to developing your leadership

Pete Hamill

KoganPage

LONDON PHILADELPHIA NEW DELHI

Publisher's note

Every possible effort has been made to ensure that the information contained in this book is accurate at the time of going to press, and the publishers and author cannot accept responsibility for any errors or omissions, however caused. No responsibility for loss or damage occasioned to any person acting, or refraining from action, as a result of the material in this publication can be accepted by the editor, the publisher or the author.

First published in Great Britain and the United States in 2013 by Kogan Page Limited

Apart from any fair dealing for the purposes of research or private study, or criticism or review, as permitted under the Copyright, Designs and Patents Act 1988, this publication may only be reproduced, stored or transmitted, in any form or by any means, with the prior permission in writing of the publishers, or in the case of reprographic reproduction in accordance with the terms and licences issued by the CLA. Enquiries concerning reproduction outside these terms should be sent to the publishers at the undermentioned addresses:

120 Pentonville Road	1518 Walnut Street, Suite 1100	4737/23 Ansari Road
London N1 9JN	Philadelphia PA 19102	Daryaganj
United Kingdom	USA	New Delhi 110002
www.koganpage.com		India

© Pete Hamill, 2013

The right of Pete Hamill to be identified as the author of this work has been asserted by him in accordance with the Copyright, Designs and Patents Act 1988.

ISBN   978 0 7494 6564 3
E-ISBN   978 0 7494 6565 0

British Library Cataloguing-in-Publication Data

A CIP record for this book is available from the British Library.

Library of Congress Cataloging-in-Publication Data

Hamill, Pete, Consultant.
  Embodied leadership : the somatic approach to developing your leadership / Pete Hamill.
     pages cm
  Includes bibliographical references and index.
  ISBN 978-0-7494-6564-3 – ISBN (invalid) 978-0-7494-6565-0 (ebk.)   1. Leadership.   I. Title.
  BF637.L4H334 2013
  158'.4–dc23

                                                                          2013000869

Typeset by Graphicraft Limited, Hong Kong
Printed and bound in India by Replika Press Pvt Ltd

*To Satu, for her infinite patience and unconditional love.
And to Richard Strozzi-Heckler for agreeing
to be my teacher all those years ago.*

CONTENTS

FOREWORD

Over 25 years ago when we, Strozzi Institute, began to deliver programmes in Embodied Leadership to organizations and in public forums, there was much cynicism and even outright scoffing at the idea of learning leadership skills and virtues through somatic practices. Our detractors paraded out the well-worn saw that it's the mind, after all, that runs the show, and their curriculum for leadership development was to read case studies and watch video tapes (no DVDs back then) of celebrated leaders, and then do what they did. What they left out was *how* to do it.

In the meantime we continued our work of creating leadership cultures through somatic practices in the business, military, government, and non-profit sectors. The initial uncertainty we encountered back then because of the uniqueness of our approach quickly evaporated as it became obvious that the results we produced were immediately actionable and sustainable. Not only were people gaining new distinctions about leadership, more importantly, they were *being* different leaders. In other words we began to build a clientele of satisfied customers. Individuals, teams, and organizations began to transform in ways that made them more successful, and more fulfilled.

Now it has slowly, but assuredly, become common sense that leadership isn't learned by accumulating more information, gaining new insights, or understanding new concepts. With recent surveys indicating that only about 7 per cent of employees trust their leaders, we can conclude there has been little pay off in the army of motivational speakers and the profusion of books that describe great leadership. If we consider that learning is the capacity to take actions that were previously unavailable to us, then this cognitive-only curriculum for leadership development has not moved us closer to a practical and wise path of how to get there. In short, we have bookshelves filled with sound advice, but no practices of how to *be* a leader, no path of how to *embody* the virtues of exemplary leadership.

In *Embodied Leadership: The Somatic Approach to Leadership Development*, Pete Hamill clearly outlines an innovative way of approaching leadership, and the practices leaders can engage in that produce mastery. In a rigorous but accessible way, Pete grounds his research in somatics, neuroscience, psychology, sociology, and his personal history of being a masterful coach and consultant. This is an elegant, forthright book that delineates how to develop leaders in a realistic, no-nonsense way.

The reach of this book, however, is much larger than leadership, coaches, and the training of leaders. Essentially, this is a book about how we can properly inhabit ourselves as we move forward into the 21st century. Pete Hamill claims that we are all leaders, and everything he offers has application to our transformation and evolution as a species. This is critically important as we move through a time of accelerated social, economic, and environmental upheaval. As we face our role in the destruction of the planet, a growing plague of senseless violence, and a radically unjust disenfranchisement, it is of utmost importance that we learn to act with greater care and wisdom. This book is not only for those who wish to take on the formal role of leadership, but for those who hear the call to action to be a contributor to a safer, healthier and more just world. *Embodied Leadership* meets the need of a world whose leaders, and citizens, embody the virtues of grounded compassion, skillful action, and pragmatic wisdom.

Embodied Leadership is the combination of Pete Hamill's study of leadership and management, his years of coaching and developing leaders, and his enduring commitment to his own growth and transformation. While Pete has a sharp, well-honed intellect, what you will find in these pages is the authentic voice of someone who has traveled the path about which he speaks. He is not an ivory tower academic commenting on the field of leadership, but someone who has been a player in this arena and learned its language, its moves, its struggles, and its possibilities. He has integrated the distinctions in this book into his professional and personal life; and he continues to learn from the inner and outer landscape that he's traveled. Pete has done the hard personal and professional work that makes this book both intimate, highly practical, and rigorous. His voice is available and handy, without losing its depth and thoroughness. I know these things about Pete because he's a Master Somatic Coach from Strozzi Institute where he's also a teacher and a member of our consulting team. Pete also lived as an *uchi-deshi*–a live-in student in the martial arts tradition – at Two Rock Dojo where he studied closely with me in somatics and Aikido. In other words, I know Pete well and can personally attest to his sincerity, authenticity, and passionate curiosity.

In order to make a more secure and healthier world for all we now need leaders and citizens who embody the virtues and ideas that they hold dear. Take this journey by engaging in the practices in this book and you will discover a new way of living your purpose.

Richard Strozzi-Heckler
Author of The Leadership Dojo *and* In Search of the Warrior Spirit
Strozzi Institute, Petaluma California

ACKNOWLEDGEMENTS

I would like to start off by thanking all those who have guided and supported me in my discovery of embodiment. Richard Strozzi-Heckler, who embodies the principles of this book, agreed to be my teacher over 10 years ago, and has been a constant source of inspiration, support and learning ever since. He integrated and developed much of this work, carrying a lineage from his teachers, and I have immense gratitude for the synthesis he developed and to him for his care and concern towards me.

In addition Mark Mooney has been a constant source of challenge and learning on my journey as I have begun to facilitate and teach embodied leadership, and has always worked to call the best out from me. I thank him for his support and friendship over many years. In addition I have been fortunate to spend time working with both Wendy Palmer and Paul Linden, two other masters in embodied practices.

I must also thank all of the participants in embodied leadership programmes with whom I have worked, and all of the people whom I have coached. Your willingness to explore these ideas, to test and play with them has provided rich learning for me in my development, and has stretched my thinking about this work. This book would have been impossible without your involvement.

My former colleagues at Future Considerations and Roffey Park Institute also deserve a vote of thanks. They supported me in my learning and development in this work, and in my efforts to bring this work to Europe. Paul Gibbons deserves a special mention for introducing me to this work initially, and Helena Clayton for her enthusiasm in bringing this work to Europe at Roffey Park Institute. In addition I need to thank Aboodi Shabi, of Newfield Network, and Clare Myatt for their tireless support of bringing this work to a wider audience and their support of me personally.

Martina O'Sullivan at Kogan Page is also due many acknowledgements. For knowing when and how to 'give me a kick' so that I moved from research into writing, for supporting this project from our very first conversation and for all your help and support along the way, I offer you my gratitude.

Until writing this book, I lived under the happy illusion that authorship was an individual and solitary accomplishment. I now know that to be completely false. I have been supported by family, friends, colleagues and clients, who have read and commented on sections, who have tolerated my periods of 'radio silence' whilst writing, and who have encouraged me through their care and concern. I wish to thank them all.

I must mention especially Martin Saville who read and commented on every chapter, as well as Richard Strozzi-Heckler and Josie Gregory for the time they spent reading and commenting on chapters. There have also been countless conversations with friends and colleagues along the way, in various parts of the world, that are too numerous to mention, but that have shaped and influenced every page of this book.

Finally, I'd like to thank my wife, Satu, for being the first person to read any chapter before it went to anyone else. She, more than anyone else, had to put up with sentences and paragraphs that didn't make sense, errors in grammar and spelling, and those moments when I just was so engrossed in these ideas that I lost the ability to think straight. I thank her for her encouragement, feedback and love throughout.

Introduction

Why another book on leadership?

I watched the recent 2012 Olympic and Paralympic games with a fair degree of awe at what human beings were able to achieve: elite athletes, at the top of their fields, pushing the boundaries of human performance and shattering record after record. They had pushed themselves extremely hard, trained and practised for many hours, days, weeks, months and years, some even for decades, and been rigorous in applying the latest research and knowledge to their training to ensure that they would be at the absolute peak of their abilities.

The progression is incredible to witness. Olympic records of 100 years ago are now high-school records, and this group of Olympians pushed the boundaries further and harder than ever before. What are the limits of human performance? Who knows, perhaps in another 100 years these Olympic records will also be high-school records!

The question I pondered whilst I watched was whether we have made the same progression in leadership, and were we as leaders pushing the boundaries in performance in the same way? I can't think of any reason why I should answer 'yes' to this question. Standing as we are at the end of a recession created in part by banks that didn't understand their own products or, it seems, the global system they were a part of, and with surveys suggesting that only about 7 per cent of employees trust their leaders, I can find no reason to believe we have made a similar progression.

I should say that there are great individual leaders out there, some of whom I have met, but that high standard is not replicated across organizations, and we do not seem to have a way of reliably producing this high standard through coaching, training and development. This has been despite countless pieces of research, PhDs, books, articles and courses on the subject.

In the world of sport we can see a stark contrast. Let's take, for example, the British Cycling Team. Dave Brailsford came in to manage the team in 2000, when the team had won four medals and only one gold medal at the Sydney Olympics. In 2008, in Beijing, the team won 14 medals of which eight were gold. The systematic and rigorous application of knowledge and research on training, and a huge amount of hard work, combined with funding from the UK's National Lottery fund ensured that a significant lift in performance was possible. Some may argue that this is different than organizational life due to the level of motivation of those athletes. However, despite this motivation they did not fulfill this potential before 2000, so the leadership had an input. Also, the leadership included both the star athletes and a range of support staff, which is perhaps more similar to organizational life.

The thing is that organizations spend significant amounts of money on leadership development programmes on an ongoing basis, and they don't get this kind of payoff. So what's the difference? Why aren't we seeing the same level of increase in performance in the field of leadership?

I believe that, on the surface, there are two reasons, and that underneath there is a deeper reason. On the surface, the reasons are that we are not applying the latest knowledge from science and research in a rigorous way, *and* when we attend such leadership development programmes we are not putting the effort, hard work and practice into our leadership development in the same way that the athletes did. At some level this is understandable, as athletes spend more time training than performing; however, this is also an excuse – in everything we do there is the opportunity to push harder and work to perform better, and this intention could be brought into our daily activities.

The deeper level, however, is where I believe the real problems lie. We need to ask ourselves why we aren't applying the latest research, and why we, as managers and leaders, are not pushing ourselves in everything we do.

In answering that question we see that our whole way of understanding what it is to be human and to be a leader is held back by some ideas that are very deeply held within our cultural thinking. These ideas are clearly flawed, yet that does not lessen the hold that they have over us; these ideas make things that don't work sensible and obvious, and other things that do work non-obvious and perhaps a little weird. So we spend time and money with people sitting in classrooms looking at intellectual models that they then 'know about', but that they are completely unable to implement when they return to the workplace and are placed into the heat of a difficult moment. And we call this leadership development.

Underlying this approach is our cultural tendency to worship the rational mind. This is the bit we need to educate with models, theories and frameworks so that we can be better leaders. And once we know that model, theory or framework, and feel we understand it, we move on and learn another one. The kind of leadership development I mentioned above makes sense when you view the rational mind as all-important. Yet is it really? And what is the mind exactly? These are not easy questions to answer, but the answer we choose to accept has profound implications for our view both of humanity and of leadership development.

In this book I put forward a different view. It is one that has its roots in understanding the flaws in the cultural veneration of the rational mind, and is supported by research from neuroscience. It also ties us into things we know but for which we don't have an easy language. We know there is more to being human than our rationality, but here we enter a murky world of emotions, moods and the felt experience of being alive – and how do we talk about this and make sense of it? The view put forward in this book is a non-obvious view, one that at some level we already know, and it leads us to a non-obvious way of developing leadership, and developing as a person.

My contention is that you, your team, your organization could achieve the kind of increase in performance in leadership that the British Cycling Team saw in cycling, over a similar time frame. Like the Olympic athletes you will have to work very hard, and push yourself to your limits; this change is possible, but it's not a 'quick fix'. This book is designed to give you what you need to make that happen.

The structure of this book

Part One of the book is designed to look at the underlying thinking we have around leadership and how we develop leaders.

What does leadership mean to you? How would you define it? In Chapter 1, I try to define this phenomenon we call leadership, which may seem easy until you try. I have structured the chapter around the ways in which I hear people in organizations talking about leadership (rather than any academic frameworks), and I look at what lies underneath each of these viewpoints and the challenges with each of them. I end with a view on what it is to be a leader that integrates these viewpoints and allows us to move beyond the challenges of each.

What has been your experience of leadership development? Has it worked – are you a significantly better leader as a result? Can you use what you have learnt when 'the heat is on'? In Chapter 2, I continue by looking at what it takes to develop this type of integrated leadership. Interestingly the research suggests that develop-ing leadership comes back to the same principles about how we get good at anything – musical instruments, sport etc – practice! It's not just practice, however; it's a particular type of practice called 'deliberate practice', which involves bringing our complete attention and presence to our practice. I outline the principles of deliberate practice in this chapter.

Who are you? What is it to be you? What is the 'self'? Is it all just our rational minds? In Chapter 3, I look at the roots of the ideas behind our culture that lead us to the idea of the supreme importance of the rational mind, and show how flawed these ideas are. In looking at this I go back to the foundation of these ideas in our culture and show how they were, and have always been, flawed but socially convenient ideas. I also review research from behavioural economics, psychology and neuroscience that shows that we, as human beings, don't really operate in this way; we just like to think that we do. I then build up a different view on what it is to be human, on which we can have a different idea of how to develop people to be leaders.

Next I explore how the brain works and what implications this has for leadership. In Chapter 4, I go on to look at research from the field of neuroscience. Through understanding the brain, the nervous system and its interactions with the body I build up a view of how we actually think, make decisions and take action in the world. This is not based on the myth of us as rational human beings, but actually rests on more solid foundations of how we experience and interact with the world.

At some level when you look around at your family and the people around you, you know that human beings are not rational – we have just created a cultural myth that when you take all of these same family members and split them into different workplaces with other people's family members, that everyone will be rational. And then we get upset when they aren't! In this chapter I build an understanding based on science of how we work, which shows that our bodies play a significant role in our thinking and reasoning, and that any view of human beings as rational minds will always be insufficient to understand us and our behaviour.

So, if we understand who we are and how we operate differently, how might we change our ideas about how we develop leadership? In Chapter 5, I complete Part One of this book, drawing together all of the themes to show how we embody our 'selves'. Building on a different understanding of human beings, I also start to explore how leadership development needs to change and be different – how it needs to include the body if it is to be successful in delivering high levels of performance.

In Part Two, I continue the story in a different way. Using the foundation of the ideas explored and developed in Part One, I use the story of two people to illustrate the principles of embodied leadership development. Through their stories, tied into the latest research and thinking on neuroscience and leadership, I show how we can go about developing a set of deliberate practices that will shape and develop us as leaders. In Chapter 6, I look specifically at the question of purpose and at developing greater choice as a leader. In Chapter 7, I continue by looking at our conditioned tendencies and how they relate to stress and conflict at work. In Chapter 8, I cover how we can give feedback and how to be mindful, rather than mindless, as a leader.

In Part Three, I step back and start to look at the wider issues facing leadership. There are many that I could choose, but for the purposes of this book, I have chosen to cover, in Chapter 9, ethical leadership, and in Chapter 10, how we can deal with the complex set of challenges facing leaders today. Chapter 9 encompasses our individual ethical principles, but also how we deal with the pressures and dilemmas of working in an organizational context, where often things no longer appear so black and white. From this I describe how we can go about ethical decision making in our organizations. Chapter 10 encompasses complexity, innovation and the responsibility of leaders to develop other leaders. Chapter 11 completes this book with some concluding thoughts and next steps for your development as a leader.

Throughout the book I develop a set of deliberate practices that you can take on to develop your leadership. You can do these on your own or with a colleague/partner, and collectively they will allow you to transform your leadership. In addition, I have included at the end of each chapter a list of books that may be interesting or of relevance to you in further exploring the ideas covered.

It is worth acknowledging at this stage that there are entire libraries exploring subjects I am covering in this book. The book moves through the fields of leadership development, psychology, neuroscience, philosophy of the mind, organizational development and complexity sciences, ethics and moral philosophy, innovation and creativity, conflict, stress, behavioural economics, and probably one or two others I have omitted to mention. I hope that individual experts and specialists in these fields will forgive my trespasses onto their territories and my inevitably (and necessarily) incomplete summaries of their fields. There is a massive explosion of information and knowledge within each of these fields, and an increase in specialism. With this increase in specialism, in my opinion, also comes an essential need to bring these fields of knowledge together and to synthesize our knowledge, and this is my intention with this book.

Mr Duffy

In James Joyce's *Dubliners*, Mr Duffy 'lived a short distance from his body'. It's a strange line, and yet we all have a sense of what that means, and whom we could identify in our lives who are like Mr Duffy. He is disconnected from himself, from his emotions and a wider sense of purpose or what he cares about. And yet this is exactly the image of the human being as rational mind that pervades our culture. It seems we venerate this in our culture, yet also we can see its limitations.

The question I would like you to consider is whether you would follow Mr Duffy as a leader. My guess is that you would be unlikely to choose to follow anyone with this disconnection.

At some level this cultural sense of disconnection is, in my opinion, at the root of many of the problems we face in the world. It is also at the root of our inability to develop leaders who genuinely inspire us and move us forward.

I hope you will join me not just on a journey of reading and understanding, but also on the journey of implementing a set of deliberate practices that enable us to live more fully in our bodies, rather than a short distance from them, and to experience that connection to emotions, purpose and our shared humanity. Through this lies the path of leadership and mastery.

PART ONE
Setting the foundations

In the first part of this book, I will show how our ideas on leadership needed to be updated if they are to be effective. Our ideas on leadership, however, sit on top of some flawed ideas on what it is to be human, and it is ultimately these that we must address if we are to understand leadership differently.

My aim with these five chapters is that you can walk away understanding why some non-obvious and, perhaps a little weird, approaches to leadership development may actually be the ones that will be most effective. From that in Part Two, we will explore in more detail how this can work in practice.

What do we mean by leadership anyway?

> *Leadership... remains the most studied and least understood topic in all the social sciences. Like beauty, or love, we know it when we see it but cannot easily define or produce it on demand.* WARREN BENNIS[1]

It feels important to begin by establishing some foundations about the concept of leadership itself, before going on to the main theme of this book, embodiment. While it would be ideal if we started with a common and agreed understanding of leadership, this may be too much to hope for, given Charles Handy's comment above. My aim therefore, is to at least begin by laying some groundwork so that you as the reader can start with an understanding of what I mean by leadership.

To begin with, it's important to understand that when talking about leaders and leadership, people are often referring to subtly different things.

- The leaders: Sometimes we are speaking of the leaders, themselves, and the characteristics or traits of those individuals.

- The position: Regularly I hear people referring to leaders, when in fact they are referring to the people who hold certain positions of power and authority in organizations or society.

- The actions and behaviours: Some people prefer to speak about leadership, rather than leaders, and here they will often refer to the actions or behaviours of individuals that constitute leadership (or not).

- The results: And finally, others when referring to leaders and leadership, will be focused on results – leadership is about results and leaders are those who achieve those results.

One of the problems I see is that when people are speaking about leaders or leadership they are often speaking from one of these different perspectives, but without realizing it. An argument or debate can easily follow just because two people are speaking about the subject with different assumptions about leadership.

Each of these ways of looking at leadership sheds light on some aspects of the subject, and equally leaves some problematic aspects in the shadows. I will consider each of these perspectives in turn, look at the implications of viewing leadership in that way, and then begin to develop a more integrated view of this topic.

Leadership: the leaders

There are many books written on leadership, and if you distil their essence much of what they write is no different from that in older texts, such as Plato's *Republic* in the West, or the *Bhagavad Gita* in the East. What these older books seek to do is describe an exemplary human being (the *Bhagavad Gita* is at times referred to as the 'manual for mankind'), and in today's world we look for many of these virtues under the label of leadership. In this way of looking at leadership, who we are defines our leadership.

In this viewpoint we are looking for exemplary human beings to lead us, and integrity and honesty become very important concepts. What sort of mood do leaders carry with them (moods are infectious in organizations[2])? What presence and gravitas do they have? Are they benevolent or malevolent as leaders? Are they able to deal with complex and ambiguous situations? All of these are core pieces that we look for in leaders.

It's also about the relationship the leader develops with their followers. What's it like to be led by you? When you are with someone, do you feel that they are really present with you, or are they trying to get something from you? Do they have an agenda? We know from many sources (from psychology to neuroscience) that human beings need connection and belonging. For much of human evolution we were potentially something else's dinner, and being excluded from the tribe was fatal. Whilst that is not necessarily true now, our entire evolutionary biology is wired for us to seek connection and belonging.

This is probably all fairly recognizable – we want leaders with integrity, who have the capacity to build relationships and bring people together. The virtues when described in this way bring back one of the oldest debates on leadership – are leaders born or made? Nature or nuture?[3] Are some people just born good at this stuff, whilst others aren't?

Nature versus nurture?

Over the past centuries, part of what has occurred has been an evolution and democratization of the concept of leadership. Many of the prior restrictions have been removed. Historically, leadership was the divine right of kings and emperors – and indeed in some parts of the world it still is. Over time there has been a movement from this to the 'great man' and 'trait' theories of leadership, which emphasized some traits that were born into a person and allowed that person to be a leader – and it was generally men (with a few notable exceptions) who were these leaders.

Today many of us live in a world where, at least theoretically, anyone can be a leader. Theoretically, anyone can become prime minister in the UK, and theoretically any US citizen can become president. China, although filled with legal complexity, inequality and Communist Party internal politics, is brimming with entrepreneurs leading small businesses and looking for opportunities. This is not to say that there is not inequality in our society – there is; women, for example, are less likely to achieve positions of leadership in many organizations – but leadership is now thought to be more available to more people.

Some people argue that there is a genetic component to leadership, and therefore some people will just be more natural leaders. A recent study on this showed that genes may account for 49 per cent of a person's qualities of transformational or inspirational leadership.[4] The study, based on surveys of hundreds of twins, showed that although a proportion may be affected by genetics, there was a vital importance in providing training to develop managers' abilities to practise transformational leadership. So even if genes do have a say, a large proportion (around 51 per cent) comes down to development, and even with 'good genes' for leadership, the study's authors conclude that development is required.

I am dubious that even 49 per cent of leadership can be put down to genetics. In coming to that statistic, the authors of the study admit some limitations.[5] The research makes the assumption that environmental factors, such as what children learn from their parents, are all basically reducible to genetics – in other words, their parents' influence over them doesn't matter as everything will be passed on through genes anyway. This undermines their conclusions, from my perspective, and means that a figure as high as 49 per cent needs to be read sceptically.

Therefore, I am very cautious about the idea that genes are responsible for even this amount of our leadership capacity. The challenge is that our genes do not completely define us, as they were once thought to do – all genetics can really say is that someone has a propensity for something, rather than being an accurate predictor.[6] There is also a (relatively) new scientific field of epigenetics, which looks at how our genes are switched on or not, depending on, amongst other things, environmental factors.[7] Therefore the idea that our genes have fixed us in some way and dictate our leadership capacity is highly dubious.[8]

I am personally very reluctant to reduce everything back to genes in some form of genetic determinism for leadership. The majority of the evidence from science, psychology and the wider social sciences points to a wider range of factors being involved. In fact, today, a genetic basis for any talent or skill (from sports and music to leadership) is highly questionable. In his best-selling book *Outliers*, Malcolm Gladwell made these ideas famous. He looks at how most Canadian ice hockey stars are born at the start of the year:

> in any elite group of hockey players – the very best of the best –
> 40 per cent of the players will have been born between January

and March, 30 per cent between April and June, 20 per cent between July and September, and 10 per cent between October and December.[9]

On investigating this, we discover that the cut-off date for age-specific ice hockey for children is in January. Therefore a boy who is 10 at the start of January could be playing with another who turns 10 in December of the same year. This creates a development gap that is significant at this age. So what happens next? The boys who play better, who will probably be the older ones who are more physically mature, get more attention, more coaching and support. Over time they are selected for more competitive games, and get more opportunities to practise and learn the skills of ice hockey. There is no astrological or genetic determinism at work, simply factors of age, attention and opportunities to practise.

A study cited by Gladwell in the *American Journal of Human Biology* showed how, when Belgium changed its cut-off date for soccer from August to January, this changed the birth-month composition of elite players, so that within a couple of years there were almost no elite players born in December.[10]

A recent study published in the UK by the Institute for Fiscal Studies, showed how birth month impacts on schooling in the UK. Children there start primary school in the September after they turn four. A similar gap develops between those who turn four in August and those who turned four in the previous September, who are in the same school year. This development gap has a negative impact upon later exam results, university admissions and self-confidence of the younger children compared with those who are almost a year older.[11]

Geoff Colvin, a Senior Editor at *Fortune* magazine, in his book *Talent is Overrated*, goes further in arguing against a genetic basis for talent:

> Some researchers now argue that specifically targeted innate abilities are simply fiction. That is, you are not a natural-born clarinet virtuoso or car salesman or bond trader or brain surgeon – because no one is. Not all researchers are prepared to accept that view, but the talent advocates have a surprisingly difficult time demonstrating that even those natural gifts they believe they can substantiate are particularly important in attaining great performance.[12]

So it seems that, although this is still an area of active scientific study, researchers are having a hard time proving innate talents or abilities in any field.

So why should leadership be any different? Yes, genes do have an influence on us and our lives, but environmental factors such as opportunities and luck, alongside a very large amount of practice, have a much more significant impact. Although leadership is theoretically available to anyone, not everyone ends up in leadership positions, but perhaps this has more to do with a lack of equality of opportunity and the choices that individuals make regarding how much they practise.

Interestingly, perhaps the reason why so many of us hold onto these ideas of leadership as some innate gift of genes or higher powers is that they allow us off the hook. If it all comes down to innate natural gifts, and I haven't discovered these innate gifts by this stage in my life, then I don't have to stand up and take leadership on the local/organizational/world issues that are important to me: 'That's what leaders are supposed to do, and I'm not a leader.'

So it seems that if we stop letting ourselves off the hook, we/you/I/ anyone can develop as a leader. This is both an exciting and perhaps a slightly scary thought, and brings up all sorts of questions, around what to take leadership on, and how to develop ourselves as leaders. I will address these questions as I go forward, but I am not quite yet finished with our exploration of leadership.

Implications of looking at leadership through the leader

Embedded in this way of looking at leadership is also a whole set of virtues, values and ethics, just as in our manual for mankind or Plato's writings. It's important to realize then, that when we describe leadership we rarely talk about 'leadership' per se; we often describe good leadership, with all the embedded aesthetic and ethical components attached.[13] If I ask you to describe leadership, it is challenging to define as an individual concept, and you would describe to me good leadership, or perhaps what it's not (that is, bad leadership). It's rare to hear someone speak about what leadership is in itself.

This is distinct from, for example, how to be an engineer, where the descriptions will have no real moral or ethical component; you can describe someone as an engineer without any reference to whether that means they are a good engineer or a bad engineer.

When I call someone a leader, there is often an implicit message that they are a good leader or a good person. If they are a bad leader, then I may rescind the label of 'leader', saying that they have stopped leading, or are merely managing. The label of 'leader' therefore flatters us, with not just the position of authority but also with the virtues, ethics and aesthetics of leadership. This can at times go to someone's head, or alternatively become a heavy burden of expectations. Also, and perhaps most importantly, when we give someone this label, we can too easily give over to them responsibility for solving problems and sorting things out. They are, after all, *the leader*, with all that this implies.

When we take expectations from actions that can be described as good (or ethical) and we put that onto individuals as an expectation of them as people, we are inevitably expecting perfection, and we will be disappointed. If you doubt that culturally we have this expectation, then just read the tabloid press whenever a leader does something 'wrong', to see how we react.[14]

The early texts mentioned above were intended for all as something to strive towards and cultivate over a lifetime, yet nowadays we have a tendency to look for our leaders to have all of the traits described in these texts, all of the time. We look for them in anyone in authority or power, and we live in a culture where we expect the leader to come in as the hero and save the day, and be perfect all the time.

Heroic models of leadership, where the great leader will appear and save us, run throughout our culture. Look at the movies and TV and you will see countless examples of such leadership. Not only that, but if we think about stories such as *The Matrix* or *Harry Potter*, we see that not only do we need heroes to lead, but that these heroes who save us are in fact told by someone else that they are the chosen one. What does this say about our own ability to be leaders – who are we to lead when no one has told us we are the chosen one?

The messages of the media pervade our thinking and are representative of it. They reinforce a mindset that leads to a culture of dependence on our leaders. This is extremely limiting to us in developing our own ability to lead, in the domain of our own lives or in the wider domains of organizations and communities. The people attracted to leadership therefore can, at times, be those who desire to be heroic leaders, and their leadership will be driven by their ego – many of us have had the experience of seeing a leader like this at one time or another.[15]

If we define leadership as a quality we see in others, and an expectation that we have of how our 'leaders' will act, then we will be perennially disappointed. Even describing someone as a leader can be unhelpful – it puts into the conversation, at a subconscious level, all of our desires and expectations of leadership.

We know today with children, that it's unhelpful to praise them for being intelligent; much more helpful is to praise the effort they expend.[16] The former is more likely to lead to less effort and fear of failure ('then I won't be intelligent anymore'), and is praise without achievement, whereas the latter rewards their hard work and is likely to make them more keen to work hard in future. To use the same comparison with leadership, to call someone a leader flatters their ego, and puts them into the cultural conversation around dependent leadership.

To conclude

It does seem to be possible to develop the traits and virtues of leadership, as with any other talent, over a period of time, so perhaps we can all be leaders. However looking at the individual leader in this way can lead us to a dependence on heroic leaders who are driven mainly by ego. So we do need to look at leadership in other ways too.

Leadership: the position

This has its roots in top-down hierarchical military models of leadership, and whilst in many organizations it is no longer politically correct to speak in such terms, many of the people I meet do implicitly see the world in this way. It's easy when you're senior to speak of 'flat hierarchies' and the like, but often our sense of leadership and seniority comes from the position in that hierarchy, and people at the bottom of the hierarchy rarely describe it as flat in my experience.

This often leads us to equate leadership with position and the people who occupy that position. We start to refer to 'the leaders of, or leadership in this organization'. This belies the fact that anyone at any level can exercise leadership, although often at lower levels this leadership can be directed against the organization, as with union leadership. This is a form of leadership, but one designed to protect those at the bottom of the hierarchy, and can be very antagonistic.[17]

Leadership at all levels in organizations?

This has caused many organizations and leadership writers to think about how such antagonistic leadership could be put to use in service of the organization. Joseph Raelin is a writer who coined the term 'leaderful organizations', the idea being that the organization has leaders at every level.[18]

A leadership programme that I worked to develop with a UK National Health Service Trust had these ideas at its core. The chief executive of this Trust was clear about wanting people to step up to leadership at all levels, and part of the programme involved participants tackling real issues. The participants were told to list the issues where they regularly found themselves saying, 'Someone [or "they"] should do something about that,' and then choose one as a project. A senior executive team member took on a project to develop a knowledge management strategy for the Trust, something she felt was crucial for the organization going forward, whilst a district nurse took on stock rotation at their local surgery.

The team of district nurses worked in the community, but had a central surgery where they co-ordinated their activities. The store of medical supplies in that surgery was managed jointly, which often meant that it was unmanaged – messy and with little stock rotation going on, resulting in medications going out of date. The district nurse, in taking on this project, had to overcome his peers' perceptions of him taking leadership ('Who does he think he is?!'), and his own perceptions ('Who am I to do that?'), and get others to buy in to his ideas and work with a new system. Together with the other district nurses, on the project he led, they managed to save that Trust a significant amount of money every year on out-of-date medicines.

Was this leadership, and if so why? I'd say it was. He stuck his head above the organizational parapet and took responsibility for something that wasn't in his job description – something that everyone at his level knew about, complained about, and blamed senior management for not sorting. Stepping up in this way, he made himself a target, which is often the case where leadership is concerned (we'll come back to that theme later).

The problem with seeing leadership as a position in the hierarchy is that it ignores this leadership that is available throughout the organization. It also reduces leadership to something that is about power, salary and perks (and the ego boosts we get from promotion), rather than a wider concern or commitment to achieving something. Leadership can become an end rather than a means.

End or means?

When I speak to executives and leaders in organizations, part of the problem they face is a problem of purpose. Why are they doing what they are doing? Some do not know and often, in an attempt to resolve and answer these questions, they will resort to the safe haven of family – mortgage, school (or university) fees and quality of life.

This is a de facto admission that they have no real sense of purpose in their work. Often they have pursued senior positions in their organizations because of the status, power and salaries that come along with them – the leadership positions themselves have become the end, the goal or the purpose.

I maintain, from my perspective, that someone is not a leader on the basis of their position in the world, but rather on the basis of what they do, build, create or change in the world. It is this desire to create a different future that is the starting point of leadership. Then the next question we need to ask is: what position do I need to get into, to create this new future? Who do I need to lead to create this future?

Sometimes that will involve becoming senior executive director or equivalent in the organization, sometimes it will involve community or political leadership, and sometimes it can be achieved from all sorts of other positions within organizations, or by campaigning for change on the outside. The great leaders I meet, in small or large organizations, all have a clear sense of purpose: what they are in the job to do or achieve.

A true sense of purpose or calling is relatively rare amongst senior executives; indeed it is more often associated with medicine, teaching, not-for-profit or charitable work, or other caring professions. Yet if such a sense of purpose is not there, why do we do what we do? There are a range of reasons, from falling into careers, expectations of parents to 'get a career', wanting to be well off, enjoying the sense of competition to get to the top, and so on.

There is a substantial challenge with the competitive urge, which is common among men, and therefore most of the people currently occupying positions of leadership in our society, which is that when you have reached the top your sense of purpose disappears. When getting to the top is the purpose, there is often an 18-month honeymoon/proving yourself period, after which the leaders can start to feel directionless. There can be a mild sense of depression or listlessness that comes with achieving the goal and not knowing what to do. Sometimes the answer is to find a new top job to compete for – a bigger organization, a chairmanship rather than CEO or executive director position, or bigger bonuses. This is just a game for our ego, which is never satisfied, of competing for who has the biggest job/status/_____ (or perhaps you should just fill in the blank!).

When commentators look around and speak of a lack of leadership, or of a need for more leadership in our organizations or society, they are looking at the people in leadership positions and making a judgement. They are suggesting that those who are in these positions aren't fully stepping up to leadership. This is not to say that they don't work hard, or that they don't care about what happens to their organization – having met some of them I know that they do care and they do work very, very hard. However it's rare that they are living their leadership through a clear, compelling purpose.

Interestingly, this may be less of an issue in Asia, than in the West. Tsun-Yan Hsieh an observer of Asian leadership, writes:

I have been impressed by two things Western companies can learn from Asian companies. One is the level of aspiration. Asian CEOs have lofty aspirations and dream big dreams. I wish some Western CEOs would get a piece of that magic...

In many cases the personal visions of the Asian CEOs are less self-centred and more selfless than those of their Western counterparts. The Asian CEO has a very attractive vision because it is for a noble, higher purpose – for society, for the country, for the collective.[19]

It seems from this that perhaps this particular style of positional leadership is more of a 'Western' phenomenon, and I hope that, unlike many other 'Western' ideas, this one doesn't spread!

It does, however, bring up a question about whether these 'leaders' at the top of the hierarchy are actually leading. If they are not clear on a purpose and direction, they are not leading people to a clear destination, and one could argue that they are merely managing. This is something that is often suggested by those below them in many organizations.

Do the people at the top actually lead?

Some participants in workshops I have run say that there are no leaders in their organizations, only managers. In doing so they are taking away the term leader from the people at the top of the organization, and instead making leadership a concept that is much more based around the actions of those individuals – actions they perceive are sorely lacking.

This brings up a subtle but important issue in speaking about leadership. If we look at the paragraph above, we can see that leadership is also about our actions and behaviours – someone can do something that is leadership, and also something that is not. This brings us to the next way in which we can look at leadership: actions and behaviours.

Leadership: actions and behaviours

An alternative is to look at the actions someone takes, and then to label those actions as leadership or not. This approach has its roots in behavioural psychology, or behaviourism. Here leadership is about the behaviours or actions of a leader, and therefore if we copy those actions we become leaders ourselves. It leaves out the virtues and who the leader is, and it doesn't focus on the position someone has in the hierarchy. It purely looks at the actions they take, and any leader can take actions that are either good or bad.

This seems intuitively to have solved some of the issues we have previously faced in addressing leadership. It doesn't flatter someone's ego with the title of leadership, and it is unconstrained by the traditional hierarchies. But unfortunately this way of looking at leadership, also has its shortcomings.

John B Watson, one of the founders of behavioural psychology, stated:

The behaviourist recognizes no dividing line between man and brute.[20]

This is why much of the key experimental work in behaviourist psychology is done on animals. If we reduce everything to behaviours, and thereby deny that the mind is anything else but our behaviours, then working with animals makes sense. So to understand human behaviour, experiments have been conducted by the famous American behavioural psychologist BF Skinner (and others), on rats and pigeons, and the Russian Ivan Pavlov, with his famous dogs.

Rather than being determined by our genes, as in the arguments for innate genetic leadership talent, in this view we are defined purely by our behavioural responses, and these responses can be trained into us in the same ways used for dogs, rats and pigeons. Brought to its logical conclusion this denies in humans our self-awareness and free choice – we respond purely on the basis of our conditioning.

You might think that surely behaviourism has moved on from these principles, but in most respects it hasn't. Many experiments on animals are still used, and behaviourism still aligns with these basic principles. In addition its focus on positively and negatively reinforcing responses to behaviour is found in many organizations today, as people try and motivate teams, increase productivity or embed organizational change (think carrots and sticks as a way of changing behaviour in organizations).

In this view, leadership just comes down to actions and behaviours that someone takes (or not), and if we take these actions we will be leaders. Perhaps, then, we can copy someone whom we believe is a great leader and then we will be leaders too. However, at some level we all know that this isn't good enough. We've all met people who do and say the 'right' things, but somehow we just don't trust their intentions. Intention is a product of the mind, which is not always clear in behaviour – as when people are attempting to manipulate us, involve us in their political games or con us.

This is where behaviourism as a model for leadership runs into trouble. We all know that there is a person behind the actions and behaviours, and that person can inspire great trust or distrust. As human beings we are constantly assessing each other in this domain, and it is a powerful factor. Some people can do, or say, all the right things, but if I don't trust their intentions, they won't lead me anywhere!

People who say, 'Just give me the skills and knowledge...' or perhaps talk about having more 'tools in their tool box' are clearly influenced by behaviourism. Their desire for tools or skills shows a clear bias towards behaviours, rather than addressing the person who uses the tools.

So where does that leave us? To assume it is about the person seems fraught with difficulty; the position doesn't seem to be it either; and it doesn't seem to be about the actions or behaviours. So what is leadership about then? This is often the point where people say, well it must be about the results – people who get good results get promoted into positions of leadership, so can leadership be viewed through this lens?

Leadership: the results

This would also intuitively seem to make a lot of sense. People should be promoted into positions on the basis of their results, and therefore the way we should define leadership is through the results people achieve. This focuses leaders on achieving things, rather than just on attaining positions. It incorporates behaviours and the person doing them in the outcome of those behaviours – the outcomes will only be achieved if people follow the leader; therefore it must encompass both the behaviours and the person using those behaviour and their ability to build trust.

This unfortunately also runs into a few problems. Firstly, some research shows a correlation between CEO prominence (as measured by press cuttings etc) and salary, but not between organizational performance and salary. So do we actually value results in leadership (allowing for the fact that this refers to the position of leadership)? Keith Grint, a professor of leadership at Warwick University in the UK, suggests that the success of any leader is judged on their capacity to be persuasive in a way that legitimizes their actions, rather than on any measure of their results.[21]

A second challenge to this way of looking at leadership is that it implies that those who get promoted are the ones who get the best results. Yet this is one of the most common complaints I hear from people about their organizations – the people who get promoted often do so by political means rather than through their achievements. This is in fact backed up by research; in 1988 a paper published in the *Academy of Management Executive* journal contrasted successful and effective managers – successful being the ones who get promoted and effective being the ones who have high-performing business units. It stated that surprisingly these two groups had little in common – in other words, they were distinct.[22]

Thirdly, how do we measure the impact of someone's leadership? Say, I am the new CEO of Microsoft and I institute a new strategy. The company's performance rises and we all pat each other on the backs for the success of this change. If however the company's performance declines, it's likely that in explaining this I will refer to the external market conditions and other factors outside of my control (court judgements, a competitor's new products etc). The reality is that the causality of any new strategy on organizational results is extremely difficult to prove. There are too many other factors that impact everything.

The only way we could actually know the impact of the strategy would be to have two parallel universes where nothing else was different but the strategy and note the difference in results over time. As, with current scientific knowledge, this is impossible, we really have no way of accurately accessing the impact of leadership on results.

Therefore, whilst it is tempting to view leadership through the lens of results, it proves very difficult to do this accurately in reality. That doesn't mean that we shouldn't expect results from our leaders; it is just that measuring this becomes much more complex.

So if all of these four ways of looking at leadership are flawed, how can we understand leadership?

Leadership: an integration

The answer, I believe, lies in an integration of the ways of looking at leadership described above, rather than a choice between them. It is all of these things; it is about the people who lead, and their behaviours; it's about the position that they lead from, which is appropriate to achieve what they are committed to achieve; and it is about leaders achieving those results.

So how do we bring together the internal aspects of leadership – the person, their intentions, virtues, traits etc – and the external aspects: the actions and behaviours? (This divide mirrors a deeper divide in 'Western' culture, which I will address further in subsequent chapters.) How do we bring together the means – positions of leadership – and the ends – the results achieved by the leader? And how do you develop leaders in such an integrated way?

Internal and external

The reality is that both the internal and external aspects of leadership are interconnected and intertwined, and they impact upon each other. What we do is a reflection of who we are, and who we are is the combined total of what we repeatedly do. To see them as separate and distinct is to miss the point – they are both reflections of the same underlying process. Who we are is not a fixed entity; it is an evolving process of becoming, and what we do shapes and drives that process.

This is a very important point, which I will return to later. In the West, with all our personality models, tests and instruments, we are often encouraged to think of the personality as a fixed immutable thing. However the emerging field of neuroscience has discovered that adult brains are plastic – ie changeable.[23] How this change happens we will explore in future chapters, but the message is clear: we can evolve and change; we can see ourselves as in a process of becoming who we are, rather than a fixed personality that we have become. We are more than our genes and conditioning.

However, I am aware that I could become very philosophical here, so let's take this back down to earth with a concrete example. Have you ever been in the situation where you know you should do something (eg say 'no' to some of the requests people make of you), you want to do it, you need to do it, you know how to do it (if I asked you to say 'no' without any pressure you could do it), but somehow you end up not quite able to say 'no', and you end up with another piece of work on your to-do list. So there is an action you need and want to take, know how to take in the abstract, and yet are unable to take when it matters.

Someone's action or lack of action will produce the assessment (opinion) we have about that person and their leadership. Someone who is solid and holds their boundaries will produce a different assessment than someone who gets steamrollered at the meeting and takes on the tasks no one else wants. It's not enough to say that a leadership action is to hold your boundaries and say 'no'. We must also be the person who has the capacity to take that action, and so it is with all acts of leadership.

So we can say that the actions we repeatedly take will be seen as our virtues. However, we can go further than this, and say that what we repeatedly do will become who we are, and this is where the external and internal dimensions of leadership come together. When you do something altruistic, you will feel good about yourself, and this will shape your mood and your interactions with others. As you consciously repeat this action, you will begin change as a person. As Aristotle said:

These virtues are formed in man by his doing the actions.[24]

Through repeated actions we can cultivate the virtues of leadership in ourselves. Self-cultivation is a notion that is more familiar in Eastern philosophies. In Confucianism (a Chinese philosophy from around 500 BC), leaders were expected to cultivate themselves in major virtues and to be benevolent.[25] The Japanese have the word *shugyo*. The *kanji* (the logographic Chinese characters that are used in the modern Japanese writing system) for this is made of two characters: one 'to master' and the other a 'practice'. Literally it means to master a practice; however, it is understood in everyday language as self-cultivation.[26]

This description of the concept through the characters is important. Through practising benevolence, for example, as a set of behaviours, we can begin to master that ability and develop the virtue of benevolence.

This idea is also backed up by modern-day neuroscience. Evidence shows that London cab drivers (who have to memorize the streets of London before getting their licence) have larger hippocampi (a brain region associated with memory) than the rest of us. A group of volunteers who undertook a three-ball juggling routine for three months, without any prior knowledge of juggling, had a considerable increase in the amount of grey matter found in the temporal lobes of both brain hemispheres.[27] Practising something changes our brains, and therefore changes us.

So can we act ourselves into a new way of being? Yes we can do this, and no, it's not quite that simple. In the process of taking on these new actions, we will find some that are difficult for us. We will find our lifetime of experiences and programming, the traumatic experiences and the actions that have been rewarded, will all arise in us. In developing new capabilities we must develop our self-awareness and our insight, and we must heal past traumas.

The means and the end

A commitment to achieve certain results in our organization or world – the ends – is what drives us to take these actions and to develop ourselves into who we need to be. It gives direction to our efforts in our own development and to our actions in the world. Such a commitment needs to be deeply felt, which means it emerges from inside us – from inside what we care about and what is important to us. Then we can reflect on what external position we may need to achieve in the organization or society in order to achieve that commitment.

This involves a new way of looking at results. Since we cannot predict the future, and cannot compare the impact of one strategy to another, all we can do is focus on what we are committed to achieving, and finding positions that will enable us to lead others to achieve those results.

To conclude

To understand leadership, and to become a better leader, it seems we need to change how we look at who we are as people, and how we learn and develop. In this way of looking at ourselves, who we are as a leader is developed through practice – taking the actions of leadership makes me a better leader. But as we'll discover in the next chapter, it's not just any practice that will do this; it's actually a specific type of practice that makes very specific demands of us. Having a clear sense of purpose in our leadership, being really clear on the end results we are working to create, gives us the motivation to meet those demands and develop ourselves as required.

In this chapter I have explored the concept of leadership. In the following chapter I seek to build on that understanding to explore how to develop our leadership capability. Now we know what it is (and isn't), how do we get better at it?

Recommended reading

Talent is Overrated: What really separates world-class performers from everybody else, by Geoff Colvin.

The Cult of the Leader: A manifesto for more authentic business, by Christopher Bones.

Outliers: The story of success, by Malcolm Gladwell.

The Leaderful Fieldbook: Strategies and activities for developing leadership in everyone, by Joseph Raelin.

The Leadership Dojo: Build your foundation as an exemplary leader, by Richard Strozzi-Heckler.

A Very Short, Fairly Interesting and Reasonably Cheap Book About Studying Leadership, by Brad Jackson and Ken Parry.

Seeing Systems: Unlocking the mysteries of organisational life, by Barry Oshry.

Notes

1 Bennis, W and Nanus, B (1985), *Leaders: The strategies for taking charge*, Harper & Row, New York.

2 We probably all know people, who when they come into a room affect the mood. Some people lift it because of the mood they bring with them, whilst others bring it down. Resignation and cynicism are two moods in organizations that are very destructive and infectious. How much time do people in your organization spend gossiping negatively about the organization? One of the aspects of leaders here is the capacity to be aware of the mood they carry with them and to generate moods that are more likely to lead to possibilities and success.

3 Nature or nurture was a phrase first coined by Francis Galton in the 19th century. At first Galton believed that all children were born with equal abilities. After reading his cousin Charles Darwin's writings on evolution he reversed his view and began to promote a more evolutionary take on talents and abilities – see his book *Hereditary Genius*. His influence can still be felt today.

4 Chaturvedi, S, Arvey, RD, Zhang, Z and Christoforou, PT (2011) 'Genetic underpinnings of transformational leadership: the mediating role of dispositional hope', *Journal of Leadership & Organizational Studies*, first published on 28 April 2011, doi:10.1177/1548051811404891.

5 They base their study on the genetics of 'hope' (based on other research on the heritability of hope), which they state correlates well with transformational leadership. However, they also admit that hope is something that can be learned and transferred from one person to another. This implies that environmental factors may have a significant bearing and the research does not seek to take into account these factors.

6 Not everyone who has a genetic propensity for certain diseases will develop them; often they will not even know they have such a propensity.

7 *The Biology of Belief* by Bruce Lipton goes into further details of how our genes do not define us. If you would like to know more, that is a good starting point.

8 A recent article in the *New Scientist* magazine (29 Sept 2011, pp 10–11, by Ferris Jabr) shows how environmental factors can influence the expression of our genes. The article describes how the DNA (to be exact tiny strands of RNA, called micro-RNA) in food can survive the digestion process, go into our blood stream and end

up in our cells. Here these pieces of RNA can alter the expression of our DNA, turning on or off genes. This gives us more of an understanding of why some foods will be good or bad for us, but more fundamentally it shows the degree to which the environmental factors, such as food, can change the expression of our genes, and shows that we are not defined by our genes.

9 *Outliers: The story of success*, by Malcolm Gladwell – see page 23 for this quote. The book is definitely worth reading.

10 Helsen, WF, Starkes, JL and van Winckel, J (2000) *American Journal of Human Biology*, **12** (6), pp 729–35.

11 Crawford, C, Dearden, L and Greaves, E (2011) 'Does when you are born matter? The impact of month of birth on children's cognitive and non-cognitive skills in England'. *Institute for Fiscal Studies*, November.

12 *Talent is Overrated: What really separates world-class performers from everybody else*, by Geoff Colvin. This quote originates from page 6.

13 See *Ethics: The Heart of Leadership* edited by Joanne Ciulla for more on this subject. I am indebted to an MSc student at Roffey Park Institute whom I worked with, Karen Callaghan, for drawing my attention to this work.

14 Tabloid newspapers represent the shadow side of a culture and are a useful point of reference. Few in the reserved British culture would go through someone's rubbish, take photos with a long lens etc. However we will quite happily sit on a train and openly read about it. The reactions such as those to leaders on the wrong side of ethical issues represent a reaction from the shadow side of leadership – dependence. When we give over responsibility to leaders we have a need for them to be perfect, and when they are not we react accordingly.

15 See *The Cult of the Leader*, by Christopher Bones, as an excellent discussion of this issue.

16 Professor Carol Dweck at Stanford University has researched extensively in this area. Her book *Mindset: The new psychology of success* gives a fuller description of her findings and their implications.

17 The work of Barry Oshry is very powerful in understanding the way hierarchy effects leadership and relationships across organizations. See his book *Seeing Systems* for an introduction to this work.

18 *The Leaderful Fieldbook: Strategies and activities for developing leadership in everyone*, by Joseph Raelin, gives a good introduction to this work.

19 Hsieh T-Y (2006) 'Bridging the divide: a conversation with Tsun-Yan Hsieh', *Leadership in Action*, 26 (5), pp 10–11.

20 Watson, JB (1913) 'Psychology as the behaviourist views it', *Psychological Review*, 20 (2), pp 158–77.

21 Grint, K (2005) 'Problems, problems, problems: the social construction of "leadership"', *Human Relations*, 58 (11), pp 1467–94.

22 Luthans, F (1988) 'Successful vs. effective real managers', *The Academy of Management Executive*, 2 (2), pp 127–32.

23 The term given to this property of the brain is 'neuroplasticity'. Plastic is used as a metaphor for that which is somewhat changeable and malleable, and yet also somewhat fixed.

24 *Nicomachean Ethics*, Book II, 4; Book I, 7. Often Aristotle is misquoted as stating, 'We are what we repeatedly do. Excellence, then, is not an act, but a habit.' That statement actually comes from Will Durant, *The Story of Philosophy: The lives and opinions of the world's greatest philosophers* (1926; Simon & Schuster/Pocket Books, 1991) Chapter 2: 'Aristotle and Greek science; part VII: ethics and the nature of happiness': 'Excellence is an art won by training and habituation: we do not act rightly because we have virtue or excellence, but we rather have these because we have acted rightly; "these virtues are formed in man by his doing the actions"; we are what we repeatedly do. Excellence, then, is not an act but a habit: "the good of man is a working of the soul in the way of excellence in a complete life... for as it is not one swallow or one fine day that makes a spring, so it is not one day or a short time that makes a man blessed and happy"' (p 76). The quoted phrases within the quotation are from the *Nicomachean Ethics*. The misattribution is from taking Durant's summation of Aristotle's ideas as being the words of Aristotle himself.

25 *Leadership and Management in China*, edited by Chao-Chuan Chen and Yueh-Ting Lee, gives an excellent summary of how Confucian ideas relate to leadership.

26 *The Leadership Dojo*, by Richard Strozzi-Heckler, has its second chapter on 'The cultivation of the self' that addresses this subject and it is from here that I have taken the meaning of the Japanese characters.

27 *The New Executive Brain*, by Elkhonon Goldberg (pp 237–39), gives more information on these studies and wider issues of neuroscience.

How do I get better at it?

Traditionally in organizations we attend training programmes to get better at leadership. Some organizations have a complete curriculum of such programmes, which are tailored to and address different levels in the organization. Some people may also have mentors, and typically as we get more senior in organizations we stop attending such programmes and we may be able to get access to coaches. (There are obviously lots of exceptions to this, but this is a broad path that I see across a range of organizations.)

These efforts tend to focus on three mains aspects:

- theories and models through which we make sense of business and organizational life, and potentially applying these to case studies;
- developing skills and behaviours;
- self-awareness (through feedback, personality questionnaires or psychometric instruments, reflection etc).

Different courses will focus on different aspects to differing degrees. A strategic leadership course may pay more attention to models of strategic planning and case studies, whereas a first-line manager course may pay more attention to skills and behaviours. Programmes of a more reflective nature will pay more attention to self-awareness. All of this is good stuff that can form a useful part of a curriculum of development. Unfortunately when it comes to producing high performance in leadership, more is required.

Understanding what more we need to do involves understanding how anyone can develop mastery in any domain of work or life, and applying that to leadership. It involves building on the understanding of leadership that we have developed previously, and it involves paying attention to our evolving understanding of neuroscience. Having watched the 2012 Olympics recently, it is very clear that performance keeps improving across all of the sports represented, through the rigorous application of accumulated research and knowledge to training and development. This same process needs to happen for leadership and this, I believe, offers an exciting opportunity to get better at leadership more effectively than ever before.

Self-cultivation

In the course of my work I have met many people who have done much personal development work and have great self-awareness. When they enact a historical pattern, such as being overly deferential to those in authority, they can observe themselves doing it, can take responsibility for it, and they understand where the pattern comes from, for example relationships with authority figures in childhood. This is all admirable, and is the sign of having done significant development work.

But, what they often don't do is change the pattern – they still play it out time and again, without actually changing. Sometimes they have become addicted to the next great 'aha' moment of awareness and are searching for that. Sometimes they have just not been helped to actually change their behaviour and don't know how to do it. Sometimes they think that it's OK, and that if they can be aware of it they don't need to change it. Often I hear it used as an excuse: 'It's just the way I am...'

To have done so much deep and sometimes painful self-development and not to have gone to the place of changing behaviour is a pity. Their behaviour is still being controlled by their history, and while they can understand it through a range of different models, see it and apologize for it, they are still ruled by it. This is what can happen when we just build self-awareness. When developing leaders, however, it is vital that we move beyond simply being aware, to creating real and sustainable change.

On the other hand, sometimes leadership focuses solely on behaviours. Here someone works on developing skills but is often unable to apply those skills in difficult situations, because here they are triggered by some aspect of their past of which they are not fully aware. They have built some level of skill and have models that inform them about when to use that skill, but are unable to use it in the moments that count.

I can know how to say 'no' but not embody the capacity to do so under pressure, and I can know my demons and have done my personal work yet continue playing out the same behaviours that don't help my leadership. A focus on either self-awareness or behaviours on its own has limitations.

If you want to truly be a leader who can make a difference in the world or your organization, then self-awareness becomes a starting point. From here you need to build your leadership capability through practices for self-cultivation. It is therefore important to ask ourselves: who do I need to be, to be able to deliver on what I care about as a leader? If my leadership is directed to community issues, who do I need to be in order to be able to step up to community or political leadership? If it is directed to organizational issues, who do I need to be so as to be able to deliver on this? This is not about manipulating others, or pretending to be someone we're not; rather it is about the cultivation of the virtues within ourselves, so that we can lead and deliver the results we intend to achieve.

Too often self-development is seen as something that takes us away from achieving results (spending time away from the desk), but if we are in a mode of self-cultivation it becomes an opportunity to practise and cultivate what will be required of us to deliver the long-term results we really care about.

What are you practising?

What are you practising right now? Nothing would perhaps seem the most appropriate answer – I'm just reading. However you are, right at this moment, practising a myriad of things.

You are practising reading – perhaps you read critically, critiquing everything you read, or perhaps you read uncritically, ingesting everything written here without much thought. Perhaps you read for confirmation of what you already know; perhaps you read to have that challenged. Perhaps you skim, or perhaps you go slowly, searching for hidden meaning. You, we, have a way of reading that has been practised repeatedly over time, and that we have become good at. So much so that you no longer think about how you read. This is akin to driving: for those of us who drive regularly, we don't think about how we drive, just where we are going.

Perhaps in addition you are practising reading whilst watching TV, updating Facebook or Twitter, or watching the kids. Perhaps you are one of those people I see occasionally who seem able to read and walk through a city at the same time (a skill I have never mastered).

You're also practising how you sit, stand or walk while you read. You may be practising reading whilst blocking other things out, or perhaps reading whilst keeping your attention available for other things, such as an expected visitor at the door or a crying baby.

All of this goes on fairly unconsciously whilst you take in and make sense of this book.

Human beings are incapable of not practising. We practise how we get up in the morning, and most mornings will probably do it pretty much the same way. Our patterns of behaviour, the way we sit, walk, listen, read, write e-mails, co-ordinate with others, avoid difficult conversations and get upset are all things that we practise.

If you add up all of this together it creates our personality. Our personality is the series of things that we have practised and continue to practise, often unconsciously – behaviours, habits, thoughts, feelings and the like. And with practice, we have become very good at them – we are very good at being us. This does not mean that it is easy to practise something different. If you have spent years practising one particular golf swing, or tennis serve, you will find it difficult to change. If you've spent your entire life practising a particular way of speaking to people in authority, there will be a lot of work to do to develop the capacity to do something different, given the length of time involved. There may also be other issues that need to be addressed in the process of doing so, such as previous unpleasant or traumatic experiences with authority figures.

Practising is a common-sense concept in developing mastery in music, sports, public speaking and many other domains of life. For some reason this is not the case with regards to leadership and the cultivation of the self. In my opinion this is a piece that is missing from our culture.

This is not the traditional view of how we become better leaders, nor is it the traditional view of personality. It does however echo the theme of self-cultivation from Aristotle and from the Japanese and Confucian traditions explored in Chapter 1. It also reconnects us with the idea, explored in Chapter 1, that this is not about some genetically inherited natural talent.

Deliberate practice

First, say to yourself what you would be, and then do what you have to do.

Epictetus[1]

Many of the ideas that I explore here have their roots in the research and thinking of Anders Ericsson and his colleagues. Ericsson is Professor of Psychology at Florida State University, and is an editor of the *Cambridge Handbook of Expertise and Expert Performance*. His work has been heavily focused on understanding how expertise and high-level performance is developed.[2]

Ericsson defines 'expert performance' as objectively measurable superior performance, which is reproducible for the representative activities that define the essence of accomplishment in a particular domain.[3] Basically what Ericsson is saying here is that domains can be broken down into representative activities, and that superior reproducible performance can be measured in these activities. There are inevitably challenges in the leadership domain in objectively measuring superior performance, but the consistency of results across a wide range of domains of expertise gives this research significant validity.

The *Cambridge Handbook*, mentioned above, includes contributions from more than 100 leading researchers who have studied top-level performance in a range of fields, and: 'Consistently and overwhelmingly, the evidence showed that experts are always made, not born.'[4] So if expertise in any field is made, how do we make ourselves into experts in leadership?

The research provides answers, and it turns out that practice does indeed make perfect (or at least expert). However, it is a particular type of practice, which Ericsson christened 'deliberate practice', that makes the difference.[5] Therefore, practice and experience are not the same thing. One can have years of experience and not have engaged in significant deliberate practice.

In a Harvard Business Review article, Ericsson and his colleagues write:

> To illustrate this point let's imagine that you are playing golf for the first time. In the early phases, you try to understand the basic strokes and focus on avoiding gross mistakes (like driving the ball into another player). You practice on the putting green, hit balls at a driving range, and play rounds with others who are most likely novices like you. In a surprisingly short time (perhaps 50 hours), you will develop better control and your game will improve. From them on, you will work on your skills by driving and putting more balls and engaging in more games, until your strokes become automatic: you'll think less about each shot and play more from intuition. Your golf game now is a social outing, in which you occasionally concentrate on your shot. From this point on, additional time on the course will not substantially improve your performance, which may remain at the same level for decades.[6]

This parallels the process of learning to drive. After a period of time driving becomes automatic; we focus on where we are going, and our driving performance does not substantially improve. In fact, we can often pick up bad habits in driving, which would mean that we wouldn't pass the test again were we to take it, so for some of us it could be argued that our driving skill decreases. This parallel is seen in the medical profession, where younger doctors can at times outperform more experienced ones in diagnosing rare diseases, as they have more recently learnt about them and can more easily remember them.[7]

So, say I want to improve my golf game, and I go to the driving range and spend an hour hitting a bucket of balls down the range. I know that it's important to keep my head still during the swing and to choose a target. I go through a range of clubs and hit the balls, some better than others. I then go home feeling virtuous about having practised. However, according to the research this will not substantially improve my performance – I have more experience of golf, but I have not engaged in any deliberate practice.

What this lacks are the clear structures of deliberate practice that have been outlined by Ericsson and that are understood, at least implicitly, by top performers.

Designed activities to improve performance

Top performers work with a series of activities that are designed to improve their performance, most often by coaches or teachers. The design of the activity has to take into account the pre-existing knowledge of the learner and stretch them appropriately. Too much stretch and there is the risk of disillusionment; too little and there will not be significant progress. The activities take some aspect of the person's current ability and stretch it to correct some weakness or improve performance in some way.

It is interesting that in nearly all of the top performers studied, teachers and coaches play a significant role. They have devoted time and attention to the development of these performers, and have designed activities that produce the appropriate stretch. Additionally, many of these top performers have worked with a number of teachers and coaches over their career; as they have developed they have found new teachers capable of stretching them further.

In the domain of leadership, most people are not qualified to design activities that will stretch their learning – most managers know about their domain of expertise, such as marketing, or their industry, but not how to develop leadership. So as with other domains working with a teacher or coach can be invaluable.

Daniel Coyle, in *The Talent Code*, lists 'master coaching' as one of the keys to developing talent, stating that if you remove this, progress slows. In his book *Mastery*[8], George Leonard describes having instruction, as one of the keys to developing mastery in any domain. He goes further, describing the attributes of a good teacher, encouraging us to look at the lineage of the teacher (who was their teacher, and their teacher's teacher, etc), and also the relationship they have with their students (is there a relationship of mutual respect?). He makes the point that today's great tennis professionals may, or may not, be tomorrow's great tennis coaches – the skills required are different – so someone's credentials may look great, but we should look beyond these.

Repeated practice

Mastering these activities to improve performance is accomplished through hours of repeated practice. To reach a level where one can win international competitions, in several domains, it is estimated that 10,000 hours of deliberate practice is required.[9] Other research suggests a minimum of 10 years to develop expert performance in any domain.[10] This implies a commitment to consistently returning to designing activities that continue to stretch us over around 10 years.

The good news is that, unlike chess, sports and music, few people start the deliberate practice of leadership in their childhood years. This means that there are few child prodigies to catch up with, and each of us has the same opportunity to develop into a great leader.

Feedback on results

Feedback on results is an essential component to these practices. Sometimes this feedback is easily received – a golf shot goes in the right direction or not. However, this can also be achieved through coaches or teachers who are capable of giving constructive, even painful, feedback. It seems that high performers deliberately choose coaches or teachers who will challenge them and be capable of driving them to higher levels of performance.

Having a clear sense of results gives these high performers the ability to know what corrections are required and how they can focus on practising something that works effectively. They can figure out things that don't work and engage in problem solving, either individually or with their coach, to find approaches that do work.

Concentration and mental demands

A study of singers taking singing lessons showed that amateur singers experienced the lesson as self-actualization and an enjoyable release of tension, whereas professional singers increased their concentration and were focused on improving their performance.[11] This shows an important distinction in how each was relating to their practice. It's easy to practise songs or music that we already know; it can be fun and enjoyable. However, deliberate practice is about constantly focusing on how we can push ourselves further and improve – this requires a level of mental concentration above that of doing what we know.

Even if I do know how to sing or play a song well, the expert performer is constantly looking for improvements. How can I get just that little bit better? How can I bring more of myself into the music so that it is more moving and powerful. High performers may sing or play the same piece of music as someone else, but they are constantly searching for the improvement.

What this requires is fighting off the temptations of automaticity. When we learn to drive it becomes automatic for us, and we focus on where we are going. And for many of us this is enough when it comes to driving. However, if I want to be a Formula 1 champion, I need to go beyond this, and it turns out that running on automatic is a problem. When I go to automatic I am no longer clear and focused on my learning. I am repeating and reinforcing what I already know – I am reinforcing that which I do well enough to do automatically. This is the experience of playing more rounds of golf, described above, without deliberate practice.

Bringing our attention and full concentration to our practice is essential for it to be worth our while. In his *Harvard Business Review* article, Ericsson cites the famous violinist Nathan Milstein:

Once when I became concerned because others around me practiced all day long, I asked [my mentor] Professor Auer how many hours I should practice, and he said, 'It really doesn't matter how long.

If you practice with your fingers, no amount is enough. If you practice with your head, two hours is plenty.'[12]

It turns out that this type of concentration is very tiring. Those who do it, build up their capacity to concentrate in this way, starting with a small amount of time and building up. The top performers in any field seem to put in a maximum of about five hours of deliberate practice a day. This seems to be about as much as any person can do, and they often report taking additional naps to recuperate from this process.

This aspect of concentration, of overcoming automaticity, is a crucial one for the development of leadership, and for distinguishing between experience and deliberate practice. There are many managers whom I meet who have many years of experience, but who are also running on automatic in regards to how they lead. Often they are completely unaware of the areas in which they could improve and how to go about doing so. Being mindful (rather than mindless) about our actions is an excellent starting point.

Coyle refers to this as a need to struggle. In *The Talent Code* he describes how neuroscience research shows that struggling – pushing yourself to the edge of your performance, making mistakes, slowly figuring how to correct those mistakes, and then pushing some more – wraps more myelin around our neurons. Myelin acts like insulation around the neurons and enables them to process signals more effectively. In fact it seems that increased myelin around the neurons can increase the speed of transmission of signals in our brains by up to 3,000 times.

This is how we develop skills – it seems that one of the key ways we develop the capacity to take actions more effectively is through increasing the efficiency of signal transmission in our brains. It also seems that this is only generated by such deliberate practice and struggle, where we pay mindful attention to pushing our edges and correcting mistakes.

Interestingly, the research on such concentration or mindfulness goes much further. In 1995 a neuroscience researcher, Alvaro Pascual-Leone, experimented with volunteers practising a five-finger piano exercise. One group did the exercise, whilst the other group practised it in their minds, focusing on the movement of each finger in turn, essentially playing the piece in their minds. The physical practice produced changes in the motor cortex of the volunteers' brains, but perhaps surprisingly so did the mental process of concentration.[13] This shows the clear power of concentration or mindfulness in learning, a theme I will return to in Chapter 8.

Not about fun

Constantly pushing the boundaries of what you can do is not necessarily fun. It's probably more fun to play music you know and play well. It's probably more fun to stay within your comfort zone and play for self-expression or self-actualization, as the amateur singers did above. However expert performers know that this is not what will drive continued improvement in performance.

A study of children in the US National Spelling Bee showed that those who were most successful focused on deliberate practice: in this case time spent on their own, memorizing words. The amount of time spent in this way was shown to be an accurate predictor of success. It was also deemed by participants to be the most effortful and least enjoyable form of practice (compared with being quizzed by another person, or more leisurely verbal activities such as reading). In fact reading time had no predictive value for success, which relates back to our earlier distinction between experience and deliberate practice.[14]

This is not to say that these activities cannot be fun, but that they require effort and concentration, and a focus on achieving high performance. Expert performers report that they gain a sense of satisfaction from achieving these results, and that with this comes a sense of enjoyment. Their starting point is a focus on achieving that performance, however, rather than on having fun.

No upper age limit

Contrary to popular belief, research shows that there is no age limit on attaining or maintaining expertise. For some professions such as ballet dancing the structure of the hip joints is changed through practising between ages 9 and 12, as is the case with baseball pitchers' shoulder joints. For the world of business and leadership, however, such childhood adaptations of joints are not required.

For domains such as music and sports, if someone has already achieved 10,000 hours of deliberate practice by the age of 20 (not unusual in music), and is continuing to engage in deliberate practice for five hours a day, then catching up with them will be extremely difficult, if not impossible. However, we can still start at any age, and if we choose put in 10,000 hours of practice and develop expertise; it's just unlikely we will ever catch up with those who started in childhood. In leadership, people rarely, if ever, practise from childhood in this way, so the possibility of being a world-class leader is more available to someone starting to practise in adulthood.

Deliberate practice is also of key importance in maintaining expertise. Research shows that age-related performance decline is as a result of a decrease in deliberate practice rather than of aging. Myelin is living tissue that breaks down over time; the process of deliberate practice is what maintains the myelin around the neurons and maintains skill levels. In fact, in many fields we can be surprised by those who continue to operate at a high level at an older age than those around them, and the research suggests that this is possible more widely.[15]

Motivation

This is perhaps the most interesting aspect of this research. Why would someone do this? It requires extreme mental effort to constantly push yourself to the edges of your ability; it's not necessarily fun, it takes up considerable time over many years, and it requires receiving ongoing feedback, which may be tough to hear.

There is definitely a form of satisfaction that comes from achieving high-level performance, but the mystery of why we do it remains unanswered. Some would like to argue that it's genetic, others that it has a more spiritual or religious basis. The key thing is that motivation is required to achieve this, and a lot of it. Interestingly, Daniel Pink's research on motivation would argue that people derive an innate satisfaction from developing mastery, a theme I will return to in Chapter 10.[16]

I am not going to seek to solve this question across all domains of human performance, but looking at leadership brings us back in our conversation to the question, from Chapter 1, of why we lead, and of seeing leadership as a means rather than an end. What do we care enough about to take leadership? This is what could be the motivating factor for developing mastery in the domain of leadership.

This is crucial, as it asks a fundamental question of us: why should we take leadership in the first place? It is not easy to take leadership; doing so may make us a target for the dissatisfactions of others with the state of the organization or society. Developing mastery as I have described is also not always easy, and we must cultivate the ability to master these actions over time. Why do this, when we could have an easier life and let others lead?

To do this, we must care about something enough. There must be something that we wish to change, build, create or do in the world that causes us to take action and to work on cultivating ourselves to be able to take the required acts of leadership. This is the antidote to ego-fuelled leadership – actions taken for a purpose, rather than for an individual's self-aggrandizement.

Once we are clear on this, we also need to be able to declare it in a way that gets the attention of others. This is another act of leadership. When, in your organization, the CEO (or another senior manager) stands up in front of staff and says that there is a bright new future that they are excited about, does the collective audience get excited or cynical ('Yeah right, we've heard that before…'). Does that senior manager have the ability to declare a new vision of the future in a way that builds commitment and engages those listeners in taking actions towards that vision?

Sadly this ability is all too lacking in organizations, often because managers who are trying to lead skip the first step of being clear on what they care about, and make statements from which they are completely disconnected, and it shows. They make the mistake of not feeling emotively the truth of what they say, something that was recommended in the first century AD by the great teacher of oratory, Quintilian.[17] The skill of declaring a new future that's important to you is another action that can be practised and cultivated in leadership.

Being clear about what you truly believe is important, and being able to connect to this is a large part of what gives you the motivation to do what is required, to be who you need to be, and also to inspire others to follow you.

Maximum performance?

Before Roger Bannister ran the four-minute mile, there were those who said that this couldn't be done – it was impossible for a human being to run that fast. Today amateur runners run marathons in times that would have won Olympic medals in the first half of the 20th century. In the 13th century Roger Bacon argued that it would be impossible to master mathematics in less than 30 to 40 years, yet the roughly equivalent material (calculus) is taught today in schools around the world. Pieces of music that were considered unplayable by the best musicians in the 19th century are readily mastered by today's performers.

Performance keeps improving as teaching methods improve. Today's mathematics students are brought through this process in a structured methodology of teaching – this is why they can learn this material so quickly. Teaching in running, music, chess, dance and just about all fields has improved and keeps on improving. And this allows human performance to continually improve. As yet we know of no end points in the development of human performance across these domains.

To keep pushing ourselves beyond our current expertise and into an ongoing path of developing mastery in any domain requires humility to let go of our current expertise so that we can develop more. If we live from an attitude of being an expert, then are we ever really open to learning more? George Leonard, a writer on mastery and human potential, encourages the master to surrender expertise:

Perhaps the best you can hope for on the master's journey – whether your journey be in management or marriage, badminton or ballet – is to cultivate the mind and heart of the beginner at every stage along the way. For the master, surrender means there are no experts. There are only learners.[18]

Embodiment and mastery

This book, ultimately, is about presenting a new model of how we can develop leadership in an attempt to move forward teaching in this domain. It is grounded in this research on developing high-performance and mastery, and has deliberate practice as a key principle. It takes time and commitment to become a leader in this way, but it leads to an embodiment of the principles and practices of leadership, much in the way masterful musicians embody their art, or martial arts masters embody the principles of their discipline.

We live in a culture where we tend to look for quick fixes. Self-help books are full of quick processes that can be applied to generate success, often assuming that someone is ready for that success and just needs to take a couple of easy steps. There are many stories about previously unknown people across wide domains having instant success that don't consider the previous work that person has done. This is not a quick fix – there is no five-point plan, no five-minute MBA or quick process that will transform you. Rather this is a process of learning and development over time. As our society moves more and more towards quick fixes, pills and a requirement for ongoing results, will you have the patience to develop masterful leadership?

We feel the need for a more masterful leadership in our society. This requires a different leadership conversation. It requires a conversation of self-cultivation through practices leading to embodiment and mastery.

Embodiment is the place of learning where we can do something different, consistently and when under pressure. There is, however, always more available to us. We can learn to embody the ability to drive a car, but there are a few levels of mastery between that and driving in Formula 1. Therefore, whilst embodiment of one level of learning can be an end if we chose it to be, it can also be the starting point for a new level of learning.

In leadership there is always the capacity to develop further. If you're a great listener, you can get better. If you're a great public speaker, there will always be new levels you can achieve. Developing mastery is a long-term process of learning that is available to leaders, so that they can continually take on greater challenges in the world, and lead on more substantive issues if they choose. Or it could mean that they get better and better at managing the challenge of being both a committed leader in the world and a committed parent at home.

Beginnings

Over the course of this book, a process of self-study can, if you wish, emerge, through which you can support yourself in developing your leadership. If 10 years and approximately 10,000 hours of deliberate practice are required to master leadership, then let's set a plan to get there.

I will assume that as you are reading this book you are not new to personal and leadership development, so that you are not starting from a completely blank slate in terms of deliberate practice. So, let's set a target of two hours of deliberate practice (on average) per day. This may sound like a lot in a busy day; however a good proportion of what we will cover here can be done whilst you are getting on with the things you do anyway. It will be a case of practising doing some of those things differently. Therefore, this will not add two hours of more work to each day.

Firstly, let's start with knowledge on leadership. The fact you're reading this book is a good start. At the end of each chapter I have placed some books that you can read to extend your knowledge in the areas concerned. Do not try and read all of them. However go online or into a book store and read about the books, and choose ones that interest you, or choose other books that appeal to you even more. Buy a couple that you think will help forward your learning on leadership. Alternatively there are the *Harvard Business Review, Strategy and Business* and *McKinsey Quarterly*, which are great publications to forward your thinking.

Now let's look at knowledge of your industry and organization.

- How well do you really understand your industry?
- Do you actually read the journals and papers that come across your desk or do they collect dust?

- Do you actively spend time researching competitors, customers, or even your own organization? (Most organizations are large enough that few people really understand how the whole thing works, so understanding this really does set you apart.)

Set yourself a practice of reading for 20 minutes every day from some of this selection. But remember, this is a mindful approach to practices. Bring your full attention and concentration to this – it's not the same as reading a novel in bed for pleasure. Do this when you're alert and can concentrate. Keep a notebook and make notes on what you are learning, and seek opportunities to apply and use the knowledge you have gathered that day. If you read it, make a note of it, and then use it that same day, it is more likely to stay with you for the long term. Begin this as a simple practice that will start you on the path.

Now, it is worth noting that animals also have leaders of herds or packs, and that they manage this without such books and journals. I don't wish to disparage knowledge – it's very useful – but there is obviously more to leadership. It should be clear right from the start that there is more to this concept and more required of us. Our culture has a tendency at times to reduce leadership to knowledge and IQ, and the next chapters will address where this tendency comes from, and what the implications are of moving beyond it.

These practices will develop throughout this book, from this first one for 20 minutes to take up around two hours a day, but please don't wait for them all and then try at the end to implement everything at once. That will be too much and is unlikely to work. Begin now, use these principles in the way you read this book and see what develops. You will start to see a difference in your leadership very quickly.

Two hours per day comes to around 700 hours per year, or around 7,000 hours in 10 years. Assuming you have already begun your development journey prior to this book, for most of you this should get you to around 10,000 hours of deliberate practice. The good news however, is that few of your peers will actually do this. Of those who read this book, many will decide that 10 years is just too long, and deliberate practice requires just too much effort, or actually that they're happy enough with where they are. Therefore, you'll begin to stand out from your peer group very quickly, and you should see a noticeable progression in your career in around one or two years. But stick with it – if you truly care about leading in a way that makes a difference, stick with the journey, and remember that deliberate practice is also required to maintain expert performance as well as to attain it.

Recommended reading

Talent is Overrated: What really separates world-class performers from everybody else, Geoff Colvin.

The Talent Code: Greatness isn't born, it's grown, by Daniel Coyle.

Outliers: The story of success, by Malcolm Gladwell.

Mastery: The keys to success and long-term fulfillment, by George Leonard.

The Leadership Dojo: Build your foundation as an exemplary leader, by Richard Strozzi-Heckler.

Notes

1 *The Moral Discourses of Epictetus*, by Elizabeth Carter, p 178. Epictetus was a Greek Stoic philosopher, who lived circa 100 AD.

2 His work has heavily influenced two popular psychology books that I would recommend if you would like to explore this further: *The Talent Code*, by Daniel Coyle, and *Talent is Overrated*, by Geoff Colvin.

3 Ericsson, KA (2006) 'The influence of experience and deliberate practice on the development of superior expert performance', pp 683–703 in *The Cambridge Handbook of Expertise and Expert Performance*, ed KA Ericsson, N Charness, RR Hoffman and PJ Feltovich, Cambridge University Press.

4 Ericsson, KA, Prietula, MJ and Cokely, ET (2007) 'The making of an expert', *Harvard Business Review*, July–August, pp 114–21.

5 Daniel Coyle, in *The Talent Code*, uses the term 'deep practice', and acknowledges that this is basically the same thing.

6 Ericsson, KA, Prietula, MJ and Cokely, ET (2007) 'The making of an expert', *Harvard Business Review*, July–August, pp 114–21.

7 Ericsson, KA (2008) 'Deliberate practice and acquisition of expert performance: a general overview', *Academic Emergency Medicine*, November, **15** (11), pp 989–94.

8 *Mastery* by George Leonard is a wonderful discussion of the path to mastery and the cultural barriers that are present to this learning process.

9 Ericsson, KA (2008) 'Deliberate practice and acquisition of expert performance: a general overview', *Academic Emergency Medicine*, November, **15** (11), pp 989–94.

10 Ericsson, KA, Krampe, RT and Tesch-Romer, C (1993) 'The role of deliberate practice in the acquisition of expert performance', *Psychological Review*, **100** (3), pp 363–406.

11 Ericsson, KA (2006) 'The influence of experience and deliberate practice on the development of superior expert performance', in *The Cambridge Handbook of Expertise and Expert Performance*, ed KA Ericsson, N Charness, RR Hoffman and PJ Feltovich, pp 683–703 Cambridge University Press.

12 Ericsson, KA, Prietula, MJ and Cokely, ET (2007) 'The making of an expert', *Harvard Business Review*, July–August, pp 114–21.

13 Pascual-Leone, A, Dang, N, Cohen, LG *et al* (1995) 'Modulation of muscle responses evoked by transcranial magnetic stimulation during the acquisition of new fine motor skills', *Journal of Neurophysiology*, **74** (3), pp 1037–45.

14 Duckworth, AL, Kirby, TA, Tsukayama, E, Berstein, H and Ericsson, KA (2011) 'Deliberate practice spells success: why grittier competitors triumph at the national spelling bee', *Social Psychology and Personality Science,* **2** (2), pp 174–81.

15 Ericsson, KA and Ward, P (2007) 'Capturing the naturally occurring superior performance of experts in the laboratory: towards a science of expert and exceptional performance', *Current Directions in Psychological Science*, **16** (6), pp 346–50.

16 Pink, DH (2009) *Drive: The surprising truth about what motivates us*, Penguin: New York. See also his RSA Animate talk, available: http://www.thersa.org/events/video/animate/rsa-animate-drive.

17 Quintilian was a first century AD teacher of oratory (or rhetoric) who published a 12-volume work, called *Institutio Oratoria*. This is now available translated on the internet at: http://penelope.uchicago.edu/Thayer/E/Roman/Texts/Quintilian/Institutio_Oratoria/home.html (accessed 16 May 2001).

18 Leonard, G (1992) *Mastery: The keys to success and long-term fulfillment*, Plume, New York, p 88.

03

If I am to develop myself, what exactly is my 'self'?

In the last two chapters I have concluded that in order to become better leaders we need to develop the self through deliberate practice, but what is it exactly that we are developing? Traditionally in our culture it is the mind or the brain that we think of here. But what exactly is the mind, and how do we understand what it is to be human?

These are fairly fundamental questions that we need to address. If it is just the rational mind, then all we need to do is learn some models and theories and we will be a leader. If that was the case then it would be easy, and yet we all know that leadership models and theories don't quite automatically result in leadership in our organizations and the wider world.

So if we are developing the self through deliberate practice it is worth inquiring more deeply into what the 'self' actually is, in order to understand how to work with it most effectively.

Exercise

Take a moment and just feel inside yourself. Take a deep breath, relax your shoulders, jaw and stomach, whilst lengthening out your spine. What does that feel like?

It's probably hard to put into words – what you feel in that moment is what it feels like to be you. That's distinct from me, and from everyone else who reads this book. If you try to locate the sense of what that feels like, however, it doesn't exist as a thought in your head but as a 'felt-sense' – an experience of feeling your body from the inside. Scientists refer to this as proprioception, and it allows us to know where our arms (or any other body parts) are at any moment, without looking to check.

On top of this background feeling, you may also feel something else. If you're in conflict you may also feel some anger or frustration; if you're grieving then you may feel sadness, or if you've recently received some good news you may feel joy. Or perhaps you can remember a time when you had those feelings. You may notice, once again, that these feelings also do not exist as ideas in our heads but are things we experience in our stomachs, chests and the rest of our bodies. We experience them physically.

And in between the background sense of ourselves and our current emotions, there are our moods. Moods and emotions are often confused, but generally moods are seen to be longer term than emotions. Emotions are short-term reactions to events in the world, whereas moods are longer-term attitudes, often in the background and some-times out of our awareness, that influence our view of the world. Both emotions and moods alter our attitude to events and other people, and change the way we think. Optimism and pessimism are good examples of these moods. I have seen many people who live in long-term moods of cynicism and resignation regarding their organizations, often as a result of years of trying to make things better and having given up. Once again these are things that we feel physically; they are not just ideas in our heads. It you are to try to identify your mood, you will need to connect with how you are feeling, which brings us back to physical sensations and our bodies.

Can you imagine yourself without these felt-senses? The back-ground feeling of you, the foreground feeling of whatever frustra-tions or nervousness you feel from time to time, plus your longer-term moods. Who would you be? Would a disembodied you still be you, if it didn't feel like you in this way? Can you separate these feelings and sensations from the sense you have of who you are?

It's a challenging question, and most people have difficulty imagin-ing such a reality, never mind imagining who and how they would be in such a world. The idea of it feels alien and uncomfortable, perhaps almost a robot-like experience.

Strangely enough, however, our culture seems to be quite attached to the belief that who you are (the mind) is detached from the body, and therefore from the felt experience of being alive and being you. So, according to this logic, who you are is this disembodied sense, rather than an embodied feeling of being alive, and experiencing what you feel. Therefore it is as if there is a rational computer inside all of us that represents our true self, unimpeded by messy things such as feelings, emotions and moods.

This idea is represented in science fiction with the idea of someday being able to transfer our consciousness to a computer or robot, where it can live on as a rational thought process unencumbered by a weak body (the most recent form of this idea, I have seen, was used at the end of the movie *Avatar* where the hero's mind is transferred into his avatar body).[1] The idea is widely disputed in philosophy, but lingers on in the world, nowhere more so than in economics. Here, in the traditional interpretation, human beings think things through carefully and make their decisions on a rational basis as economic agents. Some groundbreaking work on behavioural economics, such as the Nobel Prize winning work of Daniel Kahneman, is rethinking this, but the ideas pervade our culture and businesses deeply.[2]

I worked for a short time in the field of strategy consultancy. If you ever doubt the idea that our businesses operate on the assumption of human beings as rational thinking machines, then you should employ a strategy consultant, or sit in on some of their meetings. It is a world of rational analyses, whilst everyone knows that what hinders organizations is not getting the right strategy but implementing it.

Millions of pounds and countless hours are spent constructing flawless intellectual and rational strategies that are never implemented – and why? Well, one client I worked with had an interesting realization when all of the executive board admitted that none of them wanted to work in the company their flawless strategy would create. They had hired consultants three years earlier who produced this intellectual masterpiece describing the market they were in, the key challenges they faced, and how they needed to develop and grow as a firm to be successful. None of the executive board had felt able to challenge the strategy because of its intellectual power and the sheer amount of data that had been collected and analysed and that sat behind it. However they all harboured doubts about whether they personally would be a good fit for the company that would be created and whether they would want to work there. Needless to say, they had made zero progress in implimenting this strategy. This to me highlights the fiction of the idea of the human being as a rational thinking machine.

For me it's a somewhat difficult conclusion that who I am is this disembodied mind, when I know how difficult it is even to imagine myself in this way, never mind to understand who I would be without that felt sense of being alive – I wouldn't be me! Intuitively I reject the idea that I am somehow separate from this embodied sense, before I even begin to martial my thoughts to generate an argument against it.

In the previous chapters I have explored what leadership is, how that relates to who we are, and how we develop as leaders. In doing so I have concluded that leadership is about a self that we are, which is cultivated through deliberate practices. If this is the case then any understanding of leadership and how to get good at it relates at a deep level to how we understand who we are. If we are just rational minds, then this implies that we should address leadership development differently.

In business today there is, despite the rise of the concept of emotional intelligence[3] (the ability to be aware of, and respond to, the emotions of ourselves and others) in recent years, a requirement for rationality and reason, and for putting feelings and emotions aside. In many respects the business world calls us to be the rational computer-like beings, maximizing productivity and profitability. I know this is to some extent a myth, given the irrational behaviour we all witness in organizations every day, but it is still rare for organizations to take into account human emotions and feelings when they conflict with profitable business decisions.

As I write this, we have had in the UK a series of ethical business issues. Barclays Bank has been in the press for fixing the Libor interest rates; HSBC and Standard Chartered have been in trouble in the United States with money laundering controls being insufficient; News

International has had to close down a newspaper, and journalists and private detectives working for the organization are facing criminal charges connected to phone hacking. This is on top of the chain of global banking activity that contributed to the current recession, and a transformation of the face of the investment banking market. It seems clear that the pursuit of productivity and profit has sat as a higher goal when any conflicts arose with any individual's emotions, feelings, values or morals in this process.

So our organizational world is built directly on top of the foundation of a self that is a rational mind, existing somewhat separately from the felt sense of being alive. This leads to a flow of business school and leadership models that speak to the rational mind, and that appear to make very limited differences to individual's behaviour and leadership capability. To address leadership in a more fundamental way, we must attack the foundational belief that we are somehow rational computer-like beings, and deal with the whole person.

In recent years there have been a series of articles and books[4] that have addressed the subject of psychopaths in the work place, and the Canadian film and book *The Corporation*[5], suggested that corporations were psychopathic by nature. The truth is that this shouldn't be a surprise to us, as the people who operate most closely to pure rationality, disconnected from the felt sense of life, from emotions, values etc, are indeed psychopaths. As the writer GK Chesterton stated:

> The madman is not the man who has lost his reason. The madman
> is the man who has lost everything except his reason.[6]

I believe it's time for a new model of leadership that builds on a different foundation of who we are, but first we must address the current foundation, understand where it came from and the flaws that exist in it. This means addressing the core philosophical viewpoints that shape our culture and ways of seeing the world.

The evolution of an idea about who we are

This is the story of an idea and its evolution, and that story could start with Plato, or even before. However this idea became firmly embedded in our culture in the 17th century, a time of great religious turmoil in Europe.

In 1633 Galileo was condemned by the Catholic Church and found guilty of heresy for believing, and writing a book advocating, that the earth moves around the sun and not vice-versa. He was sentenced to formal imprisonment at the 'pleasure of the Inquisition', which on the following day was commuted to house arrest. He remained under house arrest for the rest of his life and his offending book was banned.

This was a time in Europe in which the field of science was progressing quickly and was perceived to be threatening the authority of the Church. Science was making claims about the world that were seen to be, at times, not entirely in line with the Bible and the Church's teachings. Science was also offering an alternative source of authority in understanding and making sense of the world, and was therefore undermining the Church's power. This was taking place around a century after the Reformation, when Christianity split between Catholicism and Protestant religions, so it's fair to say that the Catholic Church may well have perceived itself as under attack, and certainly its authority was being diminished.

Against this background René Descartes emerged. Descartes was a French scientist, mathematician and philosopher, and is sometimes referred to as the father of modern philosophy. Descartes created a philosophical framework that solved the problem of his time: the clash between the Church and science. It allowed for the progression of science in such a way that it could be less threatening to the Church. For that we should be grateful to him, as it has allowed the advances in medicine and science that enhance our lives, and allow me to write this book on a computer rather than by hand.

However, his solution, which allowed progress, was deeply flawed. This was recognized by some of his contemporaries (and some speculate perhaps even by Descartes himself), but his ideas stuck, probably because they helped everyone move forward. His ideas arguably sit at the root of our culture in the West, and whilst they solved one problem they created new problems that we now face.

The reality, however, is that philosophers are still arguing today about the question that Descartes attempted to answer, along with neuroscientists and psychologists, all ultimately trying to get a handle on who we are as human beings. The answer we accept has profound implications for how we see ourselves, the world and, importantly for this book, leadership.

Understanding the root question

So what is this question? For almost all of recorded history (and perhaps longer) human beings have wondered about a particular philosophical problem: how do I know that anything is real, and not just my imagination? It's a very real problem – if you've ever witnessed anyone having an hallucination, they are in that moment as convinced about what they see before them, as you are of the pages of this book. So how do I know that what I see is real?

In fact, how do I know that everyone around me and the world I see are not figments of my imagination, and that in fact my mind is not just generating all that I see, all of the time? This viewpoint is referred to as solipsism by philosophers, and whilst it is impossible to disprove, few chose to believe it – or if they do they choose not to write and speak widely about it, for perhaps obvious reasons. It's a philosophical cul-de-sac, impossible to prove or disprove, that leaves one with no real options, and no motivation to try and change anything in the world, or do anything of any importance.

So the problem exists: if we can only know about what is out there around us because our mind perceives it to be out there, how do we know where our mind stops and the world begins? This may seem to be an abstract philosophical question but it cuts to the root of what it is to be a human being, and the answer Descartes came up with has affected much of modern society and our ideas about leadership.

Descartes' answer

Descartes, very much in the tradition of Socrates and Plato before him, believed that knowledge that had been handed down was not necessarily reliable and began a process of reasoning from first principles.

His famous phrase *Cogito ergo sum*, 'I think therefore I am', was an attempt to answer the question above. Descartes knew that he could doubt his senses and perceptions, but that he could not doubt the process of doubting – in other words, he could not doubt the existence of the doubter. And as doubting is a process of thought, there must be a thinker doing such thinking.

So, Descartes' conclusion proved to him that if there is thinking, there is a thinker. He went on to say that this also defined the nature of the 'thinker' as a thinking being. This thinking being, was in his view, an immaterial substance whose essence was thought, which was somehow tagged into the material 'real' world of our bodies. In doing this he distinguished two worlds; an interior psychological world, which perceives, decides and thinks – our minds/souls/consciousness – and an exterior world of concrete, material stuff, which exists outside of our thoughts – which includes our bodies and the physical world around us.

Descartes, therefore, separated the mind and the body. Who we are was a separate consciousness, or soul, the 'immaterial substance whose essence was thought', which was the domain of the Church; and the body, a material substance, and the material world was the domain of science. (This enabled him to persuade the Church to allow him and other scientists, to cut up dead bodies for the purposes of science, which enabled significant progress in medicine.) This separation has been referred to as 'dualism'.

Professor David Cockburn explains Decartes' ideas beautifully in the following paragraph:

> According to traditional dualism, of the kind defended by Descartes, a live human being is a compound of two, intimately conjoined, parts: a material body, which is an object in the world alongside other material things, and a non-material mind, which is an essentially thinking thing. The real me – 'the self' – is the second; and that is to say, the real me does not have a life in the normal sense. The real me does not move the furniture, dig the garden, comfort my friend who is sad or depressed, hug my wife, hide from another's anger, shout at or hit out at the one who has hurt me, and so on. Since all of these activities involve the body, and since that is not strictly part of me,

it is not strictly me that does these things. All that I, strictly speaking, do, is think – in Descartes' broad sense of that term in which it includes understanding, willing, imagining, perceiving and so on. Some of my thoughts cause this body – my body – to move in certain ways: as when, as we colloquially put it, 'I' dig the garden.[7]

This quote illustrates the Cartesian model well. The self is an abstract concept here, the disembodied mind that exists separate from the body. However this separation, or dualism, is central to the 'Western' mindset, and this has led directly to the idea of the logical and rational person described at the beginning of this chapter. In this model who I am and what's important is the rational self, and the body is the machinery to which this self is tied and that moves it around from meeting to meeting.

To some extent in the West, we have taken the ideas beyond this. The saying 'the spirit is willing, but the flesh is weak' is an example of this. Here the logical, rational mind (or spirit) knows what is right to do, but the emotions and body hold us back. In this worldview it is the role of the rational mind to bring our emotions, which we feel in the body, under control and keep them in line.

Dualism is, however, deeply flawed, and almost immediately after its conception it was contested by other philosophers. It was, however, very useful in solving the problems of its day, and has thus permeated our culture and thinking.

Probably the most fundamental problem with Descartes philosophy is to do with his basic argument. It is logical to say that because I think, there exists a thinker, but it does not necessarily follow that the being that I am is a solely thinking being. If I were to say that I feel cold, therefore I am, does that necessarily imply that I am a cold being? No, it shows that at that moment I am a being that feels cold, but no more than this. Descartes' sense of a thinking being negated many other types of being that could also be true. What would have happened if, instead of starting with a process of reasoning, Descartes had started with a process of feeling and experiencing the world, and the belief that this was the way to knowledge? He would have ended up, I suspect, with something other than 'I think, therefore I am.'

The flaw in his argument was to assume that because we think, we are thinking beings and that is all that we are. One does not imply the other, and as dualism rests on these rather shaky foundations, it gives us very good reason to doubt dualism.

A second challenge for Cartesian dualism is the problem of free will. Our world, and certainly our legal system, is based around the idea that we have choice, and can freely choose our actions. We can choose to take actions that are good or bad, legal or illegal, and so on. I can choose when playing tennis to return a shot, or let it pass me by. My mind can make these choices, and cause my body to take whatever actions are required.

So, how does an immaterial substance – consciousness/the mind – impact and cause changes in a material substance – the body – that is subject to the laws of physics? This is a tricky problem: we understand the material world, through the lens of science, and therefore we look at cause and effect. If a tennis ball flies through the air in my direction, we have an effect. The cause of such an effect is that it was hit by a tennis racket in my direction. This is simple and clear in the world of tennis balls and rackets. However, what happens when we look at me as the tennis player deciding whether to return the shot or let it pass me by?

The mind, in Descartes formulation, is something that does not occupy three-dimensional space, is not material and could not cause movement in the material world. The mind cannot impact my arm, as the tennis racket does the ball, to get it to move. Even if we take this down to the levels of atoms and particles, how can the mind – something that is not a physical substance – cause the movement of particles, which could eventually make up the movement of an arm to return the tennis ball. There does not seem to be a way for the mind, in Descartes' dualism, to cause movement over the physical body. Therefore, I cannot exercise free will to return the tennis ball.

This is a challenging thought. Descartes ideology allows no room for the immaterial world of thoughts to impact and change the material world of the body and so allow us to take actions. They are two distinct worlds and, based on our scientific understanding of cause and effect, non-material thoughts cannot impact the movement of material particles.

Descartes suggested that some kind of transformation between the world of thoughts and the material world took place in the pineal gland in the brain, a view long since abandoned by neuroscience.

There are, to be fair, quite a number of problems with Descartes' dualism, all of which I will not address here. My point is merely to show that there are problems with his ideas. That they sit at the root of modern-day conceptions of who we are is a pity and limits us in our thinking.

An alternative answer?

There is, however, an alternative philosophical view that is common today, especially in scientific fields. Here we move from seeing two worlds in dualism (the thinking self and the material world) to a single world of materialism, where everything sits in the material world.[8]

Here we reduce mind and thought to the movement of particles in the brain. States of mind, therefore, are the same as and nothing but physical states in the brain. In this view the mind disappears, as all that exists are brain states. This is often the view propagated by science, and some scientists will not use the word 'mind', claiming it is not a scientific concept; the mind as we know it is just the physical state of the brain, and this is what we need to discuss.[9]

Materialism solves some of the problems of dualism; one no longer has an immaterial mind that needs to impact the material world, but materialism also has a whole set of its own problems, and also does not allow for free will.

You see, the material world is explained by science through cause and effect. You may remember from school the basic Newtonian idea that every action has an equal and opposite reaction. Through this formulation we could, theoretically (if we had a big enough computer and enough time), track all the particles in the universe back to the Big Bang, and explain all their movements up to today on the basis of those historic movements.

Imagine it like a pool or snooker table. All the balls end up in certain positions due to the collisions that they experience with other balls and the cushions of the table. If we think about all the particles in the universe as balls on such a table (although these ones don't stop moving), then we should be able to track their positions and movements through time.

The challenge with this is that we are made of such particles. So if I raise my right arm, touch the tip of my nose with a finger, or even move my fingers to type these words, then these movements of particles are ones that are the result of a series of other movements ever since the Big Bang. They are moving because of a long chain of cause and effect interactions and not the result of free will on my part deciding to move my finger.

Free will, in this philosophical conception, then becomes the way I explain to myself my movements. Some researchers believe that this is all the conscious mind does – it makes up post hoc rationalizations to explain to ourselves why we did what we did, and we have no free will whatsoever. Free will is just something I believe about the things that I am doing, but in reality the things that I am doing were pre-determined. This is a disturbing thought for the whole concept of personal responsibility and our criminal justice systems – I can no longer be held responsible for my actions because I do not have free will.

Some would argue that quantum mechanics allows a way out of this problem, as it allows for a degree of randomness in the positions of particles. But that would produce an interesting outcome; when I want to raise my arm, does the actual raising of the arm happen randomly. When I type these words, do my fingers move randomly? (I'm not the best typist in the world, but it's far from random!) So we still have no free will in this conception.

So why is this a problem for us? Well, let's start with the fact that most of our ideas of leadership stress developing self-awareness and from this having more choice. This is a concept that relies on a philosophy of free will, yet the underlying thinking of both Descartes' dualism and materialism makes free will a very shaky concept – in dualism we can't explain how it can happen, and materialism just makes life easier by removing it from the equation. This has not stopped many people from adopting a materialist perspective, and there are neuroscientists out there basically attempting to prove that we do not have free will.

I wonder, though, if we really do want to live in a world in which no one is ever responsible for their actions and behaviours, and these are ultimately pre-determined by a scientific chain of cause and effect. Whilst it has not been possible for me (or anyone) to prove either way, in any kind of objective sense, I reject the idea that I do not have free will, and I do not want to live in a world that holds this idea as truth. My experience of life is that I can make choices and exercise free will, and that my levels of self-awareness affect my ability to do so. To live in a world where no one has any accountability for their behaviour seems to me an unpleasant and unhealthy option. Indeed there is evidence to suggest that exposure to messages that we have no free will and are not responsible increases the likelihood of unethical actions.[10]

Behaviourism, which I mentioned in Chapter 1 when looking at leadership as actions and behaviours, comes directly from the materialist worldview. In this viewpoint, what is important about someone is the concrete and measurable movement of atoms and particles through behaviour and action, and all of who we are is reducible to such movements. Ultimately this is a very mechanistic view of humans as trainable animals or programmable machines. The philosopher John Searle writes of behaviourism:

> In its crudest version, behaviourism says that the mind just is
> the behaviour of the body. There is nothing over and above the
> behaviour of the body that is constitutive of the mental.[11]

What Searle is saying here is that in behaviourism all of who we are is expressed in the actions we take, and there is nothing else that exists that is worth paying attention to.

This leaves out a lot from our experience of life. If everything of our experience is reducible to, or exactly the same as, physical processes, where does that leave the experience of listening to an uplifting piece of music or looking at a beautiful piece of art. The internal qualitative experiences of drinking beer and of looking at art are very different, but these are left out of a materialist world view.

As an example, a colour-blind neuroscientist who understands all the brain processes involved in perceiving the colour red, and understands all about light and colour spectrums, will know everything about the colour red from a materialist point of view. However, this person will never know what it feels like to see a beautiful deep shade of the colour red. This qualitative experience is an internal experience, rather than an aspect of the material world, and is therefore missing from the materialist worldview.

To take this further, imagine yourself in a room where someone is sending you questions in a Chinese script. You don't speak Chinese; however you do have a rule book that dictates a response to each of the symbols, so you look up each symbol and send a response. If you answer each question clearly and perfectly, all whilst having no idea what any symbol means, you are from a materialist point of view communicating in Chinese. To a behaviourist or materialist, the behaviours and actions count, and your behaviours and actions are equivalent to speaking Chinese – the internal experience of understanding does not exist, it is merely an illusion.[12]

Ultimately in the behaviourist view the internal experience does not have any validity. However, as in the example above, I can behaviourally appear to speak and understand Chinese, but not actually have the experience of knowing Chinese. This weakens behaviourism and materialism as a school of thought for understanding human beings. Understanding behaviour does not give you the entire person. John Searle quotes the linguist Noam Chomsky as stating:

> the idea that when we study psychology we are studying behaviour
> is as unintelligent as the idea that when we study physics we are
> studying meter readings.[13]

Of course we use behaviours to understand the mind, just as physicists use meter readings, but it's a mistake to reduce the study purely to the behaviours. They are a sign of what lies beyond.

So materialism leaves us with many challenges. Neuroscientist Jeffrey Schwartz, concluding a review of materialism, states:

> Even this abbreviated rundown of mind–brain philosophies
> would not be complete without what the Australian philosopher
> David Chalmers calls 'don't-have-a-clue materialism.' This is the
> default position of those who have no idea about the origins of
> consciousness or the mind, but assert that 'it must be physical as

materialism must be true,' as Chalmers puts it. 'Such a view is held widely, but rarely in print.' One might add that many working scientists hold this view without really reflecting on the implications of it.[14]

Materialism puts everything into the realm of science and so for scientists is an attractive point of view. Many people do seem to be attached to it, without reflecting too deeply on its implications for responsibility and free will.

Therefore, it seems that materialism comes no closer than Descartes' dualism to answering some of the fundamental questions about who we are and how the world is. The choice between the two is an unsatisfactory one, and doctor, neuroscience researcher and philosopher Raymond Tallis describes the choice between Descartes' dualism and materialism succinctly when he states:

> I implicitly dissent from two views of humans: either that they are free-floating spirits, trains of thought, only accidentally entangled with bodies [Descartes]; or that they are pieces of meat, dancing to the same tunes to which non-human pieces of meat dance [materialism].[15]

Can we find something that makes more sense?

My first degree was in physics, which was taught from a clearly materialist perspective, although I did not reflect fully on the implications of this at the time. My upbringing was clearly dualist in perspective, although once again I did not reflect fully on this at the time. Now, I look at both with a sense of dissatisfaction. Neither appears to me to be fully satisfactory in making sense of what it is to be human.

It seems clear to me that we have minds and a rich internal experience, which is part of what it is to be human – to deny that seems to be foolish. However, in saying this, I do not seek to sneak in dualism by the back door – that is too flawed a philosophy. We need another option to these two ideas, on which to build our ideas of humanity. This is an embodied perspective, which I will introduce here, and then I will look at the neuroscience that supports this idea in the following chapter.

Professor David Cockburn makes an interesting point about dualism and materialism. Ultimately they both share a similar perspective on the mind – that it is distinct from the bodily being that we see and touch. For dualism the mind is an entity separate from the material world, and for materialists the mind (as much as there is one) is exactly the same as brain states, and not therefore, the wider body. If we go back to our starting point of this chapter, much of how we experience ourselves in the world is through and in our bodies and their sensations. This is a piece that is missing from both of these perspectives.[16]

He brings us back, therefore to something we implicitly know; that our embodied experience of ourselves, our sensations and our emotions, is part of who we are, and it is this self that takes action in the world, such as moving the furniture, comforting a friend and so on. This brings us to the idea of an embodied mind, something that captures and includes the whole body and our bodily experience of being alive.

In including the mind in his philosophy, he is not going back to dualism, he is incorporating the mind in a different way. He states:

> To take a rough analogy, one can deny that the shape of a vase is part of the vase, or a distinct entity that sits alongside the vase in some other realm, without denying that vases have shapes.[17]

This parallels the mind or consciousness beautifully.

If we break the vase down into its scientific constituent parts there will be elements, atoms, molecules, particles and so on. An extensive scientific analysis of the constituent parts will not tell you what the shape is, but it has a shape. When we dissect or analyse the physical body or brain, we do not find a mind, and an extensive analysis of brain activity or a dissection of the brain will not tell you what is happening in the mind, but we have minds.

Neither is the shape a distinct entity that sits alongside the vase in another realm, in the way the mind does in Descartes' dualism. The mind does not need to be reduced to brain states or denied (materialism), nor does it need to be an external factor in another realm (dualism). It becomes an aspect of the full, undivided, human being.

Interestingly, this is closer to the position that some neuroscientists are coming to. The eminent neuroscientist Antonio Damasio states in his aptly named book *Descartes' Error*:

> It is not only the separation between the mind and brain that is
> mythical: the separation between mind and body is probably just
> as fictional. The mind is embodied in the full sense of the term,
> not just embrained.[18]

Another neuroscientist, Candace Pert, agrees, stating: 'I can no longer make a strong distinction between the brain and the body.'[19]

These neuroscientists, and others, are overturning the belief in the idea that the mind is just our brain states. They are coming to a more nuanced perspective inside which the body is inseparable from our thought processes, and our entire bodily experience of being alive becomes part of who we are.

Raymond Tallis, goes further in his writing:

> Those who believe that consciousness is to be found in the
> stand-alone brain subscribe to a body–body dualism with the brain
> being a 'mind–body' and the rest of the body being just a body.
> To me, this is no advance on the traditional Cartesian mind–body
> dualism... One way forward from this position is to acknowledge:
> (a) that the brain is situated in a body from which it cannot be
> separated; (b) the embodied brain is inseparable from a biosphere;
> and (c) in the case of humans, we are inseparable from a community
> of minds and the worlds that its component selves have built.[20]

Here, Tallis builds on the idea of embodied mind, and connects us back to our wider biological heritage and environment, as well as connecting us to the wider community of humanity. Dualism has enabled us over time to separate ourselves from the wider world and communities in which we live, and this has arguably enabled some of humanity's destructive behaviours. These are ideas I will come back to later in this book, in Chapters 9 and 10, as they have important implications for leadership.

Support for the idea of the embodied mind, also comes from an unexpected source – that of Artificial Intelligence. For years researchers in this field have attempted to come up with intelligent computers, like IBM's supercomputer Deep Blue, which played Grand Master Gary Kasparov in chess in 1996–97.[21] However attempts to develop such an intelligence have been plagued by difficulties, and some of the most advanced research in this field is now in the field of robotics.

Embodied Intelligence is the name of this new field, and two of its basic premises are:

> The nature of the human mind is largely determined by the form of the human body.

> Artificial intelligence can only be achieved by machines that have sensory and motor skills and are connected to the world through a body.[22]

Perhaps it will be through our research into Artificial Intelligence, and the process of trying to create new forms of intelligence, that we will come to understand the human mind and consciousness as embodied.

An embodied mind

In this section I have explored the philosophical underpinnings of how we think about who we are and how we experience and impact the world. In doing so we can return to the inquiry at the start of this chapter, where I asked you to feel what it was like to be you. There it was difficult to imagine a separate disembodied self, however much of our current thinking about ourselves and the world is predicated on this idea.

To move forward into a new understanding of an embodied mind or self, we need to rethink much of how we see ourselves in the world. The body is no longer a piece of meat or a machine that carries the head (the important bit) from meeting to meeting. In this way of looking at ourselves, the body is an integrated part of the self, of who we are.

We have separated the mind and the body, for convenience of language, and for expediency in allowing science and the Church to co-exist. To really step into a complete understanding of the embodied mind or self, we need to begin to see how the two are ultimately the same. They are intertwined, interwoven and co-exist.

The same perspective exists in physics. We have known from physics, since the days of Einstein, that energy and matter are the same thing. They are not separable – matter is energy and energy is matter – and particles can exist as particles of matter or energetic wave forms.

This provides a useful analogy for how we see the self (mind) and the body. They are one and the same, and when we speak of one, we are implicitly speaking of the other.

For leadership and the learning of leadership this has some profound implications. At the start of this chapter I stated that it is time for a new model of leadership based upon a different foundation of who we are.

If we start from Descartes' premise of the mind as a rational, disembodied entity, then we need to look for those who have minds with high IQs, who are good at rational reasoning, and we need to give them leadership models that will allow their rational mind to work out how to lead. In Chapter 1 I looked at the leader as a born heroic leader, and showed the flaws in such thinking.

If we start from the premise that it's all about brain states, and there is nothing else, then we look at behaviours and brain scans. Yet we looked in Chapter 1 at behaviourism as a way of understanding leadership as actions and behaviours, and saw the flaws in that approach.

My contention is that any leadership development approach will always be less powerful unless it embraces the embodied mind and begins to work with the whole self. This is the position of an integrated leader we arrived at in Chapters 1 and 2, where the actions we take can shape us in a process of becoming and developing: a process of self-cultivation.

An embodied self detailed above allows such a process of self-cultivation. The mind and body as an integrated unity allows the development of the self through the actions of this physical body. In the rest of this book I will explain more about how this actually happens.

However, to begin this process, start by noticing your mood at the start and end of each day, and take a note of it – you can use a notebook, your phone or whatever device you choose. Just begin by noticing what it is and where you experience it in your body. As you do this notice how your moods shape your orientation to the world and your actions and thinking. Just this simple act of noticing will increase your self-awareness, and will enable you to have more choice in your actions and words in various situations.

Recommended reading

If you are interested in reading more about the philosophy that sits behind this chapter then I recommend:

An Introduction to the Philosophy of Mind, by David Cockburn.

Mind: A Brief Introduction, by John Searle.

If you are interested in getting deeper into the philosophy behind this book, then I recommend:

Aping Mankind: Neuromania, Darwinitis and the misrepresentation of humanity, by Raymond Tallis.

Philosophy in the Flesh: The embodied mind and its challenge to Western thought, by George Lakoff and Mark Johnson.

Notes

1 Arthur C Clarke's novel *The City and the Stars* (1956) is the earliest reference to the uploading of consciousness to a machine that I have found. It is an idea that has returned in various forms throughout the years.

2 *Thinking Fast and Slow* by Daniel Kahneman serves as an excellent introduction to this field.

3 Daniel Goleman popularized this concept with his book *Emotional Intelligence: Why it can matter more than IQ*.

4 There are a range of articles, such as HBR's 'Executive psychopaths' (October 2004), 'Is your boss a psychopath' and 'Coping with psychopaths at work' from Fast Company (July 2005). Books include *Snakes in Suits: When psychopaths go to work* by Paul Babiak and Robert D Hare, and *The Psychopath Test* by Jon Ronson.

5 *The Corporation: The pathological pursuit of profit and power* by Joel Bakan, and the film is of the same name.

6 Chesterton, GK (new edn, 1996) *Orthodoxy*, Bantam Doubleday Dell, New York.

7 Cockburn, D (2001) *An Introduction to the Philosophy of Mind*, Palgrave, Basingstoke, p 142.

8 In fact, there are actually quite a few forms of materialism that have been developed over the years. I will not go into an explanation of all of them, but it's interesting that so many versions of materialism have developed – this is in essence because of the problems each version has in explaining the mind. A good review of many of these can be found in John Searle's book, *Mind: A brief introduction*.

9 Some, such as Elkhonon Goldberg, a Clinical Professor of Neurology at New York University School of Medicine, believe that any discussion of consciousness or the mind, implies a return to dualism, which the scientific community has broadly rejected. More on his ideas is available in his writing: Goldberg E (2009) *The New Executive Brain: Frontal lobes in a complex world*, Oxford University Press, Oxford.

10 Vohs, KD and Schooler, JW (2009) 'The value of believing in free will', *Psychological Science*, **19** (1), pp 49–54.

11 Searle, JR (2004) *Mind: A brief introduction*, Oxford University Press, Oxford, p 35.

12 This is the Chinese Room argument put forward by John Searle, ibid.

13 Ibid. This quote from page 37.

14 Schwartz, JM and Begley, S (2002) *The Mind and The Brain: Neuroplasticity and the power of mental force*, Harper Perennial, New York, p 46.

15 Tallis, R (2004) *I Am: A philosophical inquiry into first-person being*, Edinburgh University Press, Edinburgh, p ix.

16 Cockburn, D (2001) *An Introduction to the Philosophy of Mind*, Palgrave, Basingstoke, p 143.

17 Ibid.

18 Damasio, A (revised edn, 1994) *Descartes' Error: Emotion, reason, and the human brain*, Vintage Books, London, p 118.

19 Pert, CB (1997) *Molecules of Emotion: Why you feel the way you feel*, Simon and Schuster, London.

20 Tallis, R (2011) *Aping Mankind: Neuromania, Darwinitis and the misrepresentation of humanity*, Acumen, Durham, p 350.

21 Deep Blue and Garry Kasparov actually played two six-game human–computer chess matches. The first match was played in February 1996, and Kasparov won 4–2, losing one game, drawing two and winning three. A rematch was played in 1997 – this time Deep Blue won $3\frac{1}{2}$–$2\frac{1}{2}$, two wins for Deep Blue, one for the Kasparov and three draws.

22 Rodney A Brooks (1999) *Cambrian Intelligence: The early history of the new AI*, The MIT Press, Cambridge, MA, and Rolf Pfeifer and JC Bongard (2007) *How the Body Shapes the way We Think: A new view of intelligence*, The MIT Press, Cambridge, MA, both cited in: Embodied Intelligence Projects Joint Collaboration Website, 2007. Embodied Intelligence – Mission. [website] Available at: http://www.embodiedintelligence.eu/mission.html [Accessed 26 July 2012].

What does neuroscience have to say about the self?

04

No book on leadership, in today's world, would be complete without significant references to the brain and to neuroscience. A scan of the popular press today shows a considerable number of articles on this subject, which suggests a high level of interest in understanding this complex area. Often there are claims such as *finding the location of love in the brain*, for example, or *the molecule for morality in the brain*, and there is an overall thrust in the articles that we are not far from complete explanation of how human beings work. This suggests that all of who we are as human beings is made clear through understanding our brain activity, which is a materialist view of human beings, as discussed in the previous chapter.

I have, however, set out an alternative view; a way of looking at ourselves where it becomes clear that who we are includes our complete bodily experience of being alive, but it's important to stress that this does not remove the brain from our field of interest. Whilst the whole of who we are is not reducible to brain states, the brain is necessary for having a mind, so it is still important. In fact the brain, and its interactions, interconnections and integration with the body, becomes a field of intense interest and study, as it will give us greater understanding of how we can design and develop deliberate practices that we can use to improve our leadership.

Health warning: how to read neuroscience research

Before we do so however, it is worth making a few caveats and health warnings about how to read and understand brain research. As I mentioned above, many of the newspaper and magazine articles that cover brain research seem to suggest a materialist understanding of the brain. How does this weight of scientific research fit with the ideas about the mind and the brain presented in this book?

In many cases these articles are a long way from the original science. The researcher's work goes through the university's or institution's PR department (who are keen to ensure good PR so the institution gets more research grants), then on to a journalist, and finally through an editor, who may decide that 'Neuroscience proves women can't multitask' makes a good headline, irrespective of what the scientist's research on brain function was really saying about our attention. (The example was purely made-up, by the way.)

The headline, however, is picked up, repeated by management trainers and coaches in seminars, repeated by managers in their offices, and because it has the 'seal of science' behind it, it is unchallengeable – we must accept what this scientific study has 'proven'. Scientists are usually much more careful than journalists about their claims to proof, and the research that would have been at the root of the headline on multitasking probably originally had just a footnote about what this might mean for multitasking. This, however, becomes the focus of the journalistic piece, because it is interesting to a wider audience.

It is therefore important to be sceptical about the claims to knowledge that are made on behalf of neuroscience in the popular press and media.

Neuroscience is, additionally, not one field; it is a collection of fields. The following list is just part of the arena of neuroscience: neuroanatomy, neurochemistry, neuroendocrinology, neurogenetics, neuroimaging, neuroimmunology, neuropathology, neuropsychiatry, neuropsychology and molecular neuroscience, as well as various clinical neurosciences such as neurology and neurosurgery, and so on.[1] Therefore, we must realize than whenever anyone speaks of neuroscience, they are inevitably making a simplification and gener-alization. This is necessary given the size and scope of the field, but we should not forget that it is a simplification.

The step change in neuroscience research that has taken place in the last decades comes from the development of new scanning tech-niques to see and understand brain function. The two most commonly referenced are Magnetic Resonance Imaging (MRI, sometimes also called functional MRI, or fMRI) and Positron Emission Tomography (PET). Through these scans we can develop images of brain functioning whilst people are conducting various tasks.

If the same areas light up on many people's brains as they conduct the same tasks, we can notice some correlations between the task and those parts of the brain, using statistics. Now it is important to note that there is a difference between correlations and causations; if my sports team wins every time I'm wearing a particular pair of under-pants, then we have a correlation, not as many sports fans would like to believe, causation. But as human beings we like to see cause and effect even when it's not there, so we will often want to see causation where it doesn't exist.[2]

The statistical tools through which we measure such correlation need to be considered. Without going into detail on statistics, one of the findings of a 2009 review of neuroscience research published in the top scientific journals was that the statistical tools used to corre-late between activity in the brain and emotional states pretty much guaranteed high levels of correlation. The authors stated:

> To sum up then, we are led to conclude that a disturbingly large, and quite prominent, segment of fMRI research on emotion, personality and social cognition is using seriously defective research methods and producing a profusion of numbers that should not be believed.[3]

All this goes to show the fallibility of scientists. We are all susceptible, like the sports fan with the lucky underpants, to seeing causation when it isn't there. Many claims made that start with 'neuroscience has proven...' are overstated correlations, of which we need to be very wary.

That's all without even looking at the scans themselves, and it turns out there are a range of issues in dealing with these.

Firstly, these scans do not measure neural activity directly. They measure other aspects such as increases in glucose metabolism or blood flow, as markers or proxies for neural activity. So if I was to scan your brain right now, I would get an image that would inform me about increases in glucose consumption or blood flow in your brain, and from that I would infer that neural activity (which I can't detect) had increased. Therefore, we have to begin by understanding that we are not looking at brain activity itself, but at something we believe to correlate to brain activity.

Secondly, as we become more skilled or familiar with a task, the amount of effort expended by the brain goes down. This means that a highly automatic task will generate no detectable signal. You might conclude, therefore, that these highly automatic tasks don't take place in the brain; however, they can be affected by brain injury, so their lack of appearance on the scan does not mean they don't happen in the brain, just that we can't detect them. The majority of our brain's activity is this automatic and undetectable variety, rather than the effortful, detectable work that people are given to do inside a brain scanner, which represents only a small proportion of the brain's activity.

What this means is that if you're really good at maths problems and I give you some maths problems to solve, it will generate little or no signal, whereas someone who is poor at maths will generate a large signal in doing the same problems. The challenge, therefore, is that we only see the peaks of brain activity, but all of the other work that goes on is invisible to us. This is like trying to understand the landscape of a flooded area by looking solely at the peaks above the water – we are only guessing at what lies below the surface.

Thirdly, someone with a higher IQ will have a lower level of brain activity for certain cognitive activities. This is connected to the point above; someone with a higher IQ will be likely to be more practised at cognitive activities, and will therefore use less brain activity in completing activities in the scanner.

Fourthly, when we see a brain region active, from the markers we use, we do not know whether the brain activity may be inhibitory in nature – ie certain parts of the brain will inhibit other areas as part of normal brain functioning.

For example, our brain is divided into two hemispheres, left and right, which are connected by the corpus callosum: a band of neural tissue consisting of an estimated 300–800 million nerve fibres. This allows the two hemispheres to 'communicate' with each other, but it is interesting that the nature of this communication is primarily to inhibit the other hemisphere. Indeed a number of neuroscientists now believe that this the whole point of the corpus callosum.[4] So when we see a brain region active in a scan, is that area active because it is responsible for a certain brain function, or because it is inhibiting another brain function in the other hemisphere?

And, finally, men and women respond differently, left and right handedness may make a difference, and race and age also create differences. Individual cases can also be different because the way we experience the world individually is different. Even the same brain responds differently to the same task depending on the context. For example, if you came into a brain scan to do a series of cognitive tasks after having an argument with your spouse that morning, you would give different results than if you came into the brain scan having received news of a promotion.

In reviewing these experiments we also need to look at how the experiment was set up. One study had low-paid care workers look at pictures of people with intellectual disabilities in order to locate the brain activity associated with unconditional love.[5] This seems rather dubious, as I doubt that all of these care workers would have cared for these individuals without any salary and just out of unconditional love; I doubt that all of them consciously chose care work as a career as an expression of their love; and I doubt that all of them were able to generate unconditional love when looking at these photos. However, on the basis of this study, conclusions were drawn regarding how and where unconditional love is situated in the brain.

This is all to make a simple point. These new scanning techniques do not give us a window into understanding human beings and our minds; it is debatable how much of a window they give us into understanding the brain. They give us some clues and the results they yield need to be understood as tentative. They give us ways of measuring markers of some kind of brain activity, which we need to take great care in interpreting.

In this section I have talked about the challenges of brains scans, the design of the experiments for brain scanning and dubious statistical analyses, as well as the tendency for articles on the subject to interpret the findings to make them more interesting to a wider audience. From this you may be left feeling depressed about neuroscience research. However this is not my aim.

There is a significant amount of good work going on in the fields of neuroscience that is producing knowledge and understanding through the hard work and effort of many researchers, and is progressing at a rapid rate. There are powerful and useful conclusions coming from this work, and the most valuable work draws together conclusions from across four different streams of research:

- combinations of studies, using multiple types of scans, rather than relying on single experiments in one type of scanner;

- knowledge that comes from those who have brain injuries (such as strokes or head traumas), and understanding what brain functions remain and which are damaged;

- reports from the internal experience of people with brain injuries – what they experience as easy or difficult after the injury;

- studies of animal brains (as our evolutionary ancestors) to see what conclusions can be developed.

This is a complex and demanding field in which many of the things we thought we knew 10–20 years ago are defunct. It is also continuing to evolve extremely rapidly, so that much of what we think we know now will probably go the same way.

Whilst there are reports in the media that appear to show evidence for a materialistic interpretation of us as humans, I hope that the preceding section will provide an antidote to some of those conclusions. As always, with all research across all fields, we need to look beyond the conclusions drawn and understand the experiment and its underpinnings so that we may understand how to interpret the conclusions.

Growing a brain: understanding brain development

So neuroscience when over-simplified and poorly analysed can lead us to some misunderstandings. However, that does not mean that all neuroscience is to be ignored or discounted. Indeed, when we move beyond the simplified media version of neuroscience and explore in more depth, there is much of value to take from the field, and it will inform us in understanding how the brain and body work together, and how we can use this to develop our leadership. I make no great claims to proven knowledge in this section, but rather aim to look where the mass of evidence currently appears to be pointing.

It makes sense to start at the start, with brain development, and explore how that happens as this will give us a good foundation for under-standing the brain.[6] A new born child's brain contains somewhere in the region of 100 billion brain cells, called neurons. If we take a conserva-tive estimate of 1,000 for the number of connections, or synapses, each neuron has then we have a total of around 100 trillion connections. (In reality this number reaches much higher and is pruned during life.)

How does this happen? How do we develop so many neurons, each so well connected to the correct other neurons, that we develop a brain that works, and that doesn't accidentally wire the eyes to the part of the brain responsible for smell, and have us smell something every time we see a colour?

Well genes would be an easy and obvious answer, but it's also lack-ing. We have around 35,000 different genes, about half of which are involved in the brain, and even if each of these carried an instruction for one connection we wouldn't get very far. So it seems that genes do not provide a wiring map for the brain. They do, however, seem to encode the various stages of brain development that seem to be common across us all.

It turns out that the foetal brain operates in a very different way. It over-produces both neurons and synapses. At its peak the foetal brain has around 200 billion neurons, but not all of them make it and those that fail to form good synaptic connections vanish, leaving the new born infant with 100 billion.

Each neuron at the height of its forming connections can create up to 15,000 connections, which are then pruned down, on the basis of whether or not they are used. Jeffrey Schwartz, a research professor of psychiatry at UCLA, describes this process:

> Which synapses remain, and which wither away, depends on whether they carry any traffic. If they do not, then like bus routes that attract no customers they go out of business. By one estimate, approximately 20 billion synapses are pruned every day between childhood and early adolescence.[7]

So we are born with brains that are over-wired, and through time we strengthen some connections through using them, while others wither away through disuse.[8]

This also gives us a clue to brain functioning throughout our lives. Until recent time this plasticity (the ability of the brain to change) was thought to be limited to the child brain. But more research shows that the adult brain has this adaptability also.

In 1949 Donald Hebb suggested a process for the efficient transmission of signals across synapses (connections) between two neurons (brain cells). He suggested that over time, through repeated activation, both neurons would change, whereby one neuron was more likely to activate the other. This has been summarized as, 'cells which fire together, wire together,' and Hebb's ideas have been held up by subsequent neuroscience research.

This is a basic description of the process of learning in the brain, and is the other side of the child brain development discussed above; that addressed the pruning of unused synapses like unused bus routes going out of business, whereas this describes the strengthening of used synapses, like popular bus routes where extra buses and bus lanes have been laid on to speed up travel across the neurons and synapses.

Professor Paul Bach-y-Rita, an American neuroscientist conducted some of the early research in this field. His father had a stroke in 1958, and Paul treated him so that he was able to lead a normal life, despite the opinion of his doctors that this would be impossible. When his father died an autopsy was conducted that showed that his stroke had been a major one, damaging a large portion of his brain stem. The fact that he made such a sufficient recovery suggests that the brain had reorganized itself, providing some of the early evidence for neuroplasticity.

Today there is a considerable weight of evidence for neuro-plasticity, as mentioned in Chapter 1. We noted there how London taxi drivers develop a larger hippocampus, a brain structure presumed to be critical for learning and memory, including spatial memory,[9] and how volunteers trained in a three-ball juggling routine for three months were found to have a considerable increase in the amount of grey matter in the temporal lobes of both hemispheres and the left parietal lobe. Interestingly, when the training was then discontinued for three months, later scans revealed a reduction in grey matter in these regions.[10]

This, and considerable other research, provides important evidence for how the brain operates. Like muscular tissues, the brain develops through use, and these tissues will reduce with disuse.

So how does this happen? There are three main mechanisms for this brain development. In Chapter 2, I have already referenced one of these mechanisms, the development of myelin on neurons. This speeds up signal transmission through neurons and changes our brain when we engage in deliberate practice. Like in the juggling example above, when we stop practising the myelin breaks down.

Another way in which this happens is through a re-organization of the neural circuitry, and this is proposed as the mechanism for the change in our London taxi drivers' brains. This means that our brain structures can change in response to our experiences as adults, through the creation of new synaptic connections. So not only are we pruning unused connections as we get older; we can also create new ones through our experience.

Finally, and this is a relatively recent discovery in brain science, we have neurogenesis, the creation of new neurons in the adult brain. This was observed in the brains of other species, but in human brains only from around 1998, when Swedish neuroscientist Peter Eriksson 'demonstrated that the human hippocampus continues to acquire new neurons well into adulthood.[11] Whether this takes place more widely in the brain is still the subject of debate, but there is a long list of brain regions that are being studied for this phenomenon.

That the brain is developable and changeable seems clear from this research. What is also clear is that this development can be something we choose. We can choose to learn all the streets of London, or to juggle a 3-ball routine.[12] Neuroscience researchers, Merzenich and deCharms state:

> Experience coupled with attention leads to physical changes in the structure and future functioning of the nervous system... Moment by moment we choose and sculpt how our ever-changing minds will work, we choose who we will be in the next moment, in a very real sense and the choices are left embodied in a physical form on our material selves.[13]

This is an important and profound conclusion. Our choices can cause our brain structures and nervous systems to change and, therefore, the entire brain–body system. Choice and attention (of which I will say more later) prove to be key to being able to change, and we can choose who we will be moment by moment.

The only thing I would add to this quote is 'or not...' I add in this phrase because moment by moment we can – and often do – not choose. If we don't pay attention we will not be making such choices and will not be shaping our brains. It requires willpower and effort to do so. This is not a statement of what is morally good or bad; just think about the last time you drove, or when you got up this morning. Did you then bring your attention to these moments and choose who you would be in the next moment? Probably not, even though it was possible.

And this brings us to the big challenge of personal change – it is possible but it requires a lot of effort. We can change the patterns that we have learned in our brains, nervous systems and entire bodies, but this requires work.[14] This ties into my conclusions around the development of leadership in Chapter 2. There we saw that deliberate practice, where we practise on the edge of our ability, is key to getting better at something, and here we see how doing this actually changes our entire nervous system.

I entitled this section 'growing a brain', and I started with our more normal interpretation of this, which was around foetal and child brain development. However I have attempted to show in this section that each one of us is, in actual fact, continually growing our brain on the basis of our choices and how we direct our attention. The power of attention is something we will come back to in future chapters.

How the brain–body unit functions

In the last chapter I concluded that we needed to understand who we are, as being not some thinking self in another realm (Descartes' dualism), or as being just the state of our brains (materialism), but as a whole self including the bodily experience of being alive. We have started to understand the brain and how it can change and develop, but we need to go further and understand how the brain and body interact as a system and how this contributes to our actions in the world.

If we look at some connections between the mind and the body, there are some that we are probably all familiar with, to some degree.

Not long ago, I came across a newspaper article addressing the issue of how to develop focus, concentration and memory.[15] The first piece of advice was physical exercise, which the authors stated would improve both memory and concentration. Similar articles appear regularly in the popular press. Perhaps this is not surprising to you, as many articles will emphasize similar ideas; however, it shows that what we do with our bodies (exercise) impacts mental capacities, usually associated with the brain, such as memory and concentration.

Looking at things from the other side, the concept of psychosomatic illnesses is well known, where back pain, ulcers, high blood pressure can be connected to our mental state, for example our levels of stress. Here mental factors, usually associated with the brain, have an impact on the body.

So the relationship between the mind and the body is an intricate two-way process. Research has, of course, been conducted on these processes. Professor Bruce McEwen at Rockefeller University has studied how hormones affect the brain. He found that the hypothalamus, the region in the brain controlling hormones, sends a signal through the blood to the glands that release hormones. These hormones then affect the entire body (heart, lungs, etc) as well as triggering a feedback mechanism with the hypothalamus, which will stop hormone production when it reaches a certain level. In addition, and importantly, the hormones also affect other parts of the brain, impacting on our brain functions.

This is an interesting process. Why does the brain not send a signal to itself, rather than sending signals through the body? It is only by understanding the brain and body as an integrated system, that this makes sense. As an integrated system, why would the hormones not affect the brain? This has caused John Coates, a neuroscience researcher (and former investment banker) to state:

> In fact, it may be scientifically more accurate, although semantically difficult, to stop speaking in terms of brain and body at all, as if they were separable, and to speak instead of a whole-person response to events.[16]

So how does this integration affect us in terms of real-world issues? The work of neuroscientist Antonio Damasio is crucial to understanding this.

What was your most embarrassing moment? Think back to it and remember it – how does that feel? Chances are that doesn't feel too pleasant; just thinking back to the memory of that experience is likely to cause you to feel the pain of it again. There is an emotional component to this, and also a bodily experience – just in the memory of this you will probably feel a whole series of physical sensations including, perhaps, the desire to make yourself smaller and disappear from the embarrassment.

If I think back to an experience early in my career, I was delivering the first run of a leadership development programme for a client that I had been part of designing, and a session I delivered went wrong. The session had been shortened repeatedly but never redesigned, and numerous people gave me advice on how I should run it just before I started the session. On reflection this advice was probably unhelpful for me, and I went in trying to do the session very quickly, with a muddled up series of ideas on how to run it. The props I was using for the session didn't work, and whilst I delivered the session and got through the material, the internal experience was horrible, as I knew and the participants knew it was not working.

Even now when I think about it, I feel a hole in the pit of my stomach, my body collapses a little as my chest caves in on itself, and I feel physically the feelings of embarrassment.

This is an example of what Damasio refers to as the 'somatic marker hypothesis'.[17] There is substantial research that our memories are certainly enhanced by an emotional component,[18] but Damasio goes further with this. According to him, each event we store in our memories comes connected with a series of bodily sensations that we felt when we went through it for the first time. We then re-experience these sensations when we are in a similar situation, and this helps us to decide what action to take in that moment. For example, if your embarrassment happened through speaking up, you may avoid situations where you have to speak up. For me, when I had to deliver that session again I was haunted by the memories, and the very real sensations and feelings from the first run of the session, and it made it very difficult for me to be powerful and credible in delivering that session – in fact I avoided it for as long I could. Only by engaging with this at the bodily level was I able to move beyond the somatic markers that had been laid down from my first experience and generate something different – but more of that later.

As another example, when you watch a comedy show such as *The Office* that relies on your own experience of embarrassment, you will often cringe in response – I know I do, and rarely watch it because of the response it generates in me. In those moments you feel the cringing as a bodily response, and it's real for you. For that reason some love it, and some hate it – our somatic markers create and guide this response.

So what is a somatic marker? One way to describe it is as an emotional memory. When we are in complex and potentially dangerous situations we don't have time to reason and think through all the possible options to make a decision. So we have been provided with an evolutionary short cut. When the brain recognizes a situation that is similar to previous ones, it bypasses the reasoning process and triggers the emotional memory, causing us to feel the emotional response once more. It acts as an alarm system to move us away from negative responses, and can also encourage us to move towards positive ones. Damasio also suggests that this may be the neural mechanism for intuition.[19]

Damasio and his colleagues worked with a number of people who had damage to parts of the brain that receive and integrate information from the body. It was possible for these individuals to have all the theoretical knowledge and answer all questions directed to them perfectly, but be completely unable to master things in practice. As Damasio states:

> Personal and social decisions are fraught with uncertainty and have an impact upon survival, directly or indirectly. Thus they require a vast repertoire of knowledge concerning the external world and the world within the organism.[20]

These people were completely unable to deal with complex decisions about personal decisions and the social and political dynamics of relationships, despite in many cases having very high IQs. Part of the challenge these people experienced was being able to know what they wanted. They had good ideas and could weigh up the pros and cons of any decision, but couldn't figure out what they wanted at the end of the day. Damasio relates a story of trying to arrange an appointment with one of his patients who had this condition, who weighed up the pros and cons of different possible dates for a considerable time, but who could not come to a conclusion independently. Part of what this shows is that we know what we want because of how we feel, not because of how we weigh up rational thoughts.

Damasio's theory shows us how the body relates to our decision-making processes. The kind of situations we face in personal and social decision making involve a huge degree of complexity and many diverse factors. Were we to try and reason these situations from start to finish taking into account all of the different factors, it would take an inordinate amount of time.

For example, imagine sitting in a meeting where someone directly challenges the manager. In that moment so much happens – we often talk of being able to cut the air with a knife because of the tension that is experienced by all. In understanding what has happened and how to respond, we need to take into account all the range of social relationships in the room, as well as the group dynamics – the patterns of relationship that play out when the group gets together. There is politics to be aware of, there is the validity of the challenge, there is how the manager has historically responded to such challenges, there are alliances and allegiances within the group, and the personal perspectives of each individual in the room.

Trying to assess how to respond could take a good hour of reflection and consideration, but we don't have that time; each person has to respond in that moment. So how do we do this? Damasio explains that we do this by tapping into the felt experience of being in that situation in previous moments, and knowing in that moment how we responded. We bypass the reasoning process and 'go with our gut feelings'.

Going with our guts

So it seems that going with our gut feelings is more than just a metaphor or a common phrase; it's actually what we do. Indeed there are, in fact, more neurons in the human gut than in the whole of a cat's brain.[21] The gut is under the control of what is termed the enteric nervous system, which unlike other nerves in the body can act independently of the brain, and is one of the only systems to continue functioning if all connections to the brain are severed.[22] So how accurate is it? Can we trust it? How do we work with it? And can we train it, given that it's so essential to making decisions quickly?

The psychologist Daniel Kahneman, who won a Nobel Prize in Economics along with Amos Tversky for their groundbreaking work on behavioural economics, has written a fascinating book that addresses some of these questions. He defines a System 1 and System 2 in our thinking processes. System 1 is the automatic processes that are driven through the body – in the words we have used here, our somatic markers. System 2 is the conscious thought processes that we engage through effort and attention – in the words we have used here, a reasoning process. Kahneman states:

> The defining feature of System 2... is that its operations are effortful, and one of its main characteristics is laziness, a reluctance to invest more effort than is strictly necessary. As a consequence, the thoughts and actions that System 2 believes it has chosen are often guided by the figure at the centre of the story, System 1.[23]

Thinking things through carefully is effortful and time consuming, and in the hectic world of organizations today, how much time do we really have to do this? Mainly we have to react, and quickly, to e-mails, events, situations and challenges. In this context we often respond with System 1, which is our somatic markers; later, if someone challenges us, our System 2 will believe it has guided our actions, and post-rationalize a reason as to why we responded in that way.

This is why we often hear about how people post-rationalize their decisions. They are guided by the more automatic decision-making process, through the body, and then the reasoning process tries to take ownership of and rationalize the decision later.

Have you ever asked someone why they did something, and have them respond that it just felt like the right thing to do? This is the somatic marker, and it will just feel like the right thing to do, whether it was logically and rationally the right thing to do or not. Often if you press this person for a more logical response, you will then hear a logical rationalization for why they did what they did, but this is often a post-rationalization. An argument can often occur at this point as to the logic and rationality of the action or decision, but the real argument is with the somatic marker, not with the rationalization.

When working with a group recently, I asked group members about their actions at a particular moment, and they responded with a justification using information that hadn't come to light until after the actions had occurred. When I let them know this, they generated another explanation, and another, before being willing to look at the automatic and impulsive nature of their response. We like to believe in our rational thought processes, but that may not be what is actually going on.

Does this mean that I am now saying that we don't have free will – that we are guided by automatic responses and later post-rationalize them in a way that allows us to believe we have free will? No! Let's be clear about this – I am not making that claim. We will always have choice; it's just a question of whether we are paying attention, which will influence whether we see that choice and make use of it.

My claim here is two-fold. Firstly, that we can slow things down and be aware of our automatic responses and have choice about them (more about this later); and secondly, we can educate and train our automatic responses so that they are more useful to us.

And we can, if we choose not to become aware of our somatic markers, not train them and not pay attention to our automatic responses, live our lives without a lot of choice. In this mode we live our lives through the somatic markers laid down in our personal histories, repeating our past into the future. This is something I see regularly: people who move jobs and organizations four or five times and always have an awful boss are for me classic examples. There is one common factor in every situation, which is that person, and I am always left wondering about somatic markers that have been laid down in the past, in relation to authority figures.

In his book, Kahneman describes a collaboration with another researcher, Gary Klein,[24] who studies decision making through somatic markers – specifically looking at where it works. Kahneman has repeatedly examined where this mode of decision making lets us down in our thinking.

Klein had examples of fire-fighters, who knew instinctively to leave a building seconds before it collapsed, or chess masters who glimpse a chess board mid-way through a game and can produce the response required to win.[25] All of this happens in such a short time that one cannot deliberately and with effort use a process of reasoning to think through all possible options and come up with a reasoned answer – another process is going on to enable these people to know what to do. In fact, in his research Klein discovered that these people did not generate multiple responses to the situation at all; they generated one possible response, which proved to be the correct one.

By comparison Kahneman, in his research, shows how our automatic systems prove to be very poor at understanding statistics and probabilities, and how much of our intuitive judgement gets us into trouble. In these instances we need to use a process of reasoning to get a sensible and useful response, irrespective of the time that might take. So who's right?

What they uncovered was that they are both right. Our more automatic responses can be both invaluable, and also useless, depending on how we have educated and trained them, and on the environment we are operating in.

One of the key things required for our somatic marker responses to be successful is an environment with a certain degree of stability or predictability, although it doesn't need to be a simple predictable pattern. John Coates gives an example of an experiment in which participants were asked to predict the location of a cross on a computer screen that would appear and then disappear, only to return somewhere else. He states:

> Unbeknownst to the participants, the location of the cross followed
> a rule, so it could be predicted. However, the rule was so complicated
> that no participant could formulate it explicitly. Yet, despite their
> inability to say what this rule was, people got better at predicting
> the location of the cross. In other words participants were learning
> the rule pre-consciously.[26]

In another experiment, Damasio had participants pick cards from four decks, which either won them or lost them money. Two decks had smaller wins and losses – making or losing around $50 to $100 – but choosing from these, over time, would make a profit. The other two decks had higher amounts – making or losing from $500 to $1,000 – but choosing from these, over time, would make a loss.

Of course, over time participants discovered the pattern, but what Damasio realized, was that participants' behaviour changed before they knew why. They could not state why they had changed, but they had. Damasio was also able to identify a signal from the participants' bodies that guided their learning. Participants' skin conductance (the electrical conductivity of the skin, which increases with the amount of sweat on the skin) began to spike when they contemplated the more risky decks. Their bodies were responding to that risk with a somatic response – more sweating – and this response guided them to the safer decks.[27]

So we need an environment in which it is possible to make predictions, and our intuitive system may be able to pick up patterns, and guide our behaviours, more easily than our conscious process of reasoning.

A second requirement for somatic markers to be successful is practice and feedback. If this is starting to sound familiar then this is good, as this is exactly what we explored in Chapter 2. To become good at something requires practice, but this is a more nuanced view. What we're educating is not just our process of reasoning with models and theories with which we can think through situations, but rather we're educating our somatic markers, our intuitive capacity, which can respond to situations much more quickly.

In the case of these fire-fighters, they had quick responses to their intuition – the house collapse or not – so their feedback was immediate. In chess players, again they have a quick and immediate feedback – they win or lose the game. For leadership it is rarely so easy. So much of this is in the personal and social domain, and we can never know what would have happened had we used a different strategy. The impact of our decision may also be affected by a huge range of other issues, from competitors, government regulations, other departments, team members arriving or leaving among others. Here it is much more difficult to have any clear sense of feedback on what happens, so developing this clear sense of expertise becomes more difficult – although definitely not impossible.

Kahneman concludes that in an environment where prediction is possible, and if people have practised and received feedback, they can often use the somatic markers incredibly successfully. However, his book is littered with examples of 'experts' who have not received clear and immediate feedback on their decisions, or who have not practised sufficiently, or who are in environments that are not predictable, and who use their somatic markers to make very poor decisions.

From somatic markers to the shape of the self

Throughout our lives we have a massive range of experiences. Some positive, some negative. Some joyful, others embarrassing, humiliating or saddening. We learn from these experiences, and a big part of how we learn is through carrying the felt sense in our memories of how we experienced that moment. This means that when we recall such moments, we can feel the joy or humiliation as a set of physical sensations in our bodies.

When we encounter something in the future that reminds us of some particular experience, the felt sense arises again, and that feeling guides our actions. Without the ability to feel this, we are actually limited in our ability to take actions and make choices in the world, as Damasio showed.

As we go through our lives and we collect these experiences, we develop into who we are – our personality, which is the pattern of emotional, attitudinal and behavioural responses we typically portray. We develop our personality through our body. As we develop somatic markers, we develop responses to those markers, and then in future situations we feel the somatic marker and repeat the response. In this way we practise those responses continually, until we become expert in them – we become expert in being us. The actions we then repeatedly take are driven by the somatic markers and emotions we feel; this then sculpts our brain and nervous system as neurons fire together, connections gets strengthened and myelin is laid down on neurons.

The challenge is that not all of these patterns will be useful to us. They will shape us in particular ways, and will therefore leave some actions less available to us than others. Leadership involves stepping up in the world and making yourself more visible – if you grew up in an environment where your safety was threatened, you may have had real experiences where being visible was not safe; then the experience of being visible will bring you back to the physical sensations of danger. You will experience those sensations in your body, just as if you were actually being physically threatened, and your actions will be limited as a result. You may have been embarrassed when speaking up and now feel those sensations whenever you are in a situation where you are expected to speak up.

The reality is that we all have our own version of this: lessons learned that stay with us through the somatic markers that have been laid down, plus the sculpting of our brains and nervous systems, through practice, leading to patterns of behaviours and our personality. This is why behaviour is so difficult to change. It may be rationally obvious, but that's a process of reasoning, which is not how we actually operate.

Some psychologists (although by no means all) believe that personality is largely unchangeable throughout our lives. I believe this lies in the fact that psychology has often appealed to a process of reasoning to generate change, rather than dealing with the somatic markers that so often drive our responses. Personality is difficult to change – it requires significant effort and we will never engage in a wholesale change of who we are, but we can learn to deal with those aspects of our selves that do not serve us in our leadership.

To do this we need to become aware of and work with somatic markers and patterns that we have developed, and create new deliberate practices, along with clear feedback, to enable us to improve in our leadership. In addition to this we need to develop clear mechanisms for feedback, through others who can act as coaches, mentors and teachers to enable us to develop clarity around the impact of what we do, especially when this is unlikely to be clear and obvious for us. Finally we also need to get better at slowing down and starting to see our automatic processes, so that we can have greater choice over them, and we can know when we need to use a more thoughtful process of reasoning to arrive at a better result.

Having set a clear context for embodied leadership, understanding how to do the things listed above is what I will explore during the rest of this book.

Recommended reading

If you are interested in reading more about the ideas that sit behind this chapter then I recommend:

The Social Animal: A story of how success happens, by David Brooks.

Thinking, Fast and Slow, by Daniel Kahneman.

Sources of Power: How people make decisions, by Gary Klein.

The Mind and the Brain: Neuroplasticity and the power of mental force, by Jeffrey M Schwartz and Sharon Begley.

Descartes' Error: Emotion, reason, and the human brain, by Antonio Damasio.

If you wish to explore neuroscience research more deeply, then I would also recommend:

A General Theory of Love, by Thomas Lewis, Fari Amini and Richard Lannon.

My Stroke of Insight: A brain scientist's personal journey, by Jill Bolte Taylor.

The Feeling of What Happens: Body, emotion and the making of consciousness, by Antonio Damasio.

The Master and His Emissary: The divided brain and the making of the Western world, by Iain McGilchrist.

Self Comes to Mind: Constructing the conscious brain, by Antonio Damasio.

The New Executive Brain: Frontal lobes in a complex world, by Elkhonon Goldberg.

Notes

1 Tallis, R (2011) *Aping Mankind: Neuromania, Darwinitis and the misrepresentation of humanity*, Durham: Acumen Publishing, pp 15–16.

2 Daniel Kahneman, a Nobel Laureate in Economics, explores why this is the case in his excellent book, *Thinking Fast and Slow*.

3 Vul, E, Harris, C, Winkielman, P and Pashler, H (2009) 'Puzzlingly high correlations in fMRI studies of emotion, personality and social cognition', *Perspectives on Psychological Science*, 4 (3), pp 274–90.

4 For a wider discussion of this issue, see McGilchrist, I (2009) *The Master and his Emissary: The divided brain and the making of the Western world*, Yale University Press: New Haven.

5 Tallis, R (2011) *Aping Mankind: Neuromania, Darwinitis and the misrepresentation of humanity*, Durham, Acumen Publishing, p 74.

6 I am indebted to Jeffrey Schwartz and Sharon Begley and their book, *The Mind and The Brain: Neuroplasticity and the power of mental force*, for describing this process. This is done in much greater detail than here, in the chapter, 'Birth of a brain'.

7 Schwartz, JM and Begley, S (2002) *The Mind and The Brain: Neuroplasticity and the power of mental force*, Harper Perennial, New York, p 117.

8 This is why the childhood brain is much more resilient to brain injury than the adult brain – it has more connections available, and can find ways to rewire broken connections easily.

9 Goldberg, E (2009) *The New Executive Brain: Frontal lobes in a complex world*, Oxford University Press, Oxford, p 238.

10 Ibid, p 239.

11 Ibid, p 235.

12 Schwartz, JM and Begley, S (2002) *The Mind and The Brain*, pp 117–18.

13 Merzenich and deCharms (1996) cited in Schwartz, JM and Begley, S (2002) *The Mind and The Brain*, p 339.

14 Schwartz, JM and Begley, S (2002) *The Mind and The Brain*, p 254.

15 Helsingin Sanomat (2011) *Helsinki National Newspaper*, 31 January.

16 Coates, J (2012) *The Hour Between Dog and Wolf: Risk-taking, gut feelings and the biology of boom and bust*, Fourth Estate, London, p 31.

17 See Damasio's book *Descartes' Error* for a full description and exploration of the somatic marker hypothesis.

18 See the chapter 'Memory and emotion' by Elizabeth Kensinger and Daniel Schacter in *Handbook of Emotions* (2010) ed M Lewis and JM Haviland-Jones, Guilford Press, New York.

19 Damasio, A (2006) *Descartes' Error*, Vintage, London, revised edn pp 187–89.

20 Ibid, p 84.

21 Watzke, H (2010) 'The brain in your gut', TED Talks [online] http://www.ted.com/talks/lang/en/heribert_watzke_the_brain_in_your_gut.html (accessed 4 August 2012).

22 Coates, J (2012) *The Hour Between Dog and Wolf*, p 104.

23 Kahneman, D (2011) *Thinking Fast and Slow*, Penguin (Allen Lane), London, p 31.

24 Ibid, Chapter 22.

25 Klein, G (1998) *Sources of Power: How people make decisions*, MIT Press, Cambridge, MA.

26 Coates, J (2012) *The Hour Between Dog and Wolf*, p 84.

27 Damasio, A (2006) *Descartes' Error*.

05 **Embodying our selves**

Up until this point I have mainly taken you through a different way of understanding leadership, who we are – the self, and how we develop the self. This chapter will provide a bridge between this understanding and the rest of the book, which will be more focused on what you can do to further your development as a leader.

In the last chapter I made a claim that we can become aware of, work with and change our somatic markers, so that we can develop ourselves and, for the purposes of this book, our leadership. So how do we begin to do this? How do we develop awareness of these markers? How do we have more choice over our actions, and how do we begin to change some of these that are less helpful for us?

How somatic markers shape us

I want to make clear that many of our somatic markers are helpful to us. They give us a sense of what it is to have good manners in our culture, without many of us being able to list all of these rules. They often guide our behaviour at the pre-conscious level. Over time we have practised the behaviours that these markers guide us so much that we no longer notice them – they are unconscious to us. Shaking someone's hand, bowing or kissing on the cheeks as a greeting – what we have habitually done is a polite habit we hold deeply so that it's just normal. It's only when we encounter something different that we notice our somatic markers, as it doesn't feel quite as comfortable to us. So somatic markers are not good or a bad; they are just how we go about learning at a deep level.

Now when you are uncomfortable in life, say you are too hot or cold, what do you do? You might adjust the thermostat or add or remove layers of clothing. Rarely will you just sit there and be uncomfortable. Exactly the same process ensues with the discomfort we feel around our somatic markers. If I feel uncomfortable emotionally, I will change something so as to feel more comfortable, such as withdrawing from a potentially embarrassing situation. To understand this fully we need to understand what happens to us when we experience an emotion.

The common-sense view is that when we experience an emotion, for example joy, we have the emotional experience, which then we express through our musculature – smiling face, leaping for joy and so on. This common-sense view, it turns out, is most probably wrong. Current research suggests that actually the purpose of the muscular movements may not be to express emotions so much as to generate them.

Neuroscience researcher, John Coates, states:

> It also turns out that our muscles play an intimate role in
> our emotional expressions. When we are angry or sad or elated
> our posture changes, and muscles in one part of our body tense
> while others relax. The muscular nervous system, moreover,
> is fast enough to keep up with, even to cause, our fluctuating
> emotional feelings.[1]

At some level you already perhaps know this. If someone is depressed they tend use their flexor muscles, which contract the body, rather than their extensor muscles, which extend the body, and this causes them to cave in on themselves, make themselves smaller. They may slouch, bend their back, and cave in at the chest, and we know that just standing differently will cause that person to feel different. Perhaps no one can explain this better than Charlie Brown!

Some of the most interesting research in the field of emotional expression has been the work of Paul Ekman, who has built upon one of the less-known works of Darwin. After writing *The Origin of Species*, which gave us the principle of evolution, Darwin wrote another book, entitled *The Expression of the Emotions in Man and Animals*. In this book Darwin looks at the way emotions are

PEANUTS © 1960 Peanuts Worldwide LLC. Dist. By UNIVERSAL UCLICK. Reprinted with permission. All rights reserved

expressed physically through facial expressions, and argues that these are shared by all humans, linking this to our evolutionary heritage. The anthropologist, Margaret Mead, disagreed with Darwin and felt that emotions were expressed in our faces in culturally specific ways.[2]

Ekman picked up on this research, and went to remote tribes in Papua New Guinea, and saw that people there ascribed the same emotions to photos of faces of Americans that had been ascribed in the United States. He has continued his research around the world, and there are now five emotions that are agreed across scientists to be universal in their expression, as well as another three that are likely to be universal, although research is still being conducted.

The five that are agreed to be universal across researchers are:

- anger;
- fear;

- sadness/anguish;
- disgust;
- happiness.

The three that are likely to be universal, are:

- surprise;
- contempt;
- excitement.

Part of the research, which is most relevant to this chapter, is that when Ekman or his volunteers spent time practising different facial expressions, they would begin to experience the emotion concerned. Ekman then had volunteers move particular muscles or engage in exercises that would compose an emotional expression (such as holding pencils in their teeth in such a way as to create a smile), without the volunteer being told what that expression was, and then he tested his volunteers for their emotional state. By moving their facial muscles, these volunteers came to experience the emotional state portrayed on their face. (This brings up the interesting aside that, if emotions begin with the muscular changes in the body, then those who have Botox, which limits the movement of facial muscles, may limit their ability to feel a full range of emotions.)

The body, and the face in particular, turns out to be extremely important in how we read other people. It turns out that whilst we can lie verbally, we're very poor at doing so physically. In fact, we could go so far as to say the body doesn't lie. In Ekman's work it was found that emotions can be expressed on the face as 'micro-expressions', lasting only milliseconds.[3]

Some of us will be able to pick up on these micro-expressions pre-consciously; as for the participants in last chapter's card game where two decks of cards won money and two lost money on average, our body will spot the pattern even if we are not consciously aware. However, the ability to see these emotions accurately and consciously can be learnt, and Ekman has set up online training tools to do this.[4] These tools can be used repeatedly as a practice to develop your competence in this arena, and this is a practice I recommend working through on a quarterly basis to improve your ability to read the emotions of others.

Overtime, what happens is that the pattern of our continued emotions tends to create lines on our faces. The face of someone who has laughed a lot is different from the face of someone who has frowned a lot. This is perhaps what made US President Abraham Lincoln, reject a man for his cabinet because: 'I don't like his face.' 'But the poor man isn't responsible for his face,' responded his advocate. 'Every man over 40 is responsible for his face,' countered Lincoln.[5] The patterns of emotions that we experience through our life will be influenced by our somatic markers, so after 40 perhaps we are responsible for the contours of our faces.

But our emotions don't just create lines on our faces. Through our somatic markers, emotions create the shape of who we are. When we create a somatic marker, we create an emotional memory of, for example, the experience of being embarrassed when we spoke up, because we were laughed at or said something that wasn't taken seriously. Depending on the strength of that memory – either if we experienced it very strongly, or it was repeated over time – then we will re-experience that emotional memory in any situation that has even a slight resonance with the original one. That emotion may guide our actions, often so that we avoid the potential embarrassment by, for example, pulling away and withdrawing. We become emotionally uncomfortable, and take action to become more comfortable. Over time, as we practise the withdrawing and not speaking up, this can become the dominant feature of our personality, and our body. This shape becomes who we are.

So what shape will this be? It will probably be the shape of us sitting back, perhaps collapsing in on ourselves a little, not speaking, and watching for safety. Some people may perceive it as shyness or lack of confidence. Let's be clear, however, that different people will respond slightly differently to this stimulus, depending on how they are responding to the somatic marker, and this may look a little different in each case, although we can speak about general patterns.

Let me give another example.[6] Imagine a young child on its way out of nursery/ kindergarten, moving towards its mother, the object of love and safety. In the next garden along, there's an old dog, which is a bit grumpy, so the teachers have warned the children to stay away from it, as it might bite them. For this child, this has produced a fear of the dog.

As the child runs towards its mother, the dog starts barking. Now the mother is on her way from work, and has multiple concerns and commitments running in her head, and doesn't even hear the dog, but the child does, and starts to cry. The mother picks up the child and comforts him, trying to find out what is wrong. The child can't express what is wrong, and the dog keeps barking so the child keeps crying.

This goes on for some time and eventually the mother, needing to get on with her day, says: 'If you don't stop crying, I'll have to put you down.' The child keeps crying, and eventually the mother puts him down. (This in no way means an attack on mothers by the way – this is just to illustrate a point.)

In this moment the child is separated from safety, in what it perceives as a moment of danger, and so he learns at a deep level that he made the wrong move. He wants to reconnect with his mother, so what does he do? To stop crying, he tightens on the diaphragm, brings the breathing up into his upper chest, tightens the jaw and throat, and tightens the eyes, which stops the expression of the emotion, and as we have also learnt, the feeling of the emotion (by changing the musculature). Now his chin will wobble a little, and he may quietly sob a little, but the big emotional outburst is contained.

The mother then picks up the child, consoles him again, reinforcing the message that crying was the wrong move, and that holding in the emotion was the correct one – here there is safety from danger. If this is repeated on an ongoing basis, or happens at a particularly significant moment, then 40 years later you have the man who hasn't cried in 40 years (not uncommon in our culture, especially for men where messages such as 'big boys don't cry' are reinforced).

This man will have a long-term pattern of tightening the diaphragm, shallow breathing, holding the jaw tightly, and tightening the eyes, all of which are required to not feel and express that pattern of emotions. This is how a somatic marker moves from an emotional memory to the shape we take in the world. This is the shape that the person will develop, and is how he will hold himself, initially when he feels emotion, but eventually as he practises this it will just become a normal way of being.

If this man then becomes a manager making others redundant, then he will be uncomfortable with the emotion of the experience. He cannot be comfortable with his own emotions, and when he is being called on to empathize with another's he will be unable to. Empathy ultimately requires his ability to feel the same emotion that he has spent a lifetime restraining. He may then be accused of being brutal or unfeeling in the process.

The impact of somatic markers

The reality is that all somatic markers shape us, in both helpful and unhelpful ways. If, in my history, I was always rewarded for speaking up and never embarrassed, it may be for me that there is a somatic marker related to a feeling of happiness associated with speaking up. This may mean that I always contribute in meetings, and that I always share my ideas, which may serve me well. It may also mean that I speak first when I have little to contribute, or when it would be more appropriate for others to do so. Again, as with all somatic markers, these aspects of our behaviour happen before deliberate thought and choice and are the patterns we play out, and there is a physical shape associated with this pattern.

Our culture is passed on this way. We learn at a young age what is appropriate and inappropriate, but if asked to describe our culture we would have difficulty. The somatic markers aren't a set of rules we learnt in our rational neo-cortex (the most recent part of our brain, which allows us to deal with abstract concepts, theories and models); they are more deeply held in our bodies. Therefore, we will generally act in line with our culture, because not to do so just feels wrong. In her book *Watching the English*, cultural anthropologist Kate Fox, who is English herself, describes her experience in breaking the rules of English culture by queue jumping, a most unapproved of behaviour in England. She states:

> Just the thought of queue-jumping was so horribly embarrassing that I very nearly abandoned the whole project rather than subject myself to such an ordeal. I just couldn't bring myself to do it. I hesitated and agonized and procrastinated, and even when I thought I had managed to steel myself, I would lose my nerve at the last minute and slink humbly to the back of the queue, hoping that no one noticed that I had even been considering jumping it.[7]

She had to prepare herself for the experience by having a couple of drinks, because it feels such an unnatural and difficult thing to do – the drinks anaesthetize her to her learned somatic markers. This shows the power of somatic markers in guiding our behaviour: we can want to do something, know that we should do it, and be lost in hesitating, agonizing and procrastinating, such that we are unable to do it.

Our entire personality is expressed this way. This is why there are certain things we will never do, and certain things we will always do. If we are always the one to start a conversation, or never the one to do so, these are part of the somatic markers that have been laid down for us in the formation of our personality. There is no moral value judgement for these markers – they are not good or bad, right or wrong – they are our merely personality. The question for us all is when these somatic markers serve us in what we need to achieve as a leader and when they don't.

When you see someone's body, therefore, you are not just looking at the shape of the body; you are seeing their personality and their history expressed physically. Emotions and moods are physical phenomena that start with the body, so when you look at the body you see on the surface the current emotions. Look more deeply and you will see the moods. Look more deeply again and you will see the long-term patterns of holding in the muscles that give the shape of the personality the person is holding, in response to their somatic markers.

For example, let's go back to the example of the person who couldn't speak up because of historical experiences of embarrassment, and the development of somatic markers from these experiences. This person may be quite happy when you meet them; perhaps they have just become received some good news. You will see that in their face, primarily. If you look more deeply you will see, however, that even their expression of joy is contained to some degree – they are still making themselves smaller, and despite their joy, their movements of expression of this joy are limited to avoid attracting attention. Their overall shaping beneath the emotional expression is still one of making themselves smaller and avoiding feeling exposed or vulnerable.

In this example we can see that the person has at the surface level the emotional expression that we can see and experience through body language and facial gestures. At another level there is a long-lived structure that is the shape of the personality they have developed expressed through posture, contracting and making themselves smaller.

We can also see that the structure limits the emotional expression, to avoid visibility, and from what we have seen before, it will also limit the emotional experience – the limited physical movement of muscles into the shape of joy will limit the experience.

So we do, literally, embody our selves. And if we pay close attention to others (and ourselves) we will see that who we are at the deepest level is there inside the structure of the body. If you've done yoga, dancing, tai chi or other martial arts you will realize that there is a structure of how the body was designed to be, and with which we were born. It's aligned and balanced, it is flexible, it has an uprightness and a dignity you see in those with good postures. You'll also realize that our bodies are not like this – our bodies have a shape and a form to them that is slightly off-balanced and unaligned, and somewhat inflexible, and we spend time in yoga or martial arts classes trying to return to that basic structure we were born with.

That movement away from this basic structure is the personality that we have developed over time, through our history. It is those somatic markers and our embodied responses that give the structure (underneath body language) of the body and the self.

When you see very young babies, there is a point where often people will say that they have started to look like a person. This is the point where they have already begun to embody enough somatic markers that we start to see some elements of personality arising. If you've seen a dead body, you will also know that it's very clear that this person is dead. There is something missing; there is no animating force to the tissues, which leaves the body limp and lifeless – it is lacking the personality that was previously there. There is no mistaking it for someone who is sleeping.

At some level you already know all of this. When you walk down the street, sometimes another person will just strike you as aggressive or shy; without your having any interaction with that person you have that sense of them. Sometimes if someone comes to the door to do some work for you, you may just know that you don't want to let them in, or that if you do you'll need to keep an eye on them. Sometimes you'll also just 'know' you can trust them. The thing is we're always assessing other people, and we do that at a pre-conscious level, assessing their bodies – this is all we have to go on.

Applying this to leadership

This is all crucial to understand for leadership. For most of human evolutionary history, we lived in groups and we were also potentially something else's dinner. Being in a group provided safety, and groups required leaders who were able to lead the group to food and maintain safety. This means that leadership is connected very deeply to human survival and therefore we as human beings are always, at an unconscious level, assessing leadership in others. The fact that a survey that found that the majority of Fortune 500 CEO's are men of above average height[8] suggests that at a basic level many of us will attribute leadership qualities in the same way we would have when hunting on the savannahs – when we needed leaders who were big and strong, and could therefore provide safety and food.

That's not to say we always get our assessments right – but we are always making them. Much of the time they are unconscious to us; you will have a first impression of someone you just met, but if I asked you what that was, you would probably have to think about it and form it in language.

If you've ever seen a leader in an organization give an address to the company on the future, you will see that groups of people will be making these assessments constantly. If there is any incongruence in the leader, it shows up in the cynicism of the audience – they will think it is bullshit, basically, and will say that to each other. If the leader is talking about a great future and doesn't really believe it – that shows in the body. It would be like me giving you a presentation on stress whilst having my shoulders up to my ears and my body very tense – I am a living embodiment of a tense and stressed person. Why would you listen to me?

And it's not about trying to fake it; trying to fake being a less tense and stressed person wouldn't work, and the same goes for congruence in the leader's message. It's about dealing with the underlying somatic markers, and being authentic about what we truly believe.

So how are we going to do this? Well for many reasons it makes sense to do this through the body. The body is where we feel and experience our somatic markers. It's where the behaviour that the somatic markers guide in us is expressed. It's where the shaping that we develop lives, and it's that shaping that we need to work with. John Coates gives another argument in support of this from neuro-science. The somatic markers will be processed through the older parts of the brain – brain stem, amygdala, hypothalamus etc, known as sub-cortical regions of the brain. These regions have many neurons and connections to our neo-cortex, which is where we can engage in rational thought and planning, but there are much fewer running in the opposite direction.[9] This is why it's difficult to think our way into a change, or for a model to truly change behaviour, but why these somatic markers can profoundly impact our thinking. He suggests new training programmes and states:

> These training regimes will have to be designed in such a way that they access the primitive brain, not just the rational cortex. Since the body profoundly influences sub-cortical regions of the brain, the new training programmes may turn out to involve a lot more physical exercises than they do at present.[10]

I would go further than Coates. I would say that in the field of leadership development, not including the body is a mistake. By physical exercises he and I are not referring to the gym exercises that you may do for fitness, but rather exercises that allow us to see and experience our somatic markers, how they drive our behaviours and how we can learn to do something different.

New ideas for leadership development

Recently I was in Bali on vacation and I did a cooking course (I love food and cooking!) with a Swiss chef who had lived in Bali for 22 years and specialized in Balinese cuisine. Regularly during the course, the chef would ask all of us participants about some generally accepted aspect of cooking. For example, how hot oil needed to be for deep frying, and how you could know.

The general conclusion was that it should be very hot and that you could drop some batter in the oil to test its readiness. He asked us what would happen if the oil was too cold, and we agreed that the food would generally be oily, the batter would separate from the food, and the food would then be unpleasant.

As he did at the end of each of these questions, he then shouted loudly, 'Wrong!' He then proceeded to cook a battered banana in oil that was cool enough for us to put our fingers into, which was more crispy and less oily than just about any battered food I have tasted.

It turns out that you can put food in cold oil and heat it gently and it will be fine. The only problem is putting food in hot oil, which cools down the oil (such as with frozen foods) at which point in between the food going into the oil and the oil reheating the food absorbs oil rapidly. He explained the science behind this, which has to do with the moisture in the food, but that's not actually important for this story. (Interestingly his original French chef training would have said you needed hot oil, but our understanding has moved on.) My point is that you can deep fry food in a way that seems a little weird, but is actually very easy and much more effective. Or you can cook it in the way that is generally accepted and it won't be as good.

It's a bit like that with leadership development. We can continue to develop leaders in the way we have always done so – cramming models and theories into the rational neo-cortex, and hope that some of it makes its way down to the sub-cortical regions of the brain and the body, and it will be limited in its effectiveness. How many of us have seen people come back from leadership programmes and try to implement models and frameworks back at work? And are they successful?

The answer is sometimes. Sometimes people have the determination to work at it and achieve some benefit. However, it would be easier for both them and their organization if we started with the body. If we took the new learning we have from neuroscience, and the understanding we have from philosophy, and apply that to leadership, we would find we could produce better leaders more easily, just like the lower-temperature deep-fat frying.

So what holds us back? I saw a great quote on Twitter, for which I don't have a source, so apologies to whomever originated this comment: 'Management will continue to apply techniques which don't work, while they don't understand the techniques which do work.' I think this sums up a substantial part of the issue, and is part of my motivation for writing this book.

However these ideas are not completely new. In philosophical terms, I build here on the ideas of Wittgenstein, which have influenced Professor Cockburn, whom I referenced previously. Merleau-Ponty, the French phenomenological philosopher, who was very influenced by Heidegger but added the body as a key missing piece to his thinking, has also been influential in these ideas. These are also the ideas of Aristotle, one of the great thinkers of Ancient Greek civilization, and very influential in how we see the world today in the West. If we go East these are the ideas of Buddhist philosophy, Ayurvedic traditions and many other Eastern philosophies. They are in the ideas of method acting, and in the work of yoga, martial arts and countless forms of bodywork and massage.

They are ideas that filter through our language in countless phrases that we have come to assume are metaphor, and that we have forgotten are literal. Phrases such as:

- describing someone as a 'pushover';
- saying 'pull yourself together';
- describing someone as 'solid' and 'grounded';
- 'posturing' in a meeting;
- getting 'hot under the collar';
- describing someone as 'chinless';
- 'stiff upper lip' – usually describing the English.

So whilst these ideas are new ones in neuroscience, and new ones in leadership, they are ideas that we have always known in other domains and to which we are merely returning.

I hope in the first section of this book I have shown you that our approach to leadership development needs to change. In the second part of this book, it is my intention to give you more information on how to go about including the body in leadership development.

Recommended reading

Emotions Revealed: Understanding faces and feelings, by Paul Ekman.
The Hour Between Dog and Wolf: Risk-taking, gut feelings and the biology of boom and bust, by John Coates.

Notes

1 Coates, J (2012) *The Hour Between Dog and Wolf: Risk-taking, gut feelings and the biology of boom and bust*, Fourth Estate, London, p 97.

2 Margaret Mead's book *Coming of Age in Samoa: A psychological study of primitive youth for Western civilisation* argued that culture was the primary determinant of human emotional expression, whereas Charles Darwin's *The Expression of the Emotions in Man and Animals* took an evolutionary take on the subject, and argued that the expression of emotions was universal.

3 His work is also the basis of the TV series *Lie to Me*.

4 See https://face.paulekman.com/face/default.aspx for these online tools.

5 http://www.sermonillustrations.com/a-z/l/lincoln.htm.

6 This example is a version of one given by Richard Strozzi-Heckler in the chapter, 'Conditioned tendency', in his book *The Anatomy of Change: A way to move through life's transitions*.

7 Fox, K (2004) *Watching the English: The hidden rules of English behaviour*, Hodder and Stoughton, London.

8 'Short guys finish last: The world's most enduring form of discrimination', *The Economist*, 23 December 1995.

9 Coates, J (2012) *The Hour Between Dog and Wolf*, pp 221–22.

10 Ibid, p 236.

PART TWO
Exploring the ideas in practice

In the first part of this book, I focused on showing how our ideas on leadership needed to be updated if they were to be effective. As I have already mentioned, this book is now about to change to become more focused on what you can actually do to develop yourself as a leader. In addition, I will also change the style of writing that I am using.

I have chosen to continue this book through the stories of two people, whom I have named Jane and John. They are based upon two real people whom I have worked with over a period of time; however, I have taken artistic licence in the telling of the story, for two reasons:

- to ensure their complete anonymity and confidentiality, and that of the organization they work for;

- to produce a narrative that fits with this book, and that serves the purposes of explaining the concepts presented here.

The situations they faced and the results they were able to achieve through their continued work with embodied leadership are from real situations. I have deliberately not included information on the home lives of the people concerned, which inevitably played into the situations they were working on, to respect their wishes and ensure anonymity. I have played with the timelines a little, and each character includes some aspects of other people I have worked with, although still based heavily around one core person, in order to bring across all of the points and issues I wanted to address in this book.

Through their stories and the work they did on themselves, my aim is to show how the ideas and principles that I covered in part one of the book are brought to life, and the type of results that can be achieved through deliberate practice.

Developing choice and clarity as a leader

06

John was a senior executive in a multinational company. Whilst he'd always been ambitious and wanted to get to the top, he had expected by the time he got there that he would know what to do, and know what was going on. Privately he admitted to being worried about being 'found out', that a lot of the time he didn't really know what to do, but felt tremendous pressure from others, and by virtue of his position, to have the answers.

John had been promoted six months before, and felt like he was still proving himself. The company was going through some tough times and the CEO was putting him under immense pressure to address some of the problems. He could see that the CEO himself was also under similar pressure from the board, but that did not make it any easier for him.

John had been a rising star in his previous department, a department that he knew very well. The promotion, however, had involved a move into a department he didn't know very much about at all. The team under him were not operating as well as they needed to, but from a technical perspective they knew the job better than he did, and he would meet with walls of reasoning and arguments about technical stuff he didn't understand whenever he suggested a change or tried to get them to perform at a higher level.

He was being pushed to provide more and more interim reports on the department, to the point that he felt like he spent all his time compiling reports, trying to educate himself on the department, and arguing with the people below him. He didn't feel sure in himself, and he felt sure his staff knew this, and probably took advantage of it. They had survived the last person who had come in to run this department and they would survive him.

When he had gone for this promotion John had visions of himself as a successful senior executive, on top of the world. Instead, he felt pressured, lacking confidence in himself and his work–life balance had disappeared – in fact his wife was also pushing him to be at home more and spend more time with her and the kids. 'Doesn't she understand the pressure I'm under?' he asked himself.

John was beginning to realize that, fairly deep down, he was pretty insecure. He probably always had been, but had excelled academically and found a job in a big company after university. He was the kind of person who was comfortable at work, and in social environments where his status and intelligence were recognized – bring him into a new group of people without this, and he would struggle to know what to say and how to be. Once he had established his intelligence and career status in a group he could relax and be more at ease.

Looking back at his life John realized that he hadn't been one of the popular kids in his school days – he hadn't been unpopular, but he was just never completely at ease with himself. He had been bright and had friends, but somehow had never quite been able to fit in as well as he would have liked to. He suspected that he had never really moved beyond this schoolyard insecurity.

Now that the area at which he excelled – work – was not going as well as it should have been, it was like his self-confidence had been fundamentally shaken. At some level he still knew he was good at what he did, but he was worried and stressed. If he could just get on top of this situation then he would be back to normal, he thought.

Still, he had a plan that would come to fruition very soon, all being well. He had submitted a proposal to the CEO for a reorganization. He talked it through with the CEO, who seemed to think it was a good idea, so he put a paper together to be discussed at the next senior management team meeting. Part of his department would merge with Jane's department, and he would get part of her department inside his. It made sense in many ways – those guys in Jane's department were doing work that was closely connected with his department and this would make things much more efficient. The guys he would lose were interfacing with her department most of the time – there were many good arguments in favour of this plan.

It also enabled him to get rid of some of the difficulties in his department, by passing them on to her, and as it happened the guys he would inherit were performing really well. If he could just get this agreed then he would be able to work his way back. His confidence would come back, and he'd get to his vision of the successful senior executive he intended to be. Also he'd be able to have a better work–life balance, and that would get his wife off his back.

Jane probably wouldn't like it, but he'd sent in the plan last week, whilst she was on some kind of leadership course, and anyway she'd always been a bit of a pushover and didn't speak up in the senior team meetings. Jane was technically excellent, but he knew that he could get his way in this upcoming meeting.

The meeting

He walked into the meeting feeling positive. He greeted his colleagues, one or two of whom he hadn't actually seen for a few weeks because of travel schedules, and grabbed a coffee. Jane walked in looking a little different; he wondered casually if she'd changed her hair or glasses, but then thought nothing more of it. He prepared himself to argue his case.

As the meeting got going there were the usual ceremonies: review of minutes from the last meeting, the usual finance request for numbers and reports, people feeling pleased with themselves around actions completed, and justifications from others for actions still incomplete.

Then the CEO started to introduce his plan. 'John has put together a plan for a reorganization, which seems to have some merits, and I want to explore it with you all. You will have seen his paper in your briefing pack, but why don't we start with John giving a brief rundown of the key elements of this plan.'

John was nervous, but despite that felt he did a good job. He stated the key changes that would be required, and his arguments that, on the basis of the work people did, they would be better in the other departments. He argued that his predecessor in this role had been unsuccessful in turning the department around because the structures weren't right, and that with this restructuring, the department could be successful.

As he spoke he noticed a series of nods around the room from colleagues. He avoided looking at Jane, but given the response of the room he felt that this was definitely going to go through.

What came next shocked him. Jane spoke up. Rather than sitting back as usual, she was sitting upright, and had a strong clear voice, which she never had before. She said very directly that she needed time to review this proposal, as she had been away. The plan would involve changing her work flows and she didn't believe that John's proposal captured the full job descriptions of her staff, so it would take some time to review these and understand the implications of this proposal. In addition, she felt the staff concerned should be consulted; otherwise this decision could just breed resentment.

Finally, she turned to John directly, and stated that she noticed that this proposal would have the effect of transferring some poor-performing staff to her and some high-performing staff to him. She said that she understood the pressure he was under but felt that this was just a process of moving the problem in the organization, rather than fixing it.

This floored John, and he managed to get a few words out about how this was not his intention, and this was about logical work flows and an efficient process. Jane responded by asking the CEO for more time to review and respond more fully to the efficiency proposals, to which he agreed.

Whereas at the start of the meeting, when John spoke his peers had nodded their heads, he now noticed that all the nodding of heads was happening when Jane spoke. The rest of the meeting was a blur. He spent it silent reviewing in his head what had gone wrong. Internally he cursed Jane – how come she was so different from normal? How come she was arguing back? Was he destined to fail in this role?

At the end of the meeting he left quickly, stating he had a conference call to get to, and went back to his office, shut the door, sat down and slumped in his chair. Who knows if his plan would now go through, and he couldn't see another way to get things moving. He glanced at his computer and saw a chain of e-mails from some of the more 'difficult' members of his team, and slumped even more. He didn't want to open them, he just knew there would be more difficulty, more challenge and more problems. He leant forward, elbows on the desk, with his head in his hands, massaging his temples, and he felt very low.

Jane's initial reaction to the meeting was pretty positive. In the meeting she had just attended she had stood up for herself in a way she hadn't before. Usually she would just let the guys (and they were all men) win in these situations, but she'd done it – she'd taken a stand for herself, and it had gone well.

To be honest, she was pretty angry with John, but she hadn't let her anger boil over in the meeting. No, she'd been clear and firm, stated her position and requested time to respond to the proposal fully. She had felt furious when she saw the proposal that Monday morning in the briefing pack. The fact that it had been submitted while she was away was John just trying to take advantage of her, but she'd held her ground in the meeting – a first for her in senior management team meetings, and something she was delighted about.

She had noticed that John seemed nervous during his presentation, and that he almost collapsed physically when she held her ground. It really did seem to affect him in a big way. As she thought about it she realized that he had seemed less sure of himself since his promotion – it was a tough challenge he was facing, but his strategy hadn't been to ask for help, it had been to pass the problem on to her. No, he got what he deserved, she thought, but she did need to have a productive working relationship with him, so she would need to think about her next move.

Her mind went back to the leadership programme she'd just attended.

It hadn't been what she'd expected, at all, yet it had probably been one of the most powerful and profound experiences of her life. She'd attended with a group from across different organizations and had developed some relationships that she felt would stay with her for a long time and that would be useful to her in her career. It was an embodied leadership course; even now she still wasn't entirely sure she understood intellectually everything about how the 'the self is embodied,' but she knew at a deep level that it was true for her, and she knew how she could work to be the leader she wanted to be. The meeting she had just come from had proved to her that she could act differently (and even be different), and that 'centring' was key.

Centring

After all the usual introductions, and some initial conversation about the programme, the first exercise, or practice as they called it, that the programme had taught, was called centring. At first Jane had thought this was a technique for being more relaxed and reducing stress, which she now realized to be more of a side-effect rather than its core purpose. This seemed valuable to her, but as she went through the programme and kept on practising centring, she realized that centring was much more than this – centring was the route to more choice.

Now, if you'd told Jane before the programme that she didn't have enough choice she wouldn't have understood. She'd have thought that with all the variety of information, things to buy or do in the world, that she almost had too much choice. However that was about external choices. If you brought it back to internal choices about how she would respond to the situations around her, such as the kind of meeting she'd just attended, she didn't really have a lot of choice. She knew before that she should stand up for herself more and that she should speak out, but it didn't 'feel right' inside herself, and while it didn't feel right she wasn't able to do it.

You see, for most of us, most of the time, we respond along automatic pre-practised ways of behaving, otherwise known as our personality.

Jane was the type of person who was demure, who didn't take a stand for herself, who didn't feel comfortable 'creating a fuss' about anything and who constantly put her needs last. Whilst there is virtue in politeness, she didn't have any choice about it, and it was very frustrating to those who worked for her as she also did this on behalf of her department. A life time of experiences where any instance of putting herself or her needs forward was labelled as pushy, selfish, un-ladylike and wrong in her family had created strong somatic markers, just like the markers we all have for the embarrassing situations discussed in Part One of this book.

Jane was responding on the basis of her somatic markers, which meant that she was unable to stand up for herself, to speak out and to hold her ground in meetings. She did not have choice in those moments – she acted out her historic ways of responding, which were held in her body.

So whilst she hadn't seen herself as someone who had limited choices, while she was on the programme she began to see how she lacked choices in areas that were important to her and that held her back in her career. She also saw that knowing this didn't, on its own, help. It required doing something different – centring.

Now, after the meeting, she brought herself back through the centring practice again, very deliberately in the most complete way she could, all the time paying attention to what was required to centre herself.

Centring is about aligning the body across the three dimensions of space that we live in: length, width and depth. Firstly, Jane aligned herself in length.

To do this Jane imagined that someone was pulling on a hair on the top of her head and that as she rose up from her usual slouch, that she was putting more air between the vertebrae of her spine. At the same time she relaxed downwards, aligning herself with the field of gravity. She hadn't realized this before, but she actually used a lot of energy holding herself up – holding her shoulders higher than they needed to be, holding her jaw clamped shut, holding her stomach in, tightening her leg muscles, all to compensate and hold herself in her usual shape. By relaxing across all of these areas she really relaxed for the first time in a long time, and she had so much more energy when she wasn't trying to hold herself up.

She had learnt on the programme that she held tension in horizontal bands across the body (such as the forehead, eyes, jaw, shoulders, chest, stomach and legs) and that by scanning her body from top to bottom, she could feel and then release some of this tension. She saw that by slumping in her length and holding tension across her body she created a very familiar feeling in herself; it was what it felt like to be her – slightly demure and withdrawn, not willing to take a stand. By standing straighter and relaxing across the horizontal bands, she felt freer, lighter and much more relaxed.

When we think about length, it is worthwhile thinking about how we describe someone with good posture. When we see some-one standing tall, such as a dancer will often do, we can describe it as 'dignified'. We ascribe the quality of dignity to this dimension, and when we stand tall we can often feel more dignity, as a part of our internal experience. As Jane practised standing fully in her length, she began to feel more dignified, and also began to feel that she gave more dignity to others.

She then balanced herself across the dimension of width – left to right. We all tend to have a dominant side and so she deliberately practised balancing her weight across her feet. She had come to see this as the social dimension – the dimension of reaching out to others in relationships. Jane tended to make herself very narrow, holding her arms and shoulders in (and up) and this created very little social connection. By relaxing outwards and allowing herself to take up more space in the world, she saw that she was giving herself more permission to reach out to and connect with others. Relaxing in this way she felt much less shy.

Finally she balanced herself in the domain of depth – front to back. With the majority of our sense organs on the front of our bodies, she had been taught that as humans we have a tendency to orient to the future being ahead of us and the past behind us. Jane had a tendency to lean backwards slightly, moving away from the world. On the programme it had been pointed out to her that when she greeted someone she extended her hand in a handshake greeting, but at the same time leant backwards and away from the other person, giving a mixed message.

So Jane found herself now, fully in her length yet relaxed, balanced between left and right and balanced between her front (her future) and her back (the past), bringing herself into the present moment. She then took a deep breath into her stomach and brought her atten-tion into her body to the body's physical centre of gravity – a point one or two inches below the navel.

By doing this Jane felt very different. She was calm, although this calmness wasn't based on a damping down of her emotions, but on the full awareness and experience of her emotions without being overwhelmed by them. She was relaxed and freer than she was used to feeling, and most importantly all of the usual chatter in her head had died down. Like most people, Jane had conversations that went on in her head (if you're thinking that you don't, then that thought is the conversation I'm referring to). These conversations would involve much self-doubt, being very self-critical, and were generally not very supportive. It was these voices that would usually argue against the idea of her standing up for herself in the kind of meeting she had just experienced.

But let's take a deeper look at what happens when Jane centres herself.

Firstly, as I have already mentioned, in doing this Jane brings herself into the present. She does this in two ways. Firstly she brings her attention into her body, rather than to her thoughts. Our thoughts are extremely rarely in the present moment and place. They are memories of the past, or fantasies about the future. Even if we start with 'what should I do now?' as a thought in the present we will very quickly begin analysing different options and what the outcomes might be, and perhaps our internal worrier will start looking at all the things that could go wrong. By bringing attention to our felt sense of ourselves, we bring our attention to the present moment by feeling it. Secondly, by aligning her body along depth, a domain that we metaphorically associate with time, Jane brings her attention into the present moment, rather than the past or future.

Secondly, she brings herself into a place of choice rather than a place of being run by her historical personality. The personality is, as I have shown in previous chapters, held in the body. Our somatic markers can drive our behaviours, and we develop a shape in response to them. In Jane's case she had learnt through some early childhood experiences not to stand up for herself, not to be demanding, not to make a fuss. Over time she had begun to physically hold herself back to avoid such situations, and this became the slightly collapsed, leaning back and tense posture and body shape that she developed. This is the shape in which it doesn't 'feel right' to stand up for herself, and it's the shape that feels most familiar to her.

By centring herself, she is able to make choices. She is no longer run by her historic somatic markers, and is able to choose her responses. It's not that she no longer feels the somatic markers, indeed by centring herself she opens herself up to feeling the emotions associated with the somatic markers more fully, as she is no longer reshaping herself in response to them – the first move she makes is to face her own internal demons. In doing so, however, she discovers that the old internal demons aren't as bad as they were in her first memory of the experience – many of these experiences were from childhood, and she is now a more resourceful adult and better able to cope with the feelings they generate. Therefore she is able to take different actions and have more choice. For Jane the first step in reshaping herself was to face down her demons so that she could move forward.

Jane will still regularly fall back into her old familiar way of feeling and experiencing the world – it is well practised for her, and it feels very comfortable in its demure and retreated way, and this is why centring is something she must practise time and again. Each time she does so, she will get better at centring more quickly, and she will change her habitual shape into one that will serve her in having more choice and being able to stand up for herself.

In addition, through centring herself Jane takes a deep breath, which activates the parasympathetic nervous system, sometimes called the 'rest-and-digest' system. The rest-and-digest system counters the fight-or-flight response, relaxing and settling the body, and managing her stress levels. Here Jane can move beyond any fight-or-flight reaction she may experience, which is an almost instinctive reaction, and this will allow her to have choice over her actions (I will speak further about this stress response in the next chapter).

By making these adjustments, Jane is preparing herself for what might need to happen. From a purely physical perspective the body is balanced and aligned and can move in any direction easily. Compare this with her historic stance of leaning backwards, where any movement forwards would first have to counter this – she would start off on the back foot, both literally and metaphorically. However, as we know now, there is no such thing as a purely physical perspective

– the shaping that she had developed was the personality she had become, so by centring herself Jane had also moved into a more balanced place internally; a place where she was able to take different actions in the world.

In addition, she had started to show up differently as a result. At the start of the meeting John had wondered if Jane had changed her hair or glasses, but had been too wrapped up in his own thinking about the meeting to follow the train of thought. By the end of the meeting he had definitely noticed a difference.

We talk about people having 'presence' or 'gravitas', and yet we don't really know what that means. Let me be more precise: we know it when we see it, but find it hard to define or produce. However, let's think about what we look for in presence and gravitas. We look for a dignified posture, which Jane was now adopting. We look for someone who's comfortable in their own skin; in other words, that they are relaxed and comfortable in their movements and with themselves – the deep breaths, and the relaxation across the horizontal bands that Jane did, had produced this for her. We look for someone who is present – one of the defining characteristics of presence, for me, is that someone is completely present with me, rather than off in their thoughts evaluating or working out their response to me. This form of presence is rare, and is based upon bringing oneself into the present moment, as described above, and being mindful not to be distracted by the chain of random thoughts that stream through our heads.

In doing this centring process Jane has brought herself into the present and fulfilled the criteria for presence and gravitas. At first John notices the change and dismisses it as an outer change; however, he soon sees that there is more to it than that. A more astute observer than John (perhaps one less wrapped up in their own problems) would realize that something more fundamental had changed for Jane, but over time as Jane continues on this path, and continues to practise centring, those around her will begin to hold a different assessment about her – one that includes presence and gravitas as part of the description.

However, this is no silver bullet for Jane. It's not as simple as centring and then her work is done. Life still happens. There are times, such as in the meeting, where she had to re-centre herself continuously to hold her ground. The experience repeatedly triggered her, and at the moment before she responded to John's proposal she found herself collapsing into the old shape and almost giving in. What made the difference was, in that moment, centring herself as she sat there. She sat up straighter, balanced herself on the chair, relaxed, took some deep breaths and brought her attention into her body, as she had learnt on the programme.

In that place she didn't plan her response to John's statements in her head, she spoke clearly and directly, responding in the present moment to John's proposals with the conviction that comes when we connect to what we care about. Our emotions and sensations tell us what we care about, and we experience these in our bodies – below the chin – rather than as ideas in our heads. By centring, Jane was connecting herself to this, and speaking from this place was more powerful than any made-up and rehearsed speech from her collapsed and demure posture. We come across as much more convincing and persuasive (yet also open) when we are not 'reacting' from our historic shape, but when we are more at choice and connected to what we care about.

There will always be things that knock Jane off-centre – the question is not whether she can try to remain centred all the time, but rather how quickly she can return to centre. Centring is taught in the Japanese martial art of Aikido, and there is a story I have heard repeated in the Aikido *dojo*, in which Morihei Ueshiba, who founded Aikido, was asked by one of his students how he remained so centred all the time. He responded that he didn't, he just came back to centre before his students had noticed. Ueshiba had spent a lifetime practising centring and taught that it was an essential component to being able to respond skilfully in martial arts and in life.

If you are unconvinced by the power of centring, posture, and how that creates presence and gravitas, consider this. A study was conducted in a US prison where convicted muggers were shown films of people walking along the streets in New York. They were then asked which ones they would have mugged. In most cases, the muggers were in complete agreement with one another, and the people they chose were not necessarily the smallest or weakest looking. They were those who were in some way out of balance in their posture and walking. Those who walked in a balanced and centred manner were hardly ever chosen.[1]

My intention here is not to promise you that by centring Jane will never be mugged, but merely to show how centring can create a presence and gravitas where she is taken more seriously. It does require practice, however!

Moving forwards

As Jane thought more about the meeting she realized that she could happily have throttled John for his behaviour. She was delighted at how she had handled the meeting, but she was furious at him. Part of her wanted to retaliate. She knew she could go into the CEO and point out that John was playing politics and that she wouldn't stand for it. Yes, their departments did work closely together and some of those changes might have a small amount of merit, but how he did things was out of line. He had inherited a tough situation, but frankly she was ready to let him suffer and fail. In fact, part of her wanted to just make things more difficult for him and ensure that he failed. It would be something he deserved!

However, after having re-centred herself, Jane thought more about the future. Her department and John's did need to work together, and that meant that she needed to work with him effectively. She thought back to the declaration that she created on the programme.

Declarations, she had learned, were a statement of what someone is committed to as a leader. She hadn't really thought about it before, but it made sense that leadership relates to something a person is committed to achieving, which others help them to achieve. She hadn't thought about leadership much before; previously, when she was more junior, she'd attended management development programmes, and since she had become more senior she went on leadership development programmes, so in her mind leadership was as much about position in the hierarchy as anything else. However, now she had thought about it more, it made sense that leadership was about more than just position in the hierarchy; she had seen so many senior managers who hadn't really shown leadership and she could now see many occasions in the past where she hadn't shown leadership either.

Prior to the programme she had been asked, as pre-work, to think about what she was committed to as a leader. She hadn't put much thought into it before the programme but had decided she would just use her work targets, as that seemed to make sense. During the programme she began to understand more about the ideas of leadership and declarations. The idea of a leader being someone who was out to do/build/create or change something in the world made sense, but was challenging to her – what was she trying to achieve as a leader?

Declarations were introduced in the context of this understanding of leadership as a statement of what someone is committed to achieving. However, Jane was taught, declarations are not an aspiration or hopeful statement of the future; rather they are a statement that changes the future. When a priest or minister declares a couple man and wife, the priest is not stating an aspiration but making a declaration that changes something. It changes how the community of listeners responds to and orients with that couple.

Similarly when a leader declares a new future, it creates a new context for followers to respond to that leader. It creates a new current and future reality for each person, inside which to take actions. When the CEO of Microsoft declares that it will produce a new operating system, that declaration creates a new reality for market analysts, IT buyers and everyone who uses a PC around the world. The statement changes things and this is a function of leaders – to make declarations that change the context inside which the people around them act and, through doing so, to build a different future (ie do/build/create or change something).

In the programme the participants had been asked to state their declarations to each other in pairs, and to do so whilst centred. When she tried this, Jane had been unable to state her declaration regarding her work targets. She stumbled over the words, and she was unable to remain centred. In doing this exercise, she realized that actually achieving her targets didn't really motivate her, when she was honest with herself, she didn't really care deeply about achieving these targets. At first she felt a little guilty about this – after all her company was paying for her to be there – but with some encouragement she looked beyond this to examine what she did deeply care about.

During the programme she spent time thinking and feeling about what she cared about and in the end came up with two different declarations. The first was a declaration that she would be treated with dignity at work. She had realized that she didn't speak up for herself, didn't take a stand for what was important to her and allowed herself to be pushed around. So her starting point was a personal declaration that was a commitment to being treated differently and ultimately to treating herself differently. This would involve putting herself and her ideas forward more, fighting for her department within the organization, being willing to take a stand on issues that were important to her and holding others accountable for treating her with respect. It was this declaration that she was living when she had gone into the board meeting.

The second declaration came later in the programme. It was a declaration that was more outwardly focused, around her work. This took longer for her to come to, and she wouldn't have been able to come to this without the first declaration. Her second declaration was to inspire the company's executive team (of which she was a part) to work together to build a new future for the company. To do this she would have to take a stand within the team for a change in how they worked together. For her to be able to take that stand she needed to be treated with dignity and to treat herself differently, so it was a clear build on her first declaration, but taking it to a wider audience.

It was this declaration that was coming back to her now, as she considered how to handle John. He was in a difficult situation dealing with a series of challenges that he had inherited, and she had seen at the end of the meeting that he was not in a good place. How should she move forward with him? It was tricky; given what had happened she didn't want to give in and go along with his proposal, yet she did need him to be successful, for her own success and to achieve her declaration. She knew this was inevitably the first of many challenges she would face in working with this declaration, and she wanted to address it well.

She decided she needed to have a conversation with John. She also realized that it would not be easy. He was likely to be feeling angry after the previous meeting, but she would need to face this if she was to be successful. And she would need to centre herself repeatedly, if the conversation was to go well. She began to plan how to handle the meeting.

She decided that she would need to give him some time to be angry at her. In some respects it wasn't fair that she would have to sit and allow him to rant at her, but she knew pragmatically that until he ranted he wouldn't be calm, and that she wouldn't be able to reason with him. She also knew, after the programme, that she could stand and face the energy of someone ranting and be ok – that it didn't need to affect her.

She also decided that she would have to see his point of view. She needed to start where he was, rather than trying to get him to see her point of view. She had understood that this was not weakness, or giving in, but that by being willing to see and understand his point of view, she would actually be more powerful. As Sun Tzu wrote in *The Art of War*:

> Knowing the other and knowing oneself,
> In one hundred battles no danger.
> Not knowing the other and knowing oneself,
> One victory for one loss.
> Not knowing the other and not knowing oneself,
> In every battle certain defeat.[2]

She had a good awareness of herself after the programme – in fact, if asked before the programme she would have said she had very good self-awareness, but during the programme she had realized much that she didn't know about herself, and therefore she was much more cautious now about rating her self-awareness so highly. She realized that it is a paradox that often those who state they have very high self-awareness actually don't, whereas those who are much more humble and moderate on the subject usually have much greater self-awareness. However, her self-awareness was definitely improved, and she could now be much more aware of what was going on for her, moment by moment. To ensure 'no danger' she would need to ensure that she really understood John and his position.

From this understanding she hoped she could unite their joint concerns with her declaration for the success of the team and the company, and build an ally. It would not be easy, as there was still a part of her that wanted to have some form of revenge for what

John had done, but that wouldn't serve her declaration. When she centred herself now she was practising repeating her declaration to herself and reminding herself of what was important to her, and she realized that the real challenge in the upcoming meeting wasn't managing John, but actually managing herself, her reactions and her desire for revenge.

It's fair to say that Jane spent quite a while preparing for her meeting with John. This was time spent letting go of some of her anger and frustration at him, reminding herself what was important to her, and preparing herself for his potential reaction in the meeting. In addition she had a job to get on with whilst all this was going on and, if she was honest with herself, she procrastinated a little and found things to do that ordinarily wouldn't have been a priority, as she wasn't looking forward to the meeting. However, she was using each time the phone rang as a reminder to centre herself, and with that came a repetition of her declaration and a reminder that she would have to deal with this situation.

Applying Jane's learning

I will continue with Jane and John's story in the next chapter, and now I will look at how you can apply Jane's learning for yourself. There are two elements from this story so far that will be important to learn about for your leadership. The first is centring and the second is finding what you are committed to as a leader – your declaration. There will be some slight repetition, from Jane's experience of centring, in bringing you through the centring process, which I hope you will forgive.

Centring

I will take you through the centring process that Jane learnt quite deliberately and slowly, but you will find as you practise this that you can get very quick and centre yourself in milliseconds. I will bring you through the process standing, as in this posture you will be able to have greater physical awareness than when seated (also some chairs will push your posture into weird positions). When you have learnt the process standing you will be able to apply the same process when seated.

Having a partner to work with you in this process will be helpful – they will be able to let you know whether you are standing straight and they can read out some of the instructions so you can just focus on doing them.

The challenge you face is that your current posture is normal and comfortable to you. Most people whom I meet will associate what's comfortable with what is straight, aligned and balanced, even when their shape is very out of alignment and balance. This is because we slowly and gradually take on our shapes and we don't notice it happening. Think of it like your hair growing: day by day you don't notice it, but in a month or so it will be significantly longer. This process is extended over 20–30 years for our bodies, and when you start to reshape yourself you will notice that it may not be as comfortable as what you are used to. This will pass, if you practise!

Dimension 1: Length

Firstly, stand up, put your feet about shoulder-width apart, and let your arms hang down by your sides. Keep your eyes open while you do this. (It may be easier to do this with your eyes closed, but in the middle of an important meeting when you need to be centred you want to be able to practise centring in the moment without having to go away and close your eyes for a few seconds.)

Imagine that someone is pulling on a hair on the top of your head and let your spine stretch out upwards. Visualize it as allowing some air in between the vertebrae of the spinal column. If you have someone to work with on this, get them to let you know if you are straight or if you are still slouching. You are straight if someone can look at you from the side and can see the head is balanced on the shoulders, which are on top of the hips, down to the knees and ankles in a fairly straight line.

Be careful in this process not to raise your chin – if you do this not only is it bad for your neck, but you will be looking down your nose at people, to which people generally have a reaction. So get your partner to check if your chin is level.

Figure 6.1 shows some of the kind of postures that we can develop.

FIGURE 6.1   Common postures

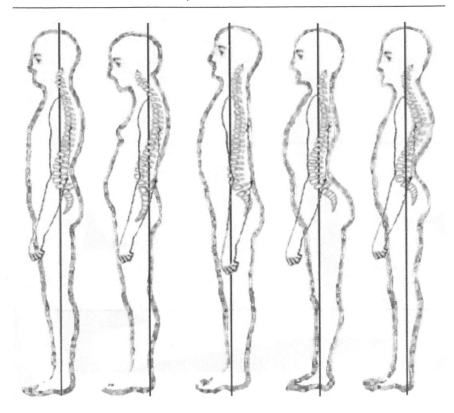

The first person (starting on the left) is pretty well aligned, with the hips, shoulders and head balanced over each other. The second is collapsed and leaning backwards a little, and is very similar to Jane's initial posture. The third is over erect, using a lot of energy to force himself upwards, with an over-projected chest and chin slightly too high. This appears almost like a military style of posture in the West (standing to attention) and is very close to our ideas of strength. This would be seen as rigid and inflexible in Eastern martial arts, and actually lacking in strength. The fourth person is out of balance at the hips and the chest, each being stuck out a little too far, and is probably about an inch shorter than they should be as a result. The final person is leaning back from a bend in the lower back, and is almost guaranteed to have back problems as a result. Try to ensure that you are as close to the first person as possible in your posture, taking into account any injuries you may have, or have had historically, that may prevent this.

Relaxing the body

Next you will need to relax downwards – this is about aligning yourself with gravity. As you go through this process start to notice where you hold yourself up, so that you can develop a sense of where exactly you need to relax in order to centre. There will be patterns of holding that you have – places where you habitually hold tension – for example you may already know you get a stiff neck and shoulders when you work, and knowing your patterns will help you to relax more quickly.

We hold tension in horizontal bands around the body. One way to think about these is like a series of belts we wear around the body from top to bottom. With our muscle tension we tighten or loosen these belts, and with that the flow of blood and hormones into the tissues is allowed or restricted. When we tighten we also limit our ability to feel – by physically reshaping ourselves we prevent the re-experiencing of the feelings that caused our somatic markers. For example, Jane had experiences that caused her to diminish herself. She reshaped herself to avoid situations where she would feel the same experience again, the memory of which was stored in her somatic markers.

So I will go through these bands from the top to the bottom starting with the forehead. Some will hold tension in the forehead by pushing the eyebrows down into an angry look and others by raising them up into a surprised look. Try to find the place in between where you can relax the forehead, releasing whatever tension you are holding. (Holding tension here can be the source of tension headaches, as well as giving others the impression of surprise or anger.)

Next the eyes. You know your eyes are relaxed when your peripheral vision is open – in other words, you can see a wider field of vision. When you harden and tense your eyes your peripheral vision closes, and you see a narrower field of vision. In addition we look to someone else's eyes when building trust. We talk about people's eyes hardening or glazing over and we have a sense of what that means in terms of that person's internal reactions, thoughts and feelings. The saying that 'the eyes are the windows to the soul' shows that the level of relaxation or tension in our eyes has a very real impact.

Going further down we have the jaw. The jaw muscle is one of the most powerful muscles in the human body, and we can hold a lot of tension here. Some people hold so much tension here they grind their teeth in their sleep and have to get teeth guards created by their dentists to protect their teeth. Relaxing the jaw means that the back teeth are not touching – believe it or not the mouth is designed so they don't touch all the time, so if your back teeth touch then you are holding them in that form. You also see many people in England (and also over the world) who hold a lot of tension around the lips and front of the mouth, perhaps the reason for the proverbial English 'stiff upper lip'.

Next are the shoulders, which is another very common place for holding tension. If you ever see pictures of George W Bush, or any gunslingers from Western movies, you'll see that their arms are regularly out from the sides of their bodies. In the movies this was often a prelude to drawing guns, and perhaps this was the image that Bush wished to portray. Doing this habitually is a sign of tension in the shoulders and it takes a lot of energy to do this. Try it if you don't already do it and you will find your shoulders quickly getting uncomfortable. To relax your shoulders first raise your shoulders up and hold them as tightly as you can for a few seconds, and then let them drop. You may need to repeat this a couple of times if you hold a lot of tension here, but you should end up with the feeling that you can feel the weight of your arms and hands at your shoulders.

Going further down we come to the chest. Here your aim is to have your chest be open and soft – perhaps imagining being open hearted will be helpful for you here. There is a soft and open way of holding your chest, in between the over-projected chest of traditional images of standing to attention, and on the other side, collapsing at the chest and losing your posture.

Moving on we come to the stomach. Holding tension here is common, as we often feel our emotions in our stomach when we feel angry or sad, so holding here can be a way to block this. It's also common because we want to have a body image like those on magazine covers (that applies to men too!). Here we need to just accept what is and relax into it. If you don't like what is, then go to the gym – holding here will only lead to stomach problems in the long term.

Then we come to the sphincters, and once again people can expend a lot of energy holding on here. There's a reason why we describe some people as anal or anally retentive, and it's a biological metaphor. There is a personality trait that is characterized by, and very often equivalent to, the biological phenomenon.

Next we come to the legs, and here we want to keep the knees soft so that the legs are relaxed. There is a place in between bent and locked, where the knees are soft and the legs are relaxed. Unfortunately, this is much more difficult in high heels, and the higher the heel the more difficult it becomes. (They may be beautiful shoes, but they really aren't good for your knees.)

Finally, there are the feet. There is a whole group of people who tense their feet, almost as if they have to hold on to the earth with their feet, otherwise they'll fall off. So relax your feet and let gravity hold you on the earth.

So you have extended upwards into your length, and relaxed downwards across the horizontal bands of the body.

Dimension 2: Width

Next is getting balance right to left. We all have a dominant side, one side where we tend to put more of our weight, so just rock back and forth and find a point where you're putting equal weight on both feet. Relax into width and feel what it is like to take up space in this dimension. Allowing your shoulders to relax and keeping your feet shoulder-width apart, rather than tightening these up, will allow you to take up space and remain balanced in this dimension. This is the social dimension – being contracted or out of balance in this dimension tends to show up in our relationships and work–life balance.

Dimension 3: Depth

Then find the balance point front to back. If you're still maintaining your posture this should just be a matter of finding a place where your weight is balanced between the balls of your feet and your heels. You're also finding a balance between the present and the future and finding that point where you are in the present. Find this point and balance yourself. You may need to just check that you've maintained your length whilst doing all of this – if you're working with a partner have them check with you on this.

Your body is now in the posture that it was designed to be in. Let me emphasize this point. This may feel like a strange posture to you, perhaps a little uncomfortable, but it is actually the posture that your body was designed to have. If this feels uncomfortable or strange in any way, it's only because you have developed a posture over time that is out of sync with how it was designed to be. Bringing yourself back into this posture moves you out of your historical somatic-marker-driven personality, and into a place of choice.

If it doesn't feel in any way uncomfortable or strange, and you haven't spent time trying working on a good posture with something like Alexander Technique or dancing, then you may not be doing it properly, so have someone check your alignment.

Bringing your attention to your centre

Now that you are aligned, take some deep breaths, bringing the breath right down into your stomach and breathing out fully. Bring your attention to the body's physical centre of gravity, a point the Japanese refer to as the *Hara*, and the Chinese the *Tan t'ien*. When I say bring your attention there I don't intend you to think about that place as an abstract concept, but rather that you feel from that place. Just like if I asked you to bring your attention to your foot you could tell me if it was hot, cold, sore, tired and so on.

Now notice what you feel from your centre. It is reasonably common for people to feel quite calm, and to notice that they don't have the usual chatter going on in their heads. Often people feel a greater awareness of themselves, others and the environment around them (birds singing outside, the room they are in, etc). Occasionally people will touch into some emotions they have been suppressing, and if this happens then just let yourself feel that emotion. Sometimes people will feel a sense of vulnerability and will want to go back to their more rigid, tense and (in their eyes) stronger state. If this is the case then just stay with the feelings you experience. For some this is a very pleasurable state, like coming home to something long forgotten.

Whatever it is for you, be with it. Remember, this is not about you trying to remain centred all the time, rather that you practise centring yourself on an ongoing basis. Stuff will still happen that knocks you off-centre – an e-mail from the boss, someone's comment in a meeting, that difficult employee and the like. However, rather than getting knocked off-centre, carrying that into the next interaction, which increases your lack of centredness, and then coming home at the end of the day in a highly tense state, kicking the cat and yelling at the kids, there is the possibility of re-centring after every interaction. Everyone I meet these days wants a better work–life balance, and it's easy to point at the hours we work; however, I believe there's another factor at play. It's about how you are when you get home, and whether you are able to be present with the people there, or are still reliving the day and taking out frustrations on those you love.

Try an experiment with yourself. Spend a week where you centre yourself every time something specific happens. It needs to be something that is fairly regular, but not so regular as to be a distraction. For example, every time the phone rings, or every time your e-mail programme pings that a new e-mail has arrived.

Practise this, noticing where you need to relax, and what adjustments you particularly need to make, in order to centre yourself. You should become quick at this, with practice, but do have someone check in with you from time to time, to check that you are still doing it properly. You can do it sitting down, bringing your feet flat on the floor, your back straight and going through the same principles.

At the end of the week notice what difference this has made to you and your week. With others who have done this, these are just some of the benefits I have seen:

- A better work–life balance – the people concerned didn't necessarily work fewer hours, they were just able to be present at home when they got there.
- A reduction in the number of antacid stomach tablets consumed.
- A greater effectiveness in dealing with conflict and difficult conversations in the workplace.
- A greater noticing of how others actually are, and therefore an ability to build better relationships in the workplace.

- Quicker telephone calls – they were centring themselves as the phone rang, and they got quicker and more effective at dealing with those calls.

Your declaration

What are you committed to achieving as a leader? What is your life's purpose, your calling? Not what your parents wanted you to do, but that which comes from the very core of your being and compels you into action. This is a remarkably difficult question to answer.

I have worked with people at the pinnacle of their careers who do not have the answer to such questions. These are people who have done what their parents, families and societies expected of them for many years. They then get to a point in their career where their family has a certain lifestyle, and they do not feel they can change anything as it may jeopardize this. Often when they scratch the surface of their feelings, they get in touch with a deep sadness and a desire to do something that they want to do, rather than what is expected of them.

Then there are others who are driven to succeed. In today's world that often means being a 'leader', and in pursuit of this they chase their way up the management hierarchy, to higher and higher levels, so as to be successful and to be a leader. All the while, they have no idea what it is they are leading people towards, other than higher and higher results; no sense of what success and leadership really means. They are unable to achieve satisfaction, as there is always higher to climb, higher results to achieve, and no real sense of why, other than the drive to succeed and to be seen to be successful. At its worst, leadership in this scenario becomes a label to satisfy the ego. These people also do not have an answer to this question of what they are committed to.

There are also others who don't feel themselves to be leaders. Who am I to be a leader? They avoid taking on leadership and in doing so live a safer life. They avoid having to stand up and say what is important to them, and whilst they may know what is important to them, there are others – the leaders – who 'should' take care of such things because, 'I am not a leader.' They live smaller lives, and even if they have an answer to the question, the answer scares them too much for them to embrace it. It would require abandoning a safe life.

To have such a deep waste of human potential and creativity is a great shame. Let's be clear, these people have not wasted their lives, and they have between them contributed much to their families and society, but they have done so at such a personal cost. Just think how much more energy would have been unleashed and how much more creativity would have been available had they aligned their work with a deeper sense of purpose.

As a book I recently came across, puts it:

> We are human beings, endowed with an incredible dignity; but
> there's nothing more undignified than forgetting our greatness
> and clutching at straws.[3]

At the end of Chapter 1, I concluded that leaders need to have a clear sense of purpose – a clear sense of what they are committed to achieving as leaders, which drives their leadership. This was part of the definition of leadership that I came to, yet it is a difficult question – there are unfortunately not many leaders whom I meet, who can answer it clearly and directly.

This is, to me, the foundational element of leadership and the development of leadership. Why should I cultivate the self, and do all of this difficult, time consuming work to be a leader, unless there is something that is important to me – something for which I am willing to stand up and be counted.

So let's begin to try and answer this question. The answer doesn't lie in rational thoughts and our head, but in our emotions and our bodies. Our emotions tell us what we care about, and it is this aspect of ourselves that we need to touch into in answering this question.

Have someone work with you for this exercise. Centre yourself, and have them ask you firstly what you care about, and secondly, why that is important to you. Speak from a centred place, and pay attention, and have your partner pay attention to whether you are able to stay centred. Don't worry about the words so much at this stage – you can have great words but if you don't believe them they will fall flat. Just try and speak from a connection to your body and what you care about. Keep going in answering both questions beyond the initial, easy answers, and start again if you begin to lose your centredness. Keep going for a while and then look at the themes that emerge. What feels important from all of this?

Try forming this into a declaration, a statement of what you are committed to. Then try speaking this from a centred place. You may need to take a couple of iterations with this process to find something that feels meaningful and important to you. Get feedback from the person you are working with – how does it feel to them? Do they believe it, or do they sense doubt? Do they feel your emotion and care about it, or does it come across flat and lifeless? The best declarations will make the hairs on the back of your partners' neck rise up – they have that intensity. Keep practising until your partner can feel your commitment when you speak it. (It's best to have a partner who can be honest and authentic with you for this process!)

Once you have something that works, integrate this into your centring practice. Every time you centre yourself, after having gone through the process, repeat your declaration to yourself. Share it with people whom you care about and ask them to help you in making it real – that could be letting you know when you're off track, or it could be about being part of helping you make it happen.

You'll know it is right when you feel it inside and it helps motivate you to take different actions in the world.

Massage/body work

For pretty much everyone I work with I would recommend some form of massage or body work (see – these practices aren't all hard work!). The point of doing massage or body work as a practice is not that they are pleasurable, although they are, but rather that you learn to relax more deeply, you start to release long-term patterns of holding in your musculature, and you learn more about where you hold tension.

Find a good massage practitioner; I would recommend deep tissue massage for relaxation of the deeper muscles, or Thai massage for flexibility. However, when you go for your massage don't just lie there – pay attention to the massage practitioners touch and to your breath. When they lean into you, breathe out and pay attention to the place they are touching. Try and relax that place just a little more under their touch. Notice where you particularly hold tension and pay attention to relaxing these areas when you centre yourself.

The good news is that having massages counts towards your 10,000 hours of practice (if you pay attention in the way I have described above). Try and fit in one or two massages a month – perhaps more if you spend a lot of time sitting on long-haul flights.

If you have trouble holding a straight posture, then you may find the Alexander Technique helpful. The Alexander Technique aims to help people to learn to stand straighter and hold less tension in their bodies, primarily to ease back pain, tension headaches and similar problems. If you have problems with developing a straighter and more relaxed posture, this will help you in that process. You can search online for teachers of the technique who can help you to learn to stand straighter.

Recommended reading

If you are interested in reading more about centring, then I highly recommend the chapter 'Center: the unity of action and being', in *Holding the Center: Sanctuary in a time of confusion*, by Richard Strozzi-Heckler. This will enhance your understanding of centring greatly.

If you are interested in reading more about commitments and declarations and how to practise speaking them powerfully, then I recommend reading the chapter, 'You are what you practise', in *The Leadership Dojo: Build your foundation as an exemplary leader*, by Richard Strozzi-Heckler.

Notes

1 Leonard, G (2000) *The Way of Aikido: Life lessons from an American sensei*, Plume, New York, p 36.

2 Sun Tzu, *The Art of War*, The Denma Translation (2001), Shambhala, Boston.

3 Kingsley, P (1999) *In the Dark Places of Wisdom*, Golden Sufi Press, Inverness, CA.

Conflict, stress and our conditioned tendencies

07

In starting this chapter we return to our story of Jane and John. We left it where Jane was preparing herself for meeting John and trying to resolve the issues they faced. We'll return to the story from John's perspective, before John and Jane meet again.

Whilst Jane was considering her next moves, John had moved through the despair he had initially felt and was angry. Who the hell did Jane think she was to block his ideas and speak to him like that? How dare she! As he ranted in his head, he conveniently forgot all about how he had timed this for while she was away and the fact that he was doing this partly to off-load some difficult staff, and instead focused on her unreasonableness in not seeing how this made logical sense. He was convincing himself that she was blocking the efficiency of the organization, which showed she lacked competence as a manager. In fact, he thought, she'd never really seemed to like him anyway – this was probably personal and she was out to get him in some kind of political move. This thought allowed him to firmly classify her as bad and wrong, and himself as the heroic victim battling against an 'evil' foe. It allowed him to let himself off with behaviour and actions that he would normally not countenance, because he was facing such exceptional circumstances.

In his head John became clearer and clearer – this was all-out war. He hadn't wanted it, or started it (so he rationalized to himself) but if that's what she wanted, then that's what she would get.

If you were to speak to John at this stage, you would hear the highly plausible story that he had constructed. You would see that at the centre was John, heroically dealing with being the victim of boardroom politics and agendas. You would hear about how he had inherited a series of problems and how his colleagues were blocking his best efforts to fix these problems, and how politics and personal agendas were destroying a company he cared about. If he left the organization now, he would recite this story in future job interviews and in reminiscences on his time in the organization.

A pity, really, that it's not actually true! There are massive gaps and holes in his story, that many would be too polite to point out, but it is this self-deception that holds him back. He cannot take powerful action for the resolution of the situation whilst he believes in this fantasy.

The reality is that I meet people in organizations who have these types of stories all the time. You might believe yours are different – *they are true*! I know that with some of the stories that my head has constructed over time, I'd like to believe they are true. However, moving back to the place of leadership requires stepping away from our simplistic stories of right and wrong, and into the reality of the situation and how we contributed to constructing it. In conflict, just like John, we live inside a story that is massively simplified, that upsets us and is part of creating the conflict, but in which we get to be 'right' (the victim battling heroically against the idiots around us). Moving to a different story that is less simple, that is ultimately likely to upset us much less and that helps to resolve the conflict, will enable us to be happier (we won't have to live with conflict), but we don't get to be right. This brings up one of the central challenges of conflict – would you prefer to be right or happy?

John hadn't made the shift away from his story yet, and if he had been asked whether he would prefer to be right or happy, he might have responded that he would prefer to be right in that moment.

There is a perverse pleasure available in righteous anger – have you ever eaten at a restaurant and known intuitively that the waiter or waitress was probably going to mess up the order, but waited until the end to complain about the awful service? It doesn't help you and your companions get the meal you wanted, but it does give the opportunity for righteous anger, as the 'customer who's always right'.

John needed to make this shift away from righteous anger – in fact not having made this shift meant that he was less powerful in what transpired next. But before we get to what happened next, let's look further at the state that John is now operating in, the stress or 'conditioned tendency' response.

Conditioned tendency response

The stress response, is sometimes referred to as a threat response, the fight-or-flight response or, as we will refer to it here, the conditioned tendency.

This response was described by the German psychoanalyst Karen Horney, who did much of her work in the United States. Horney described three categories of responses:

- Moving against: Often described as the fight response. It may show up in the workplace as competitiveness, political behaviours, challenging others in a meeting to establish authority, and engaging in conflicts.

- Moving away from: Often described as the flight response. It may show up in the workplace as an avoidance of conflict, or challenge and can appear somewhat detached or withdrawn.

- Moving towards: Often described as a 'please-and-appease' response. It is a form of self-effacement and responds to the perceived threat by making friends and forming relationships. In the workplace this can play out as working very hard to be nice to people in the face of conflict, giving them what they want, and occasionally as flirting.

Since Horney published her ideas in the 1940s we have discovered much more about the conditioned tendency response, and we also know that there is a fourth category of response, sometimes called 'freeze'. This probably has its roots in the animal response of playing dead so that a predator will move on, and can be referred to as 'tonic immobility' or as the 'fright response'.

Evidence suggests that most of us have one of these responses that we recurrently use, that we developed in childhood and that is deeply embedded. This means our conditioned tendency response is a recurrent pattern that falls into one of three general categories, although each of us develops our own unique ways of carrying out this response.

There is no right response amongst these. Sometimes participants on programmes look for which one of these responses is best, sometimes settling on 'moving towards' as preferable. However, all of these responses are limited in their effectiveness and the reality is that whichever we tend to recurrently use we are using it as a reaction, rather than as a choice. Therefore, it will at times be completely useless to us, and what is more valuable is to get into a place of choosing our responses.

John has a moving-against response. Therefore he tends to respond by fighting back, habitually his hands will close into fists, and he will move forward and challenge whatever he perceives to be threatening.

Let's look in further detail at what happens to someone when the conditioned tendency response kicks in. This response was designed, in evolutionary terms, for protection. Walking on the savannah, you might encounter a lion and your system needed to respond quickly with a response to save your life – be that through running away or fighting for survival.

The response unfolds in a number of stages. First the brain, specifically the amygdala, sends danger signals to other parts of the brain and to the heart and lungs to increase our heart rate and breathing. Blood vessels in the stomach constrict, as blood is diverted to the major muscles, giving the feeling of butterflies in the stomach. Blood may be diverted away from capillaries in the skin, causing the skin to lose colour, and the skin starts to release sweat to cool the body for the expected work it will have to do. In addition salivation will stop, to conserve water, giving a dry mouth effect. Adrenalin is then released, which prepares the body by breaking down glycogen in the liver and turning it into glucose for energy to fuel the impending exertions.

The body is prepared now for fighting with or running away from a lion, but in today's world that's not what people are dealing with. The body–brain system does not distinguish between physical threats, such as the lion, and social and political issues (perceived threats) in organizations, such as the one John faces, and so he is now prepared for fighting a lion, rather than dealing gracefully with a social and political conflict in the workplace.

Jane has a moving away response, but she is in a very different situation. During the programme she had attended she had reflected on and got to know very well her conditioned tendency. She could see how she responded to stress and had learned to feel that response at the physical level, the emotional level and at the level of the thoughts that it tended to generate for her.

She saw that at the physical level she moved away from the source of tension, often retreating physically. This was often accompanied by the emotion of fear, and the thought that repeatedly showed itself at these moments was one of her having done something wrong. She could see that this related heavily to key developmental experiences in her childhood, and was shocked to see that they were still with her and came out so strongly in these moments of stress.

However in addition to noticing what happened to her in those moments, she had learned she could have a different response. She had practised centring herself, turning to face the source of the stress and engaging with that person. This had been difficult at first, and it required her to get good at centring as her entire biology was telling her to run at those moments; however, with practice she was able to remain present and centred inside the intensity of that experience.

We now know that we can practise and train to be resilient in the face of stress. By engaging with repeated and short-lived, moderate stress experiences, we can develop a physiology better able to cope with stress. This means that the stress response will be less extreme and we will be able to have more control (and thus choice) over our reactions. Biologically, our brain–body systems will produce less of a conditioned tendency response when they are trained to be more resilient in this way. This is why different people have different stress tolerances. Research on rats also suggests that when they experience this type of 'training' they tend to live 18 per cent longer, so perhaps this can also help us live longer.[1]

Jane had gone through the experience of simulating her conditioned tendency on the programme in a very small way, so that she could know and understand it well, and so that she could train greater resilience in her biology. She had learned through centring and breathing to stimulate her parasympathetic nervous system (otherwise known as the 'rest-and-digest' system) to counter her conditioned tendency. This is the system that manages the longer-term bodily functions such as digestion, which are paused during the conditioned tendency response. Stimulating this reverses much of the direction of the fight-or-flight response, bringing blood back to the stomach and skin, reducing adrenalin production, slowing heart rate and lowering blood pressure. Here the body can be in a much greater state of balance and choice and is not set up to fight a lion or run away.

So Jane was coming into this meeting in a very different state from John. John was in the midst of a heavy stress response, whereas Jane was coming into the meeting in a much more resourceful and useful state for the challenge she faced. John was ready to fight a lion, whereas Jane was in a place of significantly greater choice.

Meeting again

This was new territory for Jane, as previously she would just have agreed to John's proposal, although she would have resented him for it later. She re-centred herself again, and then stepped inside his office. 'We need to talk,' she stated to John. John was unable to concentrate on very much, so was just sitting dealing with e-mails. He was still fuming on the inside. In a brief moment he considered telling her he was busy and sending her away, but something about her made him change his mind and instead, in a slightly passive-aggressive way, said: 'OK then, talk.' Jane's presence demanded attention and that she be taken seriously, which is why John was unable to just dismiss her.

'No, *we* need to talk,' Jane stated. There had been a little trap inside his invitation for her to talk, and she neatly sidestepped it. 'I need to understand more about your proposal and what your thoughts are,' she continued. 'Why don't you run me through it?' Her idea was just to get John talking so she could understand his point of view.

'What's the point?' asked John, 'You made it pretty clear you're going to block it at the meeting.' John was sulking slightly, and Jane saw an opportunity to make the conversation more real. 'It seems like you're pretty upset with me about what happened in the meeting,' said Jane. The honesty of this response surprised John a little, but he quickly moved beyond this into an outpouring of his anger.

'Of course I'm upset with you, actually I'm furious. What gives you the right to stand in the way of this company being successful? You're blocking my success and therefore this company's success – what did I ever do to you?' He continued with a rant that varied between commentary on Jane blocking the company and him. Occasionally he would stop after a question and pause, waiting for Jane to respond. She either maintained silence, at which point he continued, or asked him more about his perspective with a question like, 'Why do you think that?' Through these strategies she kept him going for a while, until he ran out of steam.

All the time while she was listening to this she just kept re-centring herself so that she didn't fall into her historical patterns. Jane felt her conditioned tendency response – she started to lean backwards, collapse and withdraw; she felt fear and discomfort; the familiar story in her head was that of having done something wrong, that it was her fault; and she felt the desire to say sorry, capitulate and accept responsibility just to end the meeting so she could get away. That response hadn't changed, as her system prepared itself for fleeing the situation, but by centring and breathing she brought herself back to an internal state where she could choose her response.

Finally she summed up what she'd heard: 'So, if I understand you correctly, you see me as blocking your proposals, and therefore the success of the company. You commented that we have never been close, and you're wondering if I am out to get you in some way. You're angry that I'm standing in the way of your proposals to fix a department that has been problematic for a long time, and that your predecessor was unable to fix.'

John acknowledged that this was his position and Jane stated that she could understand why he was angry, if that was his perspective. John started to see some hope in this moment: perhaps Jane was seeing how unreasonable she was being, and would agree to the proposal. Jane saw this flicker of hope across his face, and moved quickly stating that she wasn't here to agree to the proposal, but to understand more about his proposal and how they could work together more effectively.

She was tempted to respond by reminding him about his timing of the proposal and of how he was conveniently moving all of his difficult staff to her department, but she realized that she wanted to do this as a retaliation for his rant, and that this would just re-ignite John's anger. She then suggested they go for a coffee for him to talk more about his proposal and why he felt it was important. She felt that getting them both moving and changing the location of the meeting would be a good thing in moving the conversation forward and building a relationship.

Over the course of the coffee Jane was able to get John to speak about his proposal and the problems in his department. She was able to get a good understanding of the issues he was facing and to show him that he was understood. For most people, most of the time, really knowing that we are understood by someone else makes a huge difference to us. By starting with a clear understanding of him, she would be able to build a different relationship with John.

As she centred herself she made herself present. By being curious about, and trying to understand, his point of view, she was able to be open to his perspectives and the challenges he faced. Because of her presence and openness, and her desire to understand him, she made a connection with John. Being present, open and connecting with others, was something she had practised repeatedly on the programme and she was able to do this easily with John once his rant had finished. It is this connection that would enable her to move forward effectively with John.

Although John hadn't managed to persuade her to go along with his proposal he was feeling massively relieved. Just having talked with someone about the pressure he was feeling and how difficult he was finding things was a weight off his shoulders. This was literally true; Jane had noticed his shoulders going down as he relaxed the tension in this area during their conversation. She had really listened to him, and he found himself being more open with her than he had expected. At the end of the conversation, although nothing had been decided or agreed, he felt that Jane was not his enemy and that he could trust her.

Blending

Let's look at what Jane has done so far. She has a conditioned tendency of 'moving away', which means that she is likely to withdraw from sources of pressure and stress. This will happen physically through retreating, and it will also happen through giving in and accommodating others' needs. Historically it was predictable, although not inevitable, that she would have given in to John's proposals.

Here she did something very different that I will refer to as 'blending'. In the meeting that has just taken place John has pushed into Jane energetically through his rant. He hasn't physically pushed her, but he has been pushing. People don't get physically pushed around in most workplaces (although I have seen one or two where that has happened), but people still get pushed around, and there are some people whom we know are pushovers. Jane had historically been a pushover, and that's why John had targeted her – people who are consistently pushovers will make themselves targets.

Whilst John is not physically pushing her, the body and self reacts in the same way as if he was – the mind–body system reacts in exactly the same way to the energetic push in the workplace, as it would to the physical push. Indeed somatic markers generated in the physical process of being pushed around in the school playground may create some of the responses we have to being pushed around energetically at work.

Jane, when she is sitting in the face of John's energetic push, feels this just like a real push. Through centring herself, facing and entering into relationship with John she counters her automatic desire to run away and stays in the conversation. Next she does something very important – she moves herself to see his point of view. His energy is coming at her at full force and she does not try to oppose it, however tempting that may be; rather she starts with where he is and what his concerns are. In doing this she gives up nothing of herself, and does not give in; she is merely allowing herself to understand John.

This is important to emphasize: in blending she does not give in, and neither does she fight back. Rather she opens herself to seeing the world from his perspective. Blending is a subtle art – if she is not willing to be influenced by John, then she is no longer open to him, and he will feel that and there will be no blend. If she tries to use it as a technique to manipulate him, then she won't truly be open and it will also not work. In fact they will be back in conflict. If you have ever had an argument with someone who is completely closed to being influenced by you, you will know that it's a frustrating experience. If someone closes up completely the argument just escalates, or ends with people walking away frustrated.

So blending is a more subtle place of genuinely being open to another person, being willing to see and understand their views and perspectives, yet not giving in and capitulating to those views. It is about really getting someone's concerns and seeing the world through their eyes. There are many roots in our culture suggesting that we do this. The Native American saying 'Never criticize another man until you've walked a mile in his moccasins,' speaks to the same idea.

It is also fundamental to some of the Eastern martial arts, such as Aikido, where the blend comes from receiving the energy of the attack, moving with that energy and then starting to guide it and direct it. Whilst Jane did not learn martial arts on the leadership programme, she did engage in physical exercises where she practised blending. Learning to centre on the programme, face stressors and blend with them physically, enabled her to face all of the challenges she faced when dealing with stressors in the workplace without being overwhelmed by her conditioned tendency response.

In repeated practice Jane was able to generate a level of competence in responding differently, and it is this different response that she has brought to the conversation with John. In doing this she has built trust with him, truly understood his world, and has allowed herself to be open to the challenges he faces and to be touched by the difficulty of his situation. She has built a genuinely deeper relationship with him.

I meet many people who want to be able to get to this place, but from a more objective and less involved perspective. They want the trust in the relationship, but don't want to be touched by someone else. They want to be able to have the influence, but keep themselves safe and immune in their own world – this they often believe has a strength and power to it, as they are solid and unshakeable in their beliefs.

In reality it's a massive source of weakness, as they are unable to build genuine and strong relationships. Life and engagement with others requires entering fully into the relationship without knowing where it might go, and still having confidence in yourself that you will not lose yourself in the process. Fear is what keeps people in the objective, distanced and uninvolved place where they can analyse others but be unscathed and untouched in the process. Life is messy and it impacts us emotionally, and only by fully engaging with this and learning to be centred (present, open and connected) inside this can we be powerful and take leadership.

I once had someone ask me, without irony, if I could teach them to fake authenticity, as they didn't want to do all this work and to be open in this way. If we aim to do this, we aim to engage in life from that distant place but fool others that we are fully engaged with them – to try and play them in our mind's game, whilst remaining untouched by the messiness of life. In reality it is manipulation and the only people who can do it very well are psychopaths.

By the end of their coffee, Jane is in a different position. She sees that John is in a very difficult situation, and is receiving no support. She can see that he could very easily be replaced soon, just as his predecessor was, and that he is facing mounting pressure from the CEO. Something does need to change, she believes, for John (and therefore for herself) to be successful. That doesn't equate, for her, to John's proposal, but some change does clearly need to happen.

John is also in a different place. He has someone he can trust on the team – an ally. The specifics of the proposal don't seem very important any more, and he is starting to feel hopeful again for the future.

At the end of the conversation Jane addresses the one thing that's left that is impeding their relationship. She, and John, have not yet faced the truth of what happened in the original meeting and the development of John's proposal. They could go on without addressing this, but Jane knows that ultimately without being honest about this, the relationship will always be limited. If she is never fully honest about it, there will always be a part of her that is resentful. While he doesn't face the honest truth of it, John will never fully respect her as an equal.

So Jane centres herself and addresses the easier of the two aspects of the proposal – its timing. She tells John that he should know that the timing of the proposal was unreasonable given that she was away. This is an easy one for John to accept, and he acknowledges the timing didn't work and apologizes stating that he was just feeling the pressure to move things forward. This is true, but is also a little white lie, as he was trying to take advantage of Jane being away. However, Jane does not want to re-ignite conflict so she politely accepts the apology. She does however request that he doesn't repeat the behaviour in the future, to which he agrees.

Then she addresses the more difficult issue for her, that of the impact of the proposal in transferring difficult low-performing staff to her, and transferring high performers to him. She acknowledges the pressure he is under and then lets him know that the fact that the proposals he presented so conveniently transfer staff in his favour, and were presented while she was away, left her with the assessment that he was trying to take advantage of her.

John was a little embarrassed at the directness with which she addressed this issue – he really did underestimate her, he thought. At first he tried to push it away – she was overreacting and that hadn't been his intention, he said. However she held her line, and told him that whether it was his intention or not, he needed to understand the impact of his behaviour. Given the fact of the timing, and that he was transferring staff in a very favourable way to him, he needed to understand the impression that this created.

Jane avoided the trap of being righteous about John's intention – *the reality was she had no idea of his intention.* All she could comment on was the impact of what he did, and she stuck to letting him know that. The rest would be up to him – he chose in that moment not to be honest about his intention, but after sitting with it for a period of time, he did come back to her around a month later and gave a fuller apology and admission. However, if she had pushed at the time, he would have just fought her, and the reality was she didn't know whether it had been his intention or not, so arguing with him about it would not have served her.

We can never know someone else's intention (and they may not be fully aware of their intention either), and this is the source of much conflict in organizations (and relationships in general). Jane had her beliefs about John's intentions, just as John had his beliefs about her intentions in blocking his proposal – as human beings we create these meanings. The reality is that often people are responding with their somatic markers as described in Part I, which means if we challenge them about why they did what they did, they will often post-rationalize a response. They will have responded in the way that just 'felt right' to them in the moment. Therefore engaging in the arguments over intentions is largely a waste of time on both sides – all John needs to know is the impact of his actions, on whatever basis he chose to take them, so that he can learn from the experience.

Jane went on to acknowledge that previously she was the kind of person who would have just gone along with such things, and that perhaps that meant that she had created the impression that she would not need to be consulted. However, she said she had changed and that she was now willing to stand up for herself, and not just say yes to avoid confrontation.

John apologized for the impact on her, without fully acknowledging that he had hoped to take advantage of her, and Jane was satisfied as she had made her point and John knew he had to respect her.

They completed the conversation with Jane sharing her declaration for the executive team with John, and they spoke about how they could work together going forward. They agreed to meet again to look at what needed to change across the team and how they could support each other going forward.

John's stress

For John this whole process was a massive relief. He now had someone he could talk to about the challenges he faced, and this eased his stress massively.

In discussing John's state I have so far focused on his conditioned tendency response. The reality, however, is that he was suffering from a much longer-term stress response that had been ongoing for many months. Our stress response is designed for a short-term challenge – fighting or fleeing from a lion, for example. The kind of work and social challenges we face in today's world, however, can be much longer in duration, and these stresses have some pretty remarkable impacts. They can change us beyond recognition, causing us to act in ways that we wouldn't normally consider appropriate, such as the way that John acted at the start of this story.

John's initial conditioned tendency response began not long after he started in the new role. Initially the stress response had been moderate and the adrenalin had felt good. His body had also released small quantities of cortisol, a stress hormone, which gave him a good feeling. However, as he had struggled with his new position and been put under more and more pressure by a CEO impatient for results, his stress levels continued to rise. As time went on and he made little progress, while the external market and financial environment for the company went from bad to worse, and so his stress levels went through the roof.

This was because John wasn't centring himself during this process and engaging the rest-and-digest system, so the stress kept building. He carried his stress and off-centredness from one incident to the next, all the time increasing his stress levels. He worked longer and longer hours to deal with the challenges he faced, but became less and less productive.

Long-term impact of stress

When the body realizes that the situation is not going to resolve itself swiftly, it releases large quantities of cortisol. This is designed to prepare the body for a long-term challenge – the fight with the lion has taken longer than expected, so the body prepares itself for a longer fight. The cortisol, which in small quantities gave a pleasant buzz, in large quantities shuts down many of the long-term processes of the body, such as the immune system, and maintains high blood pressure and heart rate. It also breaks down pretty much anything the body can use as an energy source to prepare the body for its long-term struggle. In large quantities it no longer produces a pleasant buzz and it has a negative impact on the entire body–mind system.

The prolonged exposure to cortisol began to impair his ability to think straight. In fact, prolonged exposure to cortisol can alter people's moods and their actions. This is why, despite working longer hours, John is less effective, and it is probably why he tried to take advantage of Jane whilst she was away, at the start of this story.

An interesting thing to note is that when under a lot of stress we can become accustomed to it, and stop noticing. John Coates, who's an investment banker turned neuroscientist, has shown that traders in an investment bank environment are very poor at noticing their stress levels, but that their cortisol levels match very accurately with their profits and losses in trading – as their losses increase so do their cortisol levels.[2] What this means is that we become accustomed to stress and no longer believe we are experiencing it, but our bodies are still suffering the effects of long-term cortisol exposure. This is not only bad for thinking and performance in the organization, but is extremely bad for our health. This means that asking people about their stress levels can actually be a very poor measure of how stressed they really are.

For John, having the conversation with Jane has changed some of this. Jane's centredness has affected John, in the same way that some people can walk into a room and lift the mood and others can walk into a room and the energy is sucked out. This is a process known as structural coupling, and is a biological process.[3] As biological systems, when we engage in interactions, we align with each other – we relax more around people who are relaxed, and tense up around those who are tense. This probably had evolutionary advantage when we were living under threat from predators; when someone spots a predator their tension can be transmitted to the rest of the tribe very quickly. This phenomenon has produced a change in state for John and he is more centred and less stressed as a result.

This is a key element of leadership, and one not often discussed. Too many leaders inspire fear when they walk into the room, but what if leaders could bring a sense of calm and centredness with them that infected the mood of the organization? This is what Jane is beginning to do through her interaction with John.

Ultimately John would need to learn to manage his stress levels and centredness for himself, but after this meeting he was able to be more productive and went home earlier than usual and in a better mood.

Applying this learning

The starting point in applying this learning is to identify your own conditioned tendency response. For some people this is easier than others. From the descriptions in the story so far, you may be clear on your conditioned tendency. For some it may take more time. Either is fine, and the following should help you to clarify which of the responses you habitually use.

For many, although not all people, an awkward social moment can trigger a conditioned tendency response. Try and identify yourself in this story. Imagine that I have invited you to a party, where you know no one else. At the party is a famous author whom you admire greatly, and who is the centre of attention. Unfortunately I have not arrived at the agreed time and you arrive on your own. Do you:

- Stand at the side of the room, get a drink, snack and watch the proceedings, check your mobile phone/e-mail, perhaps engaging with another person in the same situation?
  This is the moving-away response.

- Go up and introduce yourself to the author and tell them how much you love their work? This is the moving-towards response.

- Go up and introduce yourself to the author and tell them that you enjoyed their book, but there's something you weren't sure about and wanted to question/challenge?
  This is the moving-against response.

- Find you don't know what to do and do nothing, therefore ending up being governed by others interacting with you?
  This is the freeze response.

This example will work for many people; however, it doesn't work for everyone as some people are very comfortable with social situations and this doesn't provoke the conditioned tendency response. If that doesn't work for you, perhaps consider this story, which is a true one. A former colleague of mine is South African and whilst still living there she found herself in a situation where her car was hijacked. A guy with a gun got into her car. What would you do? My former colleague has a moving-towards conditioned tendency response, and so she started to try and build a relationship with the hijacker by appeasing him. At a deep level this is driven by a sense of safety through building relationship; very simply the logic is, 'if you like me you won't hurt me.'

What would your response be? Would you respond as my colleague did, would you be out of the car very quickly (moving away), would you fight for your survival (moving against), or would you freeze?

Even with this story it can be difficult to be sure for yourself which you do. So, the next test is for you to notice what you actually do in life. Start to pay attention to what happens to you when you are knocked off-centre. Notice what happens when the boss asks to see you in his office, or when you get that e-mail that just winds you up. Start to pay attention to these moments and look for what happens at three levels:

- What happens physically? The conditioned tendency actually starts here with the physical reactions and sensations, although if you're not used to paying attention here you may not notice this first. Do you clench your fists, project your chest and lean forward? Do you lean away, slump and withdraw? Do you lean forward, extend out and try to make contact if the person is in front of you? Do you freeze (ie hold your breath and stop all movement)?

- What happens emotionally? Alongside the physical response (as we have seen in the first part of this book) there is an emotional response caused by the physical response. What do you notice here? There can be a wide range of responses – like Jane's response of fear or John's response of anger.

- What happens at the cognitive level – what stories or memories are triggered by the experience? Jane had a response of a story that she had done something wrong – a narrative that had its roots in her past. What stories, memories or narratives do you see as a recurrent pattern when your conditioned tendency is triggered?

We divide these three aspects as a convenience of language – in reality they are all one and the same response in the brain–body system, which we experience in three different forms. Getting familiar with each of these aspects is important: knowing them well gives you good insight into your reactions and where they come from, which is an important way to build self-awareness. Additionally, if you know your response at these three levels you have a greater possibility of seeing and spotting it early, so that you can choose to do something different.

Another route that may help in identifying your conditioned tendency is to ask people whom you trust – your partner, family members or key colleagues at work. It needs to be someone who can be honest with you, and they may be able to give you some feedback on how they see your reactions. If you do ask them, be prepared for them to tell you whatever their opinion is, and listen to that without getting into any arguments! In fact, if you find yourself tempted to react and argue, you are in your conditioned tendency response (probably of moving against), so pay attention to it and notice your reaction.

It's worth taking some time to identify this carefully and to get to know it well so that you can spot it quickly. Keeping a journal where you reflect on instances where your conditioned tendency has been triggered and recording your reactions and thoughts in those moments is something I recommend, as you will get clearer and clearer on your reactions and the unique way in which you play out your response. Whilst you and I may have the same conditioned tendency response, we may enact it in slightly different ways, so getting clear on how you do it is really very important.

Once you have spent some time identifying and getting familiar with your response (perhaps around two weeks), you can then start to practise doing something different. This relies on you also having been practising centring, as suggested in the last chapter.

This is a process that cannot really be short-circuited; however, it is through this process of paying attention and practising different responses that we change and develop ourselves. This is the key difference between self-awareness and self-cultivation mentioned in Chapters 1 and 2.

The first part of changing your response is to practise centring when your conditioned tendency is triggered. This may initially be difficult. You may find that you centre yourself, and then are immediately triggered again, and then need to re-centre. This may be a process that recurs time and time again. However, the job here is to use the awareness you have developed of your conditioned tendency, alongside the ability you now have to centre yourself quickly, to give you space to choose your response.

From this you can begin to work on seeing the other's point of view and building a real connection with them. This is the place where you build deeper, stronger and more trusting relationships, which is the foundation of good leadership.

There's a process that often happens when we develop self-awareness. We start off by seeing that we're doing something, such as our conditioned tendency response, in hindsight. This can at times produce some frustration, as people can see behaviour that they wish to change only after they have done it. If, however, we spend time getting familiar with our responses, and continue to pay attention to them by using the journalling process described above, we can start to see our responses as they happen. Once we get to this point we can start to choose different responses. If we continue to pay attention further, we can develop foresight and start to see situations where our conditioned tendency may be triggered in advance, and choose different ways of acting that pre-empt the triggering.

Stress

It's ironic that people who come on programmes often want to learn two things: to improve their influencing skills to get others to do what they want, and to be able to say 'no' more often. Usually they fail to see the irony in what they want. Overall it suggests a desire to move to a place of being more in control, and yet the reality of life is that when we engage with others we don't get to be in control – no matter how high up the ranks in an organization we get. I think the answer we need is to get more comfortable with lack of control and ambiguity, rather than trying to find more sophisticated methods of being in control.

Many managers whom I meet in organizations seem to believe (or act as if they believe) that fear and panic is useful as a way to run an organization. This is also a rather fruitless attempt to gain a greater degree of control in an out-of-control world. It is also massively destructive in organizations, as it increases stress levels and lowers motivation.

It seems that three aspects of the situations we encounter trigger our physiological stress response – those are the aspects of novelty, uncertainty and uncontrollability. An interesting example is that of Londoners during the Second World War.[4] Those who lived in central London were exposed to regular daily predictable bombing raids, whereas those who lived in the suburbs faced much less bombing, but it was completely unpredictable. Those in the suburbs suffered higher stress as measured through gastric ulcers.[5]

The reality is that we face a world in which there is significant ambiguity and complexity – I see the request to help managers deal with ambiguity and complexity regularly in organizations' requirements for leadership development programmes. However, through trying to be better at influencing and saying no (at the same time), or through creating a culture of fear, we are not becoming better at handling ambiguity and uncertainty; we are merely trying to minimize it. The only way to truly become better able to handle this is through working with our conditioned tendencies and experiencing the kind of training Jane did, where she was able to safely stimulate her conditioned tendency repeatedly, in a very minor way, so that she could get to know it, learn to centre after it, and build her resilience.

Research on monkeys shows that when put under stress dominant monkeys will start to bite lower-order monkeys, and that this has the impact of reducing their cortisol levels. This may be the origins of the culture of fear that begins to start in organizations that are going through challenging times. Managers are imposing fear to control others and reduce their own cortisol levels.

If you are stressed in this way, often it will be suggested that you should go on vacation, travel and explore. This is in fact usually unhelpful as it introduces new uncertainty and novelty. In these moments what you need is actually familiarity and stability. Spending time with family, being at home and around close friends is much more useful. With centring and, when you are ready for it, the kind of resilience training described in this chapter combined, you will be able to come back stronger and more able to cope with the effects of cortisol on your mind–body system.

Working with, understanding, getting to know, and learning to centre in our conditioned tendencies should be part of every manager's and leader's learning from my perspective, for the health of both ourselves and our organizations.

Conflict

Implicitly and explicitly, in this chapter, I have been addressing one dimension of conflict.[6] Many people in organizations treat conflict as if it is something to be removed, reduced or restrained – even if they speak of conflict as being potentially creative and helpful, this is often how they actually act. Others I meet in organizations see the value of creative conflict, but want it to be controlled, ordered and processed and to happen when they are ready for it. Often they will divide conflict into two categories – task conflict and relationship conflict – with task conflict being good and productive, and relationship conflict being bad and unproductive.

Indeed some research would back this up, stating that relationship conflict should be avoided because it is less productive, whereas task conflict can be valuable (although it is worth noting that this is based upon opinion surveys rather than correlations with actual work performance). The trouble with this research is that there is other research that shows that task and relationship conflict tend to occur at the same time, so they are basically inseparable, and it takes no account of whether or not the people concerned have been given support or training in dealing with conflict.[7]

An incomplete, yet useful way of thinking about conflict is:

relationship conflict = task conflict + conditioned tendencies

We may have a debate around the technical issues of a new product that's being launched, which could be seen as a task conflict. It becomes a relationship conflict when, although we're having this task debate, my conditioned tendency has been triggered and I also believe that you're a political player in the organization who's out to get me in some way. The pathway to this belief inevitably involves some instance where my conditioned tendency has been triggered. I may be explicitly fighting you, or it may be that I am avoiding conflict with you (although probably talking to anyone who'll listen about how awful you are), depending on my conditioned tendency, but the conflict is alive and well either way.

When you see people arguing over a product launch or any other such issue, you will know whether this is genuinely a task conflict or there are other layers to it – you will feel it, and be responding to it at a visceral level. Trying to avoid, reduce or restrain conflict is a fruitless activity. Task conflict abounds in all organizations because there are limited resources and many ways of dealing with anything. That won't go away. Our conditioned tendencies will be triggered – that piece of human evolution is not something we can remove through any training programme or pill.

This makes conflict – which can be difficult and painful – an inevitable reality. We need to engage with conflict and we need to be better at handling it. This requires us to, as Jane did, manage ourselves, and it is a focus on managing ourselves rather than the other person that is essential in dealing with conflict productively and yet so very rare. Addressing such conflict is not a distraction from the 'real work' of the organization – think about it: an organization is not a noun (a thing), it is a verb, and the work of organizing is the work of dealing with conflict.

To do this well we must all be familiar with and able to deal with our conditioned tendencies. We must be able to manage ourselves so that we can actually sit in the face of conflict and our own reactions to it, and be able to work it through, all the while being able to choose our responses. Arnold Mindell (a great writer on conflict) states this beautifully when he says:

> Yet enforcing order does not stop riots, hinder war or reduce world problems. It may even kindle the fire of group chaos. If we don't permit hostilities a legitimate outlet, they are bound to take illegitimate routes.
>
> … engaging in heated conflict instead of running away from it is one of the best ways to resolve the divisiveness that prevails on every level of society – in personal relationships, business and the world.
>
> … The fire that burns in the social, psychological, and spiritual dimensions of humanity can ruin the world. Or this fire can transform

trouble into community. It's up to us. We can avoid contention, or we can sit fearlessly in the fire, intervene and prevent world history's most painful errors from being repeated.[8]

As you practise centring and once you are clear on your conditioned tendency, be willing to sit in conflicts that emerge. Remember to re-centre yourself as you are in the experience, and if you find yourself reacting and unable to centre, suggest a break in the conversation. Write your journal after each experience and reflect on your learning. This is difficult and important work, so it may take years (depending on the frequency of conflicts you experience) for you to get to a place where this is easier for you. It will happen, however, and your competence in this arena will, perhaps more than any other, allow you stand out as a leader in your organization.

Recommended reading

If you are interested in reading more about the conditioned tendency, then I highly recommend the chapter 'The conditioned tendency', in *The Anatomy of Change: A way to move through life's transitions*, by Richard Strozzi-Heckler. This will enhance your understanding of the conditioned tendency greatly.

If you are interested in reading more about conflict then I recommend *Sitting in the Fire: Large group transformation using conflict and diversity*, by Arnold Mindell.

Notes

1 Coates, J (2012) *The Hour Between Dog and Wolf: Risk-taking, gut feelings and the biology of boom and bust*, Fourth Estate, London, p 234.

2 Ibid.

3 Maturana, H and Varela, F (1987) *The Tree of Knowledge: The biological roots of human understanding*, revised edn, Shambala, Boston.

4 Coates, J (2012) *The Hour Between Dog and Wolf*, p 203.

5 Gastric ulcers can be caused by the reduced blood flow to the stomach when the body is under the conditioned tendency response.

6 I say one dimension, because it is a one-on-one conflict, rather than a group conflict, and I am addressing here individual responses to conflict, rather than group behaviours or processes in dealing with conflict, which could be a whole book in itself.

7 Edmondson, AC and McLain Smith, D (2006) 'Too Hot To Handle? How to manage relationship conflict', *California Management Review*, 49 (1), pp 6–31.

8 Mindell, A (1995) *Sitting in the Fire: Large group transformation using conflict and diversity*, Portland, Lao-Tse Press.

Giving feedback and being mindful rather than mindless

08

John was left curious about what had changed for Jane and why she had changed, so he asked her about it, and Jane told him all about the embodied leadership programme she'd attended. It seemed a little weird to him, this whole idea of the body and leadership, but Jane seemed to have changed a lot, and in a really good way. He asked her about what his body was saying about him; how did he show up physically?

Somatic assessments

Jane had spent time on the programme practising somatic assessments. To understand this we first need to understand 'assessments'.

Assessments are our opinions, perspectives, interpretations or judgements. If you think about it, the chances are that you are paid for your assessments – they are the educated opinions that you have about your business, having spent time in the industry/organization/sector or having expertise in a particular field.

What assessments are not is facts, and this is a major source of conflict in organizations. If I observe someone yawning and looking out the window during my presentation, I may have the assessment that they are tired, bored, uninterested or any other of a variety of different assessments. Once I have the germ of an idea in my head that this person is uninterested in what I am working on, then I will start looking for evidence to corroborate that belief – human beings love nothing more than to be right!

Soon I will have more evidence – instances where the person looked at their watch whilst I was speaking, further yawning when I am speaking in meetings and so on. I will also start to block out the occasions when they do respond well to me, or explain them away as being about something else – for instance: 'They just wanted to show up well to the boss who was in that meeting.' Over a relatively short time I will have a collection of evidence that this person is uninterested in my work. If I was never really close to this person, perhaps I can then take an extra leap and say that the person never really liked me anyway.

Eventually I will have a clear perspective on this person and who they are, and often my belief about it will be unshakeable. However, this isn't true. It's not false either. It lies in the world of opinions, which are not facts and therefore cannot be true or false. You and I can go to a movie and have completely different opinions about the movie, the actors and actresses in it, the core message of the plot lines and so on. These will be our opinions and we can spend hours arguing over them, but the reality is they are not truth or falsehood – they are our opinions.

Let me give another example to help clarify this. There was snow lying in parts of Central London (something that is relatively rare) during the winter of 2010–11. For my Kenyan friend, who lives in London, this was a massive snowfall; for my Finnish wife, it wasn't even proper snow. These are the assessments that each holds for the same event, and there is no right and wrong and there is no truth in these assessments. Arguing about these would be pointless. The assessments have their roots in the backgrounds of the people concerned – a Kenyan upbringing versus a Finnish one. Assessments, therefore, can say a lot more about us than about the thing that we believe we are describing.

Underlying those assessments are 'assertions' – in the example above, for instance, that there were two inches of snow in parts of central London. These we can say are true or false, because we can measure them against an agreed frame of reference (inches or centimetres), and we can all go and measure it and agree on the same measurement.

If we go back to the example of my colleague who yawns, all we can agree on is that he yawned and looked out of the window for a short period of time (perhaps 30 seconds) during my presentation. This is something that could be agreed on by all who were present. The interpretation or assessment I come to about that is my own creation, and says something about my background and standards – just as their assessments about the snow say something about my Kenyan friend and my Finnish wife.

Our assessments reveal our standards. When we give our opinions on our businesses or organizations (strategies to choose, products to launch, trades to make, services to procure) we are paid for our educated assessments, where our standards have been educated through our experience, training and feedback over our career.

When we are dealing with people, we also have assessments. However, have we really educated ourselves in our ability to make assessments on other people? It's hard to get feedback on whether the standards through which we make these assessments are useful or helpful to us, and most of the time we do it unconsciously and don't pay much attention to it.

For example, how much attention did I pay in the process of developing my assessment of my colleague being uninterested during my presentation? It probably happened in milliseconds. Getting to the assessment of someone who never really liked me anyway didn't take that much longer – it just required that I collect a bit more evidence.

Once I have reached my conclusion, how would I react to being told that my assessment of someone wasn't true or false, but was in fact, just my opinion? I have given that feedback to quite a number of people, and I can assure you the reaction is generally not that positive. 'But you don't know this person – s/he really is like that...' is a common response. The challenge is that we don't really notice that it is not an objective truth about the person, but an assessment we have created about them. We believe that our opinion is how it actually is and we start to treat it as truth. This becomes a recipe for conflict and distrust in organisations (and in other areas of our lives as well).

The thing is that assessments are not a bad thing – it's forgetting that they are an opinion that gets us into trouble. Even if our assessments are well grounded with evidence (assertions), they are not true or false – they are still opinions we have created from the evidence. And even as I write this, I know that there will be some people reading this who believe that in their case, with the person they know, it's different and their assessment is true.

As human beings we love nothing more than being right, and having that taken away from us is a painful, and *very necessary*, process, because when we are right, we are generally making someone else wrong, and generally the other person doesn't like that too much, and misunderstanding and conflict can arise. True humility is, at least in part, being able to see one's own assessments as assessments, rather than believing them to be truths.

The reality of life is that we are all creating assessments all of the time. You will be reading this book and you will be creating assessments about me. Sometimes we call them first impressions, and as the saying goes, they do have a habit of lasting. However, over time, you will develop a sense of me and who I am that will be based on two things:

Your sense of me
= what I do or say + your opinions about what I do or say

Over time as you read this book you can develop a complete picture of me, of who I am, how I am, what motivates me and what I am like as a person. We all form assessments in this way, and can do this from even very tiny interactions – just witness the conversations people have about TV personalities, reality TV stars or actors/actresses and you will hear how they often have a complete picture of that person without having even met them. This is actually a little crazy when you think about it!

We can't stop creating assessments as human beings. It's just something we constantly do – we are assessment machines. So if we're doing this all the time about other people, and if it can be the source of significant conflict and pain, can we educate ourselves in the way that we do with the assessments we make on our organization's strategy, for example, and can we find a way to use them that its more beneficial? This is what Jane had spent time working on during her programme.

Developing our ability at working with assessments has a series of steps or processes to it.

1. Becoming aware of our assessments and how quickly we make them

When I was beginning with this work, around 10 years ago, I spent some time working with my teacher, Richard Strozzi-Heckler. Upon leaving any group he would always ask me what my assessments were about the individuals in that group. Initially I would sit back and think, going through each person in my head and trying to remember what my assessments were. However, it didn't take long for me to realize that this was going to happen every time we left a group so I started to bring my assessments to consciousness when I was with the group so that I would have them available more easily for the inevitable conversation.

You see, it wasn't that I didn't have assessments about this small group of people we might have met for a short time; it was just that I hadn't thought about them explicitly. If you met someone briefly in the last few days, you have some assessments, or first impressions, of them, but you may not have brought those assessments to consciousness, unless someone asked you specifically about your impression of the person.

What I discovered in this process is that when my assessments are unconscious, I live them as if they are true. We take actions on the basis of our assessments (eg our assessments about a publicly listed company would dictate whether we bought their stock), and when our assessments are unconscious they will drive our behaviours without us really thinking about them. When I thought about my assessments consciously and understood them as assessments, I had much more freedom in how I related to others and was able to be open to the times and places where the person did not behave according to my assessment – in other words, I was much less righteous about them. This is the first step at educating ourselves in our ability to make useful assessments, and it requires practice.

2. Owning the part of us that creates the assessment

Imagine someone who is slightly obsessive-compulsive regarding neatness – you know the type: they are chronically neat about everything and line up the tin cans in the cupboard so all the labels are aligned. Now that person has a somatic marker that generates that behaviour – they don't line up tin cans because rationally it's a 'good' thing to do. Rather they do it because they feel, physically in their bodies, discomfort with disorder and lining up the cans relieves that discomfort. Now this person will be the kind of person who will notice whether my desk is tidy or not. They will then generate an assessment about the messiness of my desk; perhaps that I am less competent as a result of being less organized. Another person, with different somatic markers, may not even notice that my desk is untidy, and therefore their assessment about me and my competence may be very different.

Therefore, what we notice, and then react to, is a function of our somatic markers and our history, and paying close attention to the sensations in our physical bodies will help us to tell which part of our assessment is about us, and which is about the behaviour of the other. When we notice this discomfort, we need to be aware of the sensation on the physical level, as well as the emotional reaction it generates and the stories or narratives that are created.

If you're a paranoid person, you will tend to generate assessments with a fair degree of suspicion. This will be a pattern for you in the assessments you create; if a couple of your colleagues are having a conversation in which you are not included, you may believe it to be about you, or a move on their part to exclude you. Some people will always create assessments where they are victims and others are to blame; others will create assessments where there is something wrong with them, or something they are not doing well. Each of us will have our own patterns, based on our individual histories and somatic markers, and it is important for all of us to see our patterns so that we can own the part of our assessments that is more about us than it is about the person we are assessing.

3. *Training ourselves to see what it is about the other person that generates the assessment*

Once we have seen what it is about us that generates the assessment, we also need to look at what it is about the other person. However, it's important not to skip the previous step and go straight to this one – always look inwards before looking outwards!

First, we have to understand that when we generate an assessment about someone we do so from their bodies. Just look at a random photograph of any person and you'll immediately have a series of assessments about them. What is happening in this process is that you are observing someone's shaping, that they have developed due to their somatic markers, and this gives you an impression of them. This is what makes an assessment a 'somatic assessment'.

It's important to remember that this impression isn't true, but if we can be conscious of our assessments and know the patterns we have in the assessments we create (which are more about us than the other), then perhaps this assessment can be useful to the other person. It says something about how they are showing up in the organization, to me at least and perhaps more widely, and will often provide them with information on how they have shaped themselves in response to their somatic markers.

To do this well we need to ground our assessments with our observations of what it is that someone is doing that produces the assessment. For example if I am slouching, looking down and avoiding eye contact, you may have the impression that I am trying to hide something, or that I am shy, depending on the assessment you choose. If it is to be valuable to me, I will need to know both the assessment it produces in you (shy or evasive) as well as what I am doing to produce it (slouching and avoiding eye contact). This gives me both a reason why I should change – not wanting to produce that sort of assessment in others – plus details of how I can change: stand straighter and make eye contact.

This requires us to be better conscious observers of how others are showing up. This means paying attention to how they hold themselves in length, width and depth, just as we did in centring, and how they hold tension in their bodies – forehead, eyes, jaw, shoulders and so on. This is what is giving you the impression you have of the person, and being able to see this means that when you share it with this person they can know what it is they are doing and how they can change to produce a different assessment.

4. Getting better at sharing our assessments

This leads us nicely to getting better at sharing our assessments. In many organizations I have seen, people rarely share their assessments with each other, but happily do so with everyone else. This is organizational gossip, and is usually toxic for an organization's health, as the gossip that travels most widely is negative and damaging.

So why would we share our assessments? Well in doing so we are providing information for the other person on how they are showing up. We are all reading each other all of the time, and so knowing more about how we are showing up to others allows us to have more awareness, and therefore choice, about the impact we have (or don't have).

There's a very senior politician in the UK who, when he gets on stage, looks like he never expected to be in the position he now inhabits. When he gets on stage he appears uncomfortable, uncertain, and looks to me as if he is trying very hard to convince me of something. These are my assessments of how he appears. Now these are not true or false – they are my opinions. Behind them is what I notice about his body – the evidence that I use to ground these assessments.

What I observe is that there is stiffness in his body and because of this his movements are jerky, sudden movements. This is what has me create the assessment of him being uncomfortable and uncertain.

He regularly raises his eyebrows and wrinkles his forehead upwards whilst he nods. This is what has me create the assessment that he's trying to convince me of something.

He also collapses his posture very slightly, caving in at his chest, and this collapse is enhanced by the fact that he regularly looks down to consult his notes when talking. The combination of all of these physical factors, combined with the story of how he got to his position, leads me to the assessment that he didn't expect to end up where he is now. Someone else may produce different assessments from the same data, so the assessments I have come to inevitably reflect me to some degree.

I also know that others whom I have spoken to share these assessments. This means that hearing those assessments may be valuable to that person in understanding the public identity he is creating, which may not be useful for his political career. (I am sure he gets this message through the media and his advisors.)

For it to really be useful to him, though, he needs to know both the assessment and what it is that he does to produce this assessment. How he holds himself, where he collapses and how he holds tension in his body. This would allow him to know what to change.

That these assessments are valuable is true for all of us as leaders – we show up in a certain way and we have a public 'identity' in our organizations. This 'identity' is the collective assessments of the people around us and it influences how they relate to us. In the case of our story, Jane's identity amongst most of her peers was previously one of being a pushover.

Changing this is, however, not just a matter of making a couple of simple changes in my posture. The reality is that our shaping is a result of our history and somatic markers, and when we begin to work with them we will be starting a long journey of development where we gain self awareness of our history, and begin the process of reshaping ourselves and relaxing in our own skin. This is a long-term, deep and transformative process.

Therefore, when we offer someone an assessment we are offering them a gateway into their deeper development. Offering others assessments, which we ground through our somatic observations in this way, is therefore something to be done with care and compassion.

In addition, in Chapter 2 we explored how feedback was essential in developing mastery through deliberate practice. Therefore, in the development of ourselves and others as leaders, giving and receiving assessments becomes an essential component.

Jane had realized during the programme that she was making assessments about other people all the time, and that she was already reading other people's bodies. As she learned to pay more attention to this during the programme, she started to see that as other participants underwent shifts in their self-awareness, she could also see real changes in them as they stood taller and relaxed into themselves. These produced very different assessments in her regarding their capability to take leadership.

During the programme Jane had also practised giving and receiving assessments. She had given and received somatic assessments (assessments grounded somatically – through the physical body) and had seen from that how she embodied being a pushover. This had been useful and valuable information for her in reshaping herself. She also saw that whilst she was happy to receive assessments from others, she was very reluctant to give assessments, even after acknowledging how valuable others' assessments were to her.

At first her mind would go blank and she would panic a little, leaning away from the person and trying to avoid the situation. She had to work on centring and grounding herself in order to be able to give assessments to others. With practice she was able to do this and give her fellow participants assessments that they found useful and valuable.

When John asked her about how he showed up physically, he was asking for her somatic assessment. This was a sign of trust, but still Jane's first response was the same – her mind went blank and she leaned back a little. She caught herself though, and before John had registered the wobble that she had distinctly felt, she centred herself and responded.

John held himself like the central figure in Figure 1 in Chapter 6 (page **131**). He was in an almost military posture, puffing his chest out and looking down his nose at others, with his chin held high. Jane told him that she noticed two key things. One was that his chest was puffed out in a slightly aggressive or arrogant way, but that behind that she felt was probably insecurity – that puffing out the chest was a means of compensating for the insecurity he felt. The second was that he was holding his chin up, almost like he was trying to keep his head above water and that it gave the impression that he was drowning in some way.

John felt the impact of those assessments physically. In that moment he realized that Jane could see right through him to what was going on beneath the surface. He was, as he had already realized himself, feeling insecure, and he did feel at the moment that he was struggling – perhaps not drowning, but definitely struggling in the current role.

Jane taught him centring and helped him to align himself to stand in a straight, balanced and relaxed way. This felt very new to him, and with it – without the puffed out chest – came a sense of vulnerability, but also strangely a calmness and self-acceptance to which he was unused. Because of Jane's work with him, John decided to attend the embodied leadership programme as well.

John's programme

John's programme was very powerful for him, although it did take him a couple of days to get used to becoming aware of and working with his body in leadership development. He started off with a declaration 'to make his department more successful than it had ever been'.

During the programme he realized that he was incredibly task focused. Whilst others were seemingly able to take account of others and how they were, he often was straight into task mode and ignored the people around him.

One exercise stood out for him particularly powerfully. It was called a Rondori, which comes from the martial arts. In a black belt test, a Rondori is where the candidate has to deal with multiple attackers who charge at them from the other end of the *dojo*. In this version of the Rondori there were no attackers or charging, but an exercise where he had to deal with multiple requests, assessments and offers (simulated through a physical metaphor) brought by the people in the group, all in very rapid succession and often at the same time. The aim was not to get this right or perfect – if there is such a thing – rather it was to see what patterns showed up when taking part.

In this exercise John got so focused on the task of dealing with all of these people that he engaged with none of them, didn't make eye contact with them, and treated some of his fellow participants a little roughly during the exercise. He just felt like he had to get through it, and so it became an exercise in getting the tasks done, but the human element he completely ignored. When John was given this feedback after the exercise he realized that this was exactly what he did at work (which had also been brought to his attention in past 360° feedback reports). Whilst he was still not sure how he could do it differently he realized that he needed to improve in this area.

He started by changing his declaration to 'creating a department that people loved to work in', and focused on exercises that would help him learn to build connection and relationship with people, whilst also accomplishing the tasks. At first he had been concerned that focusing on people would mean losing the focus on the tasks, but he learnt how to bring both of these elements together. After doing these exercises, he repeated the Rondori a few days later, and he saw that he was able to show up differently. He had moments where he was knocked off-centre by the busy nature of the exercise and went back to task mode, but with coaching he was able to re-centre himself and connect with people in the exercise.

He went back to his organization feeling more balanced and able to be more present with others. On his first day back in the office he met with his team as part of his usual weekly meeting and he realized, as he sat there, that he was leading a group of people who were hurt, angry and somewhat ashamed of their department's performance. This was the assessment he now had, which he could ground from how they stood and sat, their facial gestures and tone of voice. He wondered to himself how he had not noticed this before – it seemed so obvious now. It was also clear to him that his previous way of managing these people had not helped.

He began spending more time listening to and connecting with his staff and the department began to change. Together with his team and Jane's team they jointly worked on some proposals that they submitted to the CEO for reorganization across their departments – ideas that in most cases had been generated through the joint working of those teams.

Meanwhile, Jane continued to work on improving the way in which the whole executive team worked together and John continued to work on developing his department.

It would be great to say that everything worked out perfectly and that one of them is now a CEO and the results have been fantastic. In reality it is always more complex – the industry they are in suffered during the credit crunch and economic downturn. John had to figure out how to make people redundant whilst creating a department people loved to work in, and Jane had to figure out how to get the executive team to work together whilst the whole team was increasingly under pressure to improve performance.

It is fair to say that they have both faced their challenges, however. John is still in post – something that wasn't a certainty at the start of this story – and the department's employee engagement scores have gone up at a time that the rest of the organization's scores have gone down, and that is despite the redundancies.[1] His team is engaged and supporting him and they have much stronger relationships among all team members. They have also bought into his declaration for the department.

Jane managed to build strong relationships with all of her colleagues on the executive team, not just John. The feedback she received from them was that she had real presence and gravitas, was very authoritative and that they trusted her. She made some progress with the team as a whole, although there were some difficult relationships between two other team members that those individuals were unwilling to resolve. When I last spoke to Jane, her work had been recognized outside the organization and she had been approached for two senior jobs and was considering her options. Both are very grateful for the work that they did on embodied leadership and both are continuing their practices.

Ongoing practice

It's worthwhile at this point to return to a theme from Chapter 2 of this book – that of ongoing practising. It's important to note that Jane and John did not stop practising their new shapes and new ways of being. John continues to pay attention to being centred and focusing on the task and the person. Jane continues to work with her conditioned tendency to withdraw and not stand up for herself.

Their old behaviours, learnt during their childhood, had been practised for many years and they were very good at them – they were essentially very good at being themselves. These new behaviours, the new shape and the new state of being that resulted from them, were less practised and they had to work hard to develop and maintain these.

They developed and worked with practices around noticing and sharing their assessments. They read around the field of leadership, they got more and more familiar with their conditioned tendencies, and a lot more besides. They stepped onto a journey of developing mastery and are still on that path.

As well as adopting practices that were part of their working day, such as those above, they also developed a number of supporting practices – practices that would support them in their development and being at their best. Jane started to run after seeing data that showed that people were 15 per cent more efficient at work if they exercised regularly.[2] This also was a place where she could practise being determined and strong – not backing down – and she brought this into her work. John took up the Japanese martial art of Aikido, which focused him on connecting with and blending with his attackers in order to be successful. This supported him in applying the principles of connecting and blending with others in work.

There were a couple of supporting practices taught on the programme that they continued to use, one of which I will address here. That is the practice of sitting or attention training or meditation or mindfulness, depending on how you prefer to frame it. Now, some may feel that in going down this road I am going into the realm of the religious or perhaps just the New Age. However, neither of these is my intention – there's a good basis of scientific knowledge that sits behind the different forms of mindfulness, and the degree of benefits available from this simple (but not easy) practice may surprise you.

Mindfulness meditation

Mindfulness meditation is usually performed sitting down with the eyes closed or slightly open, and involves focusing one's attention on a simple object, such as the breath. Through this focus on an object the practice entails being present in the moment and being aware. This is in many ways very similar to the process of centring – centring is a process of being mindful in the midst of action and the long-term practice of mindfulness meditation will greatly assist in this process.

Mindfulness meditation leads to better ability to hold our attention (hence the fact that it can be referred to as attention training) and can reduce our reactivity and therefore our ability to be distracted. Reduced reactivity comes from two dimensions – one from top-down control, where I manage my reactions by having greater conscious attention, and the second from bottom-up control, because one effect of such meditation is that fewer basic involuntary automatic reactions are triggered in the older parts of the brain.[3] This may be what causes the lower blood pressure and reduced heart rate experienced by meditators, and could be why people who practise mindfulness meditation often report greater calmness.

This is accompanied by an increase in the grey matter density in the medulla oblongata (a region in the brain stem), which relays sensory inputs from the body to the brain and is involved in breathing and cardiac control. These findings, combined with lower cortisol measures in meditators, are a possible mechanism for the finding that regular meditation can develop greater resilience to stress.[4]

Other research shows that mindfulness meditation changes the structure of the amygdala in the brain, which as we have already discussed is heavily involved in the conditioned tendency response and in stress.

In addition, researchers have found that those practising meditation make more rational choices in financial decision-making tasks.[5] Mark Williams, Professor of Clinical Psychology at Oxford University, is a world expert on depression and has been using mindfulness meditation as a treatment. Research shows that this meditation alters the physical structure of the brain, and a part of the brain called the insula, thought to be key to empathy, becomes more active.[6] This may be part of the reason why people who practise mindfulness meditation generally report themselves to be happier than control groups.

Jeffrey Schwartz[7] has been successfully using mindfulness as an approach to dealing with obsessive compulsive disorder (OCD), using mindful attention to re-train patterns of thought in the brain. This has resulted in changes in the structure of patients' brains that are detectable in various scans.[8]

There is also some evidence that meditation also boosts immune response in vaccine recipients and patients with cancer, improves skin conditions, and may even slow the ageing process.[9]

So what does all this research mean when we take it as a whole?

Just as in centring, mindfulness meditation changes the way that we deal with stress and increases our resilience. In addition it has the capacity to increase our empathy and happiness, and to enhance our ability to make decisions. In connecting us to our bodies we see, feel and experience our somatic markers again, and because in the meditative process we simply sit in recognition of our discomfort, without reacting to it, we see and experience the drives and impulses the somatic markers create.

In mindfulness meditation, it is possible to realize at a very deep level that the sensations of discomfort from these somatic markers will pass. We come to see that in fact we do not need to do anything to make ourselves more comfortable other than be present with the sensation. Consider that, for example, if you have an itch on your nose it is not there for all eternity if you don't scratch it. It will pass if you just leave it, and the same is true of the sensations of discomfort a 'neat-freak' will feel as they survey your messy desk. As we let these sensations pass and develop a deep embodied knowing that we do not need to react to them, these sensations have less hold and power over us, and we cultivate choice.

Mindfulness meditation is a powerful process, as through it we can weaken the power that our somatic markers have over us and we can literally reshape ourselves. This is how we can become less reactive, and is the essence of the term mindfulness: rather than running around in mindless reactions we can learn to cultivate mindful choice.

The research also shows how repeated practice of mindfulness alters the structure of our brains. This makes sense, given that we already know from earlier chapters that repeated practice of anything changes our brain.

Mindfulness meditation, therefore, forms a supporting practice that underpins centring. Being in a mindfulness meditation practice gives a greater depth to the centring practice (and vice-versa in fact). I call it a supporting practice because it is not a practice of doing something different in the moment, like centring, but rather it is a practice where you take time out of your day, and one that supports you in being different in the world.

Both Jane and John developed and maintained a mindfulness meditation practice. It is not an instant gratification practice, and so initially both were unsure what difference it was really making to them. However they stuck with it, and after a month they started to notice the difference on the occasional days they missed their practice. They saw that on these days they were more likely to be grouchy, moody and reactive than on other days. Over a longer time period they noticed some larger differences in their overall level of reactivity, which was much reduced – some of the things that previously would have wound them up no longer had the same impact.

In addition, through this process they got to know the structure of their own minds (or body–minds to be precise). Their somatic markers became clearer to them, as did their patterns of thought. Jane saw that her thoughts were perpetually directed towards the future, specifically at trying to prevent things from going wrong. She realized she was trying to prevent herself from getting into trouble with some form of higher authority figure, even though this authority figure did not really exist in her life anymore. This was a piece of childhood learning that was still running her and she was able to see how she projected this authority figure onto her CEO and then tried to prevent problems so that she wouldn't be in trouble with him. This was putting her into a childlike relationship with her CEO, and also prevented her being upfront with him about the nature of the challenges they faced as a company. Through becoming familiar with this pattern, continuing with the mindfulness process and centring herself in interactions with the CEO, she was able to diminish that pattern of thought and its impact on her life.

This is all in addition to the greater health levels, reduced levels of stress and greater resilience that this process brought to both Jane and John.

There is also a deeper level of learning that happens through long-term meditative practice. The chances are that this is something you already know intellectually; however, it is about knowing this at a much deeper, emotional and embodied level. Through mindfulness meditation we come to know that we are not our thoughts, ideas, beliefs, emotions or sensations – that we are more than this.

This is an important realization – our thoughts run through our minds like crazy wild animals out of control. They don't stop, it's just an ongoing process, yet it's easy to begin to identify ourselves with our thoughts. In mindfulness meditation we see that there is also a part of our self that can observe those thoughts. We learn that when an event happens we have a sensation that arises in the body in response to this (driven through somatic markers), and from this we get emotions, and our thoughts that this event is good or bad. We see how this process runs, and we see that it does not need to run us, as it is not us – there is still that part of us that can observe it and have choice.

For example, when Jane was sitting with John and he was ranting at her, she had sensations, emotions and thoughts in response to this, driven by her somatic markers, that caused her to want to withdraw and retreat from the experience. There was another part of her, however, that was able to observe her whole internal experience and make choices so that she did not allow that internal experience to run her.

Earlier in this book, I described the self as an embodied self. In fact this was a slightly incomplete description, which it makes sense to complete now. I have shown that we embody our history – our historic patterns of thoughts, feelings and behaviour (some would describe this as our personality), *and* we are more than this. There is also a part of us that can observe, notice and see all of this as it happens, moment by moment inside ourselves, and that can make choices.

By practising mindfulness meditation what we do is cultivate this capacity to observe, to see, to notice what happens inside ourselves moment by moment. Once we have awareness, then we have the capacity to make different choices. Therefore, mindfulness meditation is, at its very essence, the cultivation of free will and is a lifetime's practice.

Much is written in science and social science about how human beings post-rationalize their behaviour after having taken action, and I have written about this process earlier in this book. Some would use this as an argument for human beings not having free will, which

I would contest. However, it is clear that a lot of the time our actions are driven by our history as stored in our somatic markers. This is a quick process and is, in evolutionary terms, how basic survival mechanisms were encoded into us as a species. And we also have another process – that is the process of conscious consideration and choice. However, we fool ourselves that we use the conscious process much more than we do – we like to believe we operate with free will as opposed to being so driven by our history.

Jane was surprised to learn that she had limited choice – she believed she had a lot of choice, but during her programme she came to see that much of her behaviour was driven by her history. And so it is for all of us. The process of developing the observer is therefore the process of cultivating free will. The mindfulness meditation process adopted by Jane and John, combined with centring and an ongoing process of self-cultivation, is what we need to develop leaders who can lead to a better future rather than being driven (and thus driving others) by their personal histories.

From mindfulness to mastery

We are coming to the end of Part Two of this book, and it feels appropriate to step back and look at the journey that Jane, John, you and I are on. I have written much about the value of centring as part of stepping back in the moment and being able to have choice beyond our somatic markers and our conditioned tendencies. However, there is another parallel process that is taking place, which was implicit in Part One of this book, and that I wish to make explicit now.

The practices of centring and reshaping ourselves do allow us to face the somatic markers that don't work for us and loosen the grip they have on us. This also does something else. This goes back to a fundamental principle from Chapter 2 – we are what we practise.

When we are practising a shaping in response to our somatic markers, we are practising a way of responding in the world, so we get good at this and it becomes who we are. When we practise centring, reshaping ourselves, not responding to somatic markers but choosing our responses, we are practising a different way of responding in the world. In doing this we develop new habits, backed by new somatic markers, that give us the capacity to respond differently on an ongoing basis. This can be reinforced by the positive impact of what we now do and by the feedback of coaches and others (who are also working on their development).

When I see Jane or John, or indeed anyone who has been practising this work for a number of years, and something triggers them, their first move is to centre. This is not a thought-out strategy they must remember; rather it is the results of embodying a practice. If we contrast this to those who have gone on a traditional leadership programme, when they get triggered by something, they may or may not remember the models they were taught as their bodies are playing out their conditioned tendency.

With practice, John is embodying the move of connecting with others whilst getting the task done. He no longer thinks about this, it is just a part of him. Jane no longer needs to focus so much on standing up for herself – it's just part of who she is, and her presence is such that people try to push her around much less frequently than before. She is embodying her declaration of being treated with dignity and respect.

With practice, as we discovered in Chapter 2, come many changes in the brain – myelin created on neurons, growth of new neurons and new synaptic connections between neurons. We also discovered, with the example of the experiment with music, that just going through the process of playing the notes in our minds also changes the brain structure – not just actually playing them. The two together is what creates real change and this is the essence of deliberate practice – really paying attention very deliberately and practising something new and difficult.

Mindfulness meditation, or attention training, is a process by which we develop our capacity to be able to do this. We develop the ability to be able to pay attention more closely and engage in more deliberate practice for longer periods of time. This is why this is an incredibly beneficial supporting practice to the process of change. Engaging in this process will accelerate the process of your development towards mastery in leadership.

Applying this learning

Assessments

The starting point in applying this learning is to follow the process explained earlier in the chapter:

1 Becoming aware of our assessments and how quickly we create them.

2 Owning the part of us that creates the assessment.

3 Training ourselves to see what it is about the other person that generates the assessment.

4 Getting better at sharing our assessments.

To practise this, first of all go to a cafe and do some 'people watching'. As you watch people go by, notice what assessments you generate about them. What stories do you create in your head? If people are in small groups or pairs, what is your sense of their relationship and their conversations? Capture all of this in your journal and repeat this three or four times, over a couple of months. The first part of this process is just to notice how quickly you generate these assessments. Continue to build on this, and every time you meet someone new, capture your initial assessments of them in your journal – remind yourself that they are not true or false, and use this just as a practice of developing awareness of your assessments.

After a short period of time it should be clear to you that you generate assessments very rapidly and these should be coming to your consciousness more easily.

The next step in the process is to go back through your journal and notice what patterns emerge in the assessments you generate. What are your most popular assessments? What in these assessments are more about you than about the other people? Also look for those assessments where you remember or notice that you had a clear reaction to the person (eg liking or disliking), as these are also a sure sign that there is something about you inside the assessment.

When you find this, remember back to encountering someone for whom you had this assessment. Try to bring yourself back to this place, and look at what you felt in that moment. Look for what you felt physically and emotionally when you had this assessment – any reaction you felt will be because of your historic somatic markers, so it is useful to know that this is in part about you.

Next go back to the people watching exercise and repeat this, only this time capture two extra things in addition to your assessments:

- your emotions and sensations (reactions) driving any assessment you have about the person;

- what it is you see about the person that sits at the root of your assessment.

For this second step, look to the centring process for help. Do you see them out of alignment or balance along length, width and depth? Do you see how they hold tension in their bodies? If, for example, you are left with the assessment that someone looks like a 'rabbit in the headlights' (a phrase I have heard people use repeatedly) then you may notice this person holding tension around the eyes and forehead, and perhaps the jaw. They may also have a stiff and tense posture. Start to make the connections between the assessment you have of them and the shape that is showing up to you.

Now occasionally at this point people get concerned that this is somehow judgemental or unethical. So if this is your concern, I want to remind you that you're doing this anyway, however much of the process is below the level of your consciousness. You then act towards these people as if they are the way you unconsciously assess them to be. By doing this we are practising becoming aware of our assessments as 'assessments' (ie not true or false), which allows us to have more choice in how we interact with others so that we have greater self-awareness. In addition, we are becoming aware of what parts of ourselves get in the way of how we see others, and we are doing all of this so that we can get better at making these assessments and offer them to others as helpful for their development. At some level my response to those who have this concern is that to not do this is probably more judgemental and unethical.

Finally, after practising with this process for some time, you can begin to share some of your assessments with others, where this may have value and where you feel that it is not just about you. Now, this is not about offering 'drive-by' assessments to people who have irritated or annoyed you. Doing that will only distance you from those people. My experience is that people can hear almost nothing in feedback when I am irritated or annoyed, as they respond to my irritation or annoyance. However, if I give assessments from a place of genuine care and concern, where I am centred and my intention is to develop the future of our relationship, then people can hear almost anything.

Take this process slowly and carefully. Pick apart those bits of yourself that get in the way of seeing others and be mindful of them in any feedback you give. Always be open to there being other bits of you that you haven't yet seen, that are obscuring your view of others. Never start with the most difficult, challenging and important relationship in your life – start where it's easier and practise with smaller issues. In doing so you will develop your capacity to give assessments well.

Finally, and perhaps most importantly, if you decide to do this, get someone else involved whom you trust and practise both ways with that person. That way you will also practise receiving assessments, and you shouldn't be giving them if you're not willing to receive them on a regular basis.

Mindfulness meditation

There are many forms of meditation that exist, and the one I describe here is a simple breathing meditation, sometimes called 'Anapana'.[10] As already noted, this is a simple, but not an easy process.

Decide for how long you will meditate. You can sit on a chair or on the ground cross-legged, as you prefer. Either way, sit with your back straight, and if on a chair, with your feet flat on the floor. Close your eyes, or have your eyelids lowered and your eyes unfocused (so that you are not distracting yourself with what goes on around you), and bring your attention to your breath as it comes in and out of your nostrils. Do not try and control your breath, just pay attention to the sensation of the breath coming in and out. As you do this for a period of time you may notice the air coming in is a little cooler than the air coming out.

When you do this, almost inevitably you will find that your mind starts to wander, and you will have difficulty focusing on your breath.

Thoughts will fly through that lead to other thoughts and so on. Very quickly your time may be up and you may realize you haven't spent much time with your attention on your breath.

The practice here is to notice when your attention drifts off (and it will) and bring it back. It's important to do this without beating yourself up for the fact that you drifted off – the point of this practice is that this will happen, and you 'gently escort yourself back to your breath', as a colleague of mine puts it. Often people give up this practice because they believe they 'aren't doing it well' because their attention is often away from their breath. What they don't realize is that this is just part of the human condition, and that the process of bringing their attention back and focusing is a large part of what they are practising. It is the equivalent of lifting weights in a gym, with the process of bringing your attention back onto your breath being the heavy lifting – every time you bring your attention back is equivalent to a repetition at the gym.

Occasionally I meet people who say that they were able to keep their attention on their breath for the entire time. I then ask them what they were thinking about during the time they were sitting, and they give me a long list. Just to be clear, if they can do that, they do not have their attention on their breath. When your attention is on your breath, you are paying attention to that breath completely, and not caught up in thoughts or ideas.

Start off with around 10 minutes of mindfulness meditation per day and after a few weeks gradually raise this up to 20 minutes per day. You can use kitchen timers, alarm clocks or phone timers to let you know when your time is up. Some people prefer to do this first thing in the morning, while there are others I know who prefer to do this as an interruption between work and home so that they can be more present with their families. The timing is your choice, but do try and retain a regular practice in your schedule – it is easier for many people to do this at the same time every day, but this may not be possible with your work–life schedule.

Maintaining this practice will give significant benefit to you in your leadership, your wider life and, importantly, your health.

Recommended reading

If you are interested in reading more about mindfulness meditation, then I recommend *The Miracle of Mindfulness: A manual on meditation*, by Thich Nhat Hanh.

To understand the research behind mindfulness meditation, I recommend *Buddha's Brain: The practical neuroscience of happiness, love and wisdom*, by Rick Hanson, PhD and Richard Mendius, MD.

Notes

1 Like many organizations, the company that Jane and John worked for conducted employee engagement surveys. These look at whether employees are engaged (willing to give extra discretionary effort), not engaged or actively disengaged.

2 Morgan Clendaniel [online] http://www.fastcoexist.com/1680481/ working-out-doesnt-just-make-you-stronger-it-makes-you-smarter (accessed 12 September 2012).

3 van den Hurk, PA, Janssen, BH, Giommi, F, Barendregt, HP and Gielen, SC (2010) 'Mindfulness meditation associated with alterations in bottom-up processing: psychophysiological evidence for reduced reactivity', *International Journal of Psychophysiology*, 78 (2), pp 151–57.

4 Ibid.

5 Coates, J (2012) *The Hour Between Dog and Wolf: Risk-taking, gut feelings and the biology of boom and bust*, Fourth Estate, London, p 240.

6 Lofthouse, R (2012) 'Power of the mind', *Oxford Today*, 24 (3), pp 30–34.

7 Schwartz, JM and Begley, S (2002) *The Mind and the Brain: Neuroplasticity and the power of mental force*, Harper Perennial, New York.

8 Schwartz refers to this as self-directed neuroplasticity.

9 Marchant, J (2011) 'Heal thyself: meditate' [online] http://www.newscientist.com/article/mg21128271.900–heal-thyself-meditate.html (accessed 17 September 2012).

10 This is a term from the Pali language, meaning respiration.

PART THREE
The wider implications for leadership

In this final section of this book I leave behind the stories of Jane and John and instead turn my attention to two of the wider issues that leadership needs to address in the modern world. To be honest I could have chosen a very wide number of issues to address, but these are two that feel like they are important ones at this moment in history:

- Ethics: Trust in business has been shaken by the recent credit crunch, followed by a long series of financial scandals and business issues. Add to this a decreasing trust in politicians and the media, and you have a vacuum of leadership (leadership is difficult without trust). Ethics needs to be core to the development of any leader – in fact, I will argue that leadership and ethics are in many ways synonymous. This is linked to wider issues of corporate social and environmental responsibility, which is now part of how the ethics of organizations are assessed.

- Leading with the series of complex challenges we face in the 21st century: We live in a complex, dynamic, non-linear world often best described by 'chaos theory', yet most of the models and frames of reference used by managers and leaders I meet are linear ones. We need to move beyond this and learn how to engage with a more complex reality. To do this we must have creativity and innovation embedded in our organizations, which it turns out is pretty much identical with leadership. I will argue that this returns us to the idea of leaders at all levels of an organization, and that ultimately the responsibility of leadership is to develop leaders.

Just like everything else in this book, I will be engaging with these concepts from an embodied perspective. In fact the body has much to say about each of these issues, and it is from this perspective that I believe these themes can be further cultivated.

Ethical leadership

09

> *I'll keep it short and sweet – Family. Religion. Friendship. These are the three demons you must slay if you wish to succeed in business.*
>
> **MONTGOMERY BURNS, *THE SIMPSONS*, TWENTIETH CENTURY FOX**

Most people I meet seem to believe that they don't really need to think about or study ethics – the study of right and wrong. For most of us, surely our sense of being a good, upstanding and moral person, combined with life experience and common sense, should carry us through ethical challenges without needing to study ethics. Shouldn't it? Besides, some of the core texts written by ethicists and ethical philosophers are abstruse and difficult to read, so why bother?

If we have a group of well-intentioned, good people in our organizations then they will behave ethically, won't they? And if there are any ethical issues that will be because of a 'bad apple' in the barrel: someone who wasn't a good, well-intentioned person. The reality that I see is much more complex. I see groups of good, well-intentioned people coming together and, through a combination of social pressures, rationalizations and a lack of understanding of ethics, together co-creating outcomes that none of them would want to create.

Consider the case of Nestlé, the Swiss-based Corporation. As *The Economist* described a situation they faced:

> the firm was caught in Africa and elsewhere promoting its milk powders so aggressively that they did, in fact, replace mother's milk inappropriately – hurting the health of babies and, when the powder was mixed with unsafe water or in too weak a dose, leading to malnourishment or death. The firm insists it has mended its ways.[1]

I'm quite sure the individuals concerned did not go to work every day with the intention of killing and causing illness to babies. The idea is just too awful to really consider – so what did happen that caused this type of horrible consequence?

If I am successful in this chapter, after finishing it you will want to study ethics. You will see that it is actually an essential component of your own development as a leader. That is my aim and intention, as I do not believe common sense, experience and good intentions are enough. Moral and ethical reasoning is a skill that is unfortunately not taught in our society. At times we are taught to follow ethical rules or codes of conduct, but following rules does not lead us to a greater understanding of ethics and ethical dilemmas. In some respects, while useful to create boundaries during our childhood, rules can limit our capability to genuinely engage in ethical reasoning, as boundaries don't really force us to think things through for ourselves.

The impact of this lack of training in ethical reasoning is seen every day in our world. How do so many good people go to work and collectively produce organizational impacts that have negative consequences? We can cite the recent credit crunch, or any of a number of financial or corporate scandals to look for examples of such behaviour. It is easy to vilify some of the key people involved and make it all about these individuals, but in reality an entire organizational system contributed towards these situations, with many people participating or, at the very least, looking on and allowing it to happen. Many of them good, decent people.

In one of the programmes that I run with a client, there is a competitive and highly charged exercise in which participants regularly break agreements with each other, mislead each other and lie in order to get a greater financial return. Often the response from participants is: 'If we hadn't done it to them, then they would have done it to us, and we would have suffered.' If there is a 'Golden rule' of 'doing unto others as you would like them to do unto you', then the situation in the exercise above is what ethicists Ronald Howard and Clinton Korver refer to as the 'Iron rule: Do unto others before they do unto you,' where our anticipation of the other person's unethical behaviour weighs more heavily in our consideration than our own ethical behaviour.[2]

These are not individuals who are in some way unique or attending remedial training – in fact they are high-potential future leaders in their organization. So what is happening that is causing this group of intelligent and moral human beings to act in ways that could be seen as 'unethical'? There are a number of elements that form part of this story, but the first place to start is with social psychology and understanding what motivates human behaviour when we come together in groups.

Understanding group behaviours

As human beings we like to believe (especially in 'the West') that we are individuals: autonomous beings who operate and make decisions in an independent manner. Now this is true; however, it is only a partial truth, a half-truth at best, which distorts and interferes with our view of the world. A more complete picture is that we have the capacity to act as individual, autonomous beings, and that we are part of an intricate network of community and social relationships that has a significant impact on our decisions and behaviours. In fact, whilst we have the capacity to act as individual autonomous beings, we do this much less often than we like to believe.

In Chapter 3, I cited Raymond Tallis, when discussing the nature of the self, where he stated:

> Those who believe that consciousness is to be found in the stand-alone brain subscribe to a body–body dualism with the brain being a 'mind–body' and the rest of the body being just a body. To me, this is no advance on the traditional Cartesian mind–body dualism… One way forward from this position is to acknowledge: (a) that the brain is situated in a body from which it cannot be separated; (b) the embodied brain is inseparable from a biosphere; and (c) in the case of humans, we are inseparable from a community of minds and the worlds that its component selves have built.[3]

So far in this book I have explored the brain and the body interconnections. Tallis also mentions the impact of being part of a community of minds, which we must also address to understand how our individual behaviour is affected by the collective behaviours of groups and organizations.

Earlier in this book, I described how we acted from our somatic markers on the basis of what felt right, and later post-rationalized some form of logical reason for what we did. The social impact of being part of a community of minds works in exactly the same way. We adapt ourselves to the social impact of others' behaviour to fit in with, or at times to rebel against, the group norms. Just look at a situation where a group is meeting for the first time and each person introduces themselves. The chances are that the group will respond to the precedent set by the person who speaks first, such as their decision whether or not to mention their family or home life in their introduction. Someone may choose to step outside of this, but that will be a risk taken by that individual, which will often make it easier for others to take such risks.

If you are not sure of the impact of this, then there is a video clip on YouTube that I encourage you to watch.[4] In this clip, from the TV show *Candid Camera*, people get into an elevator with a number of actors who stand in the same direction facing the back of the elevator, or facing one side, and even changing directions. The innocent individuals who get into the elevator end up changing direction to fit in with the behaviour of everyone else. It's a very funny piece of TV, and also a demonstration of how much we respond to the behaviour of others.

We adapt – it's that simple. We believe we live independent lives and make independent decisions, but in reality we are constantly adapting ourselves to group behaviours, usually to align ourselves with others so as to 'fit in' and belong, just as the people did in the elevator. Then, just like with our somatic markers, we post-rationalize a logical reason as to why we did what we did.

For example, let's return to the idea of introducing ourselves to a group of new people. If someone goes first and introduces themselves professionally, you are likely to do the same. If I asked you why you introduced yourself that way, you are likely to post-rationalize and tell me that this is how people introduce themselves in your organization, or that it was appropriate for that type of meeting. If the person going first introduces themselves including their home or family life, you are also likely to do the same, and if asked why would give very similar post-rationalizations. You may not like this idea, but experiment after experiment has shown that this is what we humans do.

So why do we do this and what impact does it have?

Professor Philip Zimbardo, at Stanford University, is one of the key researchers who has studied social psychology. Early in his career he conducted the now famous Stanford Prison Experiment in 1971. Seeking to understand the mentality of prisoners and correctional staff, as well the critical features in the psychological experience of prison, Zimbardo set up a prison in the basement of the psychology department at Stanford University and had volunteers take the role of prisoners and guards.

The experiment was due to run for two weeks but was finished after six days due to the level of abuse the guards were inflicting on the prisoners, some of it sexual in nature and reminiscent of some of the images seen more recently at Abu Ghraib in Iraq. Zimbardo states:

> It's hard to imagine that such sexual humiliation could happen in only five days, when the young men all know that this is a simulated prison experiment. Moreover, initially they all recognized that the 'others' were also college students like themselves. Given that they were all randomly assigned to play these contrasting roles, there were no inherent differences between the two categories. They all began the experience as seemingly good people. Those who were guards knew that but for a random flip of the coin they could have been wearing the prisoners' smocks and been controlled by those they were now abusing. They also knew that the prisoners had done nothing criminally wrong to deserve their lowly status. Yet, some of the guards have transformed into perpetrators of evil, and still other guards have become passive contributors to the evil through their inaction. Still other normal, healthy young men as prisoners have broken down under the situational pressures, while the remaining prisoners have become zombie-like followers.[5]

This happened in six days to a group of young men, who were college students and who had all tested psychologically healthy (across a range of tests and instruments). They were divided up at random between prisoners and prison guards, and over the duration of the experiment they went from normal healthy human beings to abusive guards and submissive prisoners.

Now statistically most people when they read about something like this believe that they would be the exception – that if they were in that situation they would be different. However, time and again experiments in the field of social psychology show that most of us go along with group behaviour if the conditions are right. This has caused Zimbardo to conclude:

> 'Bad systems' create 'bad situations' create 'bad apples' create 'bad behaviours,' even in good people.[6]

When we enter into a group, any group, we experience a biological, evolutionary need to belong. The strength of this need for each one of us varies, but we all have it, as at some point in our evolutionary history being excluded from the group meant death. This means that we are profoundly impacted by group behaviours. A recent review of 100 years of social psychology concludes that there is a significant and reliable impact on our behaviour from social situations.[7] In some instances these situational forces are a better predictor of behaviour than our personalities.

One of the most basic drives we have as human beings is to belong. For example, imagine or remember yourself on the first day of a new job. You'll want to fit in, make a good impression, be accepted and so on. Consciously you may notice how people dress and appear, and adjust your dress to the same level of formality, be that sharp business suits or more relaxed clothing. However, unconsciously you will be noticing so much more. How do people interact? How do they behave towards the boss or other authority figures? Who is popular and seems to have influence over the group? Who is more marginalized and has less influence? All the while you will be noting what it is to be accepted and liked in this community and will be adapting your behaviour appropriately (your adaptation may not always produce the results you intend, but the important point here is that you are adapting).

Now say in that early time in your new job you see someone not following the organizational procedures properly, which were explained to you in your induction. Let's also say that this happens quite publicly and a lot of people see this and no one comments on it or says anything. The chances are that you won't say anything either – nobody seems to think that it's a big deal, and you don't want to be the new person telling them how to do their jobs. In fact, as you sit there thinking about it, you become more unsure of your own knowledge about the detail of the procedures and you begin to doubt yourself.

This goes on for a period of time and you see greater and greater variation from the procedures, but these people have accepted you now – you're a friend. Perhaps you bring it up jokingly and are told: 'It's no big deal. No one really worries about the procedures, as actually they just get in the way of getting the job done. The person who wrote them never understood the job. Besides the bosses don't care; they just want results.'

What do you do now? Do you fight with your new-found friends on this point, about a job you're still learning, or do you go to the boss and potentially get them or even yourself in trouble? You realize that in your own interactions with the boss they've never actually mentioned procedures, only results. They must have noticed that no one's following the procedures and yet they don't seem to mind. Maybe it's not a big deal.

What I describe above is not atypical. The impacts can be relatively small, such as when we don't speak about a manager bullying staff members, or large, as with a client that I have worked with, where a collective unwillingness to speak up about safety procedures not being followed caused an explosion (thankfully no one was injured, because it happened at night). The details are removed, but this story line can be the process by which accidents happen and lives are lost in industrial accidents. It can be how banks end up losing millions through internal 'rogue traders', or contribute to the crashing of economies with innovative new mortgage-backed securities. And all the while many people conformed to group behaviours and watched it unfold, knowing that it was wrong somehow, but not feeling that they had the ability to bring it up or, in the worst cases, blow the whistle.

Now imagine what it would take to stop things earlier in the story and say that something's wrong. You might have to go up a couple of levels in the hierarchy to make that happen. You might need to make yourself a potential target inside the organization or of your boss. Your colleagues may thank you for what you've done, but the story that will be running around in your head will be one of being 'scapegoated' and vilified for rocking the boat; of bosses who will punish you for embarrassing them, and of colleagues whose working lives you have made more challenging.

This is true for everyone in the scenario – the other peer-level colleagues are feeling the same pressure, and the boss is probably feeling similar pressures, alongside the pressure of comparison with other departments and teams, and the need to hit whatever targets exist. All the while, each good moral individual probably assumes some version of the idea that, 'as no one else seems to be worried about it, it's probably not a big issue.'

So how does this happen and why are we not more conscious of it? Well, the fact that we are not conscious of it gives us a clue where to start in our exploration. It's not about the conscious mind, so our discussion and explanation needs to start somewhere else, and in this case with the body.

We feel these social pressures as sensations of discomfort that sit in our bodies – discomfort as our bodies try and warn us that we need to belong, that being excluded is dangerous. Our bodies are uncomfortable, because the somatic marker for inclusion is very deep inside us and at a deeper level equates exclusion with death. This is why it is so hard to intervene in this story. Our brain then creates the story of scapegoating and vilification as a rationalization for the action we are unable to take. All of this happens subconsciously and very quickly, and some of you may not even notice it.

Then later, after the accident or rogue trade, we all blame senior managers (or better yet 'senior management' generally so as not to personify the blame) for creating a culture of fear inside which people couldn't speak up. This is why the same story line, with a different set of details, keeps playing out time and time again, in organization after organization.

The key thing to notice is that every situation we enter exerts a pressure on us. Different situations will do this differently, which is partly why you will behave differently with your family than at work. It is also why, if you have ever gone back to a school reunion you may find yourself behaving weirdly, like you have regressed back to childhood. The people you meet will treat you the same way as they did when they last knew you, and the pressure of that will cause you to behave more like your teenage self than like the person you know yourself to be now.

These pressures are not exerted as people physically pushing us, but we do feel them in our bodies in much the same way. Sometimes we notice them most when we leave an organization; there can be a relief and relaxation in no longer having to conform to these pressures that can feel almost like being released from a prison of sorts.

Therefore, how this entire process works is that we feel these pressures as uncomfortable sensations within our bodies, to which we attach emotions and meaning (stories), and we take actions to make ourselves more comfortable. This move towards comfort can be extremely useful, but it can mean that we allow something to happen that has serious and negative long-term consequences.

Being aware of these processes and paying attention to them requires a high level of awareness, and paying attention to what is subtle and implicit, both within ourselves and externally. It starts with an awareness of what is happening inside us in response to the events that take place outside. That will allows us to understand what we are observing and experiencing.

So in the example of introducing ourselves to a new group, we would start by noticing our desire to be accepted and a part of the group, and from this the discomfort we feel and the subsequent pressure to conform to group norms. We could then centre ourselves and make a choice about the way in which we want to introduce ourselves, which would be most effective in that moment based upon what we are there to achieve.

Centring ourselves inside our experience becomes a way of tapping into the sensations and feelings generated in our bodies in response to these experiences. It is also through centring that we can have the presence of mind to engage in ethical reasoning.

Ethical reasoning versus rationalization

It is important to be clear about the distinction between reasoning and rationalization. Reasoning is a process of careful consideration where we analyse something to form a judgement. In addition reasoning is a process that includes our emotions and the body, which you may remember from an example I gave in Chapter 4, of one of Antonio Damasio's patients.[8] Without being able to engage with his bodily sensations and emotions, this person was unable to make a choice – all he could do was list the pros and cons of any decision for eternity, but without coming to any conclusion. To truly engage in a process of weighing up the options and forming a conclusion, a process of reasoning, we need a connection to our emotions and bodily sensations. Without connection to what we care about (emotions tell us this), how can we come to a decision about anything?

Ethical reasoning is, therefore, never a purely rational thought process, and to try to engage in it as such is an error. It involves engaging, at a fundamental level, with our emotions, as these tell us what we care about and what we value. Yet we need to engage with them from a centred place where we can feel them and not be overwhelmed by them – where we can still make a choice. Our emotions can at times overwhelm us, and many people have this as a concern or worry they experience when they connect to their emotions. Being centred allows us to experience our emotions without being overwhelmed and losing our ability to choose our response.

Rationalizing, on the other hand, is a process of constructing a justification for something we want to do (often based on short-term self-interest) that is at some level something we suspect to be wrong. This can happen after the event, as noted above, or it can happen before the event as we create a story in which we can take action. Howard and Korver, ethicists whom I mentioned earlier, state about rationalization:

> When we rationalize, we devise specious but self-satisfying reasons for acting. Or ascribe our actions to high-mindedness when our motives are actually otherwise. Or employ a faulty analogy or wishful thinking. In effect we create a story that holds together but, upon examination doesn't hold up.[9]

They go on to give an example of such rationalization: 'When we double-book ourselves and then tell a client we have to break the appointment to see a doctor, we tell ourselves the story that the mistruth preserves an important relationship.'[10] This is despite the fact that when we are on the receiving end of such excuses, they often lack power and alter our perceptions of the person giving them.

If you think back to the situation described before of starting a new job and the dilemma of whether to raise the issue of not following procedures, it is the same process of rationalization that occurs, which provides the justification for not raising the issue and which allows the consequences to emerge. This form of rationalization is very common in our society, and for me represents a disconnection from our embodied experience. It is our embodied experience that connects us to what we care about and what is important to us, and a disconnection from this is the first part of allowing ourselves to act in ways that are not in line with our values, and that's how unethical behaviour starts to emerge.

If we were to connect to our embodied experience, we would acknowledge both a fear of the consequences of our actions and also our values about what it important. Experiencing and feeling our emotions in this way is a good thing to do – when we disconnect from our emotions they have a tendency to drive our behaviours; it is only through connecting and experiencing them that we can have choice in our actions.

Zimbardo's research into social psychology shows how we are all susceptible to such behaviour – we can all experience the social pressures and rationalize actions to ourselves that we would not otherwise do. This is the root of many corporate scandals, industrial accidents and, whilst I haven't studied this case, I would bet is at the root of much of the actions taken by people within Nestlé that I described at the start of this chapter.

Our inclination when we see these events is to explain them away purely at the personal level, and make it about a few individuals being dishonest or somehow deviant. A more complete explanation looks at the entire social system in which a large group of people sit and the impact that this has on all of those people, as well as the actions of the few. There is always a large group of onlookers in any corporate scandal, and their inaction and failure to speak up will often be seen as an acceptance of and agreement with that behaviour, and will make it more difficult for others to speak up.

However, even with centring, there is still a process of reasoning to engage with. So this leaves each individual with a dilemma. I see someone not following an organizational procedure, and what do I do? What are the long-term consequences of not following that procedure? Is it even a 'good' procedure? What will happen to me if I speak up about it? How do I reason my way through all of these questions and come to a conclusion.

There are therefore two further things that it will be helpful to discuss: ethical frameworks and ethical dilemmas.

Ethical frameworks

There are a number of ethical frameworks that sit underneath the way we make ethical judgements. Two main ones are referred to as action-based ethics and consequence-based ethics. In action-based ethics the action, in and of itself, has an ethical value and it is on this basis that we should make our ethical decisions. In consequence-based ethics, it is the consequence of the action that should drive its ethical value. So in the example of speaking up, in action-based ethics you speak up (or not) because the action is the right thing to do, where as in consequence ethics you would weigh up the consequences of speaking up with the consequences of inaction.

The problem with not being clear on these distinctions is that depending on which framework you look at you may come to different decisions. Not recognizing this, we may select whichever school of thought is most convenient to the action we wish to take and use it as a way to rationalize our response.

Action-based ethics has its roots in the philosophies of Immanuel Kant. His idea was that you should act as if you would be happy for your action to be turned into a universal law for everyone to follow. Under this philosophy if you decide not to lie as an ethical rule, then you would always be bidden to tell the truth, no matter what the consequences. Problems crop up with this when you consider such thoughts as, 'Would it be ethical to lie to prevent a murder?'

This brings us to consequence-based ethics, where the value of the action lies in its consequence. Here an action is ethical if it results in the greatest good for the greatest number of people.

This can lead to a whole different set of questions. For example, would lying to your spouse about an affair, thereby keeping the family together and not upsetting people, be a greater good than splitting up the family and upsetting everyone through telling the truth? Would it be ethical to steal a small amount from one rich person to be able to buy your children Christmas presents – what would be the greater good for the greater number?

The problem with consequence-based ethics as a viewpoint is that it is largely an intellectual fantasy. We have big brains with large neo-cortexes that love to consider all this stuff, but we don't ever know if our lying would prevent a murder. We don't know what the outcome of being honest would be to our spouse. We don't know if those kids having presents is genuinely, for the long-term, the greater good.

Thought experiments are proposed as a way to justify consequence-based ethics. For example, imagine that terrorists are threatening to kill a plane full of people unless you kill one person. Would it then be ethical to kill a person to save the lives of everyone else? The argument is that killing one person would be better than everyone dying. However, even if we put aside the fact that this is a somewhat fanciful scenario, we can never know what the terrorists will do after we pull the trigger. They may or may not kill people either way.

Another such thought experiment is the question whether, if you had a time machine, it would be ethical to go back and kill Hitler. Surely that would be ethical? Stephen Fry's novel *Making History* considers this very idea, and ultimately points out that even if Hitler had been killed, strong feelings of anti-Semitism and hatred were floating through the culture of Europe at that time. The treaty of Versailles was still punishing Germany after the First World War and engendering resentment among Germans towards the rest of Europe. Capitalizing on these feelings of resentment and anti-Semitism could easily have been taken up by someone else. That person might have been strategically better at fighting the Second World War and could potentially have won that war, with the consequence that we would currently live in a very different world. It's a possible outcome of killing Hitler and, you could argue, is equally, if not more, probable than saving the lives of millions.

Consequence-based ethics involves us entering into an intellectual fantasy. Inside this we can construct any number of possible consequences of our actions and inactions, and the danger of this is that it allows room for our rationalization to take over and drive us towards actions that we want to take, or are afraid not to take. We can engage in the flawed belief that we can predict the future and design our actions on the basis of that predicted future.

If we come back to the real world, from fantasy situations of terrorists and time machines, the only things we can take responsibility for are our actions, and we must start here. We cannot take responsibility for the future actions of others, as we can never know what they will be. This is not to say that thinking about the consequences of our actions is a bad thing; it's just to say that this cannot be the sole basis on which we make our decisions, as we are too apt to engage in cognitive fantasies and rationalization.

Understanding these ethical frameworks gives us a way of resolving the question we started with regarding whether to speak up. If we are using consequence-based ethics, then the question is about finding a way to ensure the greater good by balancing the consequences of acting and of not acting. This is a limited strategy from my perspective.

If we are using action-based ethics we must address the nature of the action. This will then involve understanding whether the procedure is ethical and whether it is ethical to speak up about the procedure not being followed. To do this we must be clear on what we believe is ethically important, and centring is crucial in that process to connect us with what we care about. We can still, however, face ethical dilemmas, where we face a difficult choice between two options that both have negative outcomes, so I will explore that next.

Ethical dilemmas

Imagine yourself in this situation. You are a consultant and you have a range of clients, some of whom carry out research into cancer. When winning work with these clients you gave assurances to them, at their request, that you did not work with tobacco manufacturers, which you weren't doing. You are currently struggling to get new clients because of a downturn in the market and you are approached by a tobacco manufacturer for some work that will be quick, relatively easy and well paid.

So this issue has an ethical dimension to it. You could rationalize that at the time you gave the assurance to your cancer-researching clients you were not working with tobacco, so it's ok to take the work, ignoring the implication that your clients didn't want to work with anyone who worked with a tobacco manufacturer, and that you would probably never be able to tell them you took on this work. You can rationalize a way to take the money.

This issue also has an economic benefit element to it. You are short of money and this is a way to help you through a difficult economic time.

Is this an ethical dilemma? I would argue that it isn't. You see an ethical dilemma for me is where two ethical principles conflict and we have to decide between two ethical wrongs, whereas this is a case where the ethical dimension of an issue conflicts with the economic dimension. This essentially asks you: for how much will you sell your ethical principles? True ethical dilemmas are much rarer and involve us choosing between two things we consider to be ethically important. They are most often seen with troubled action heroes in movies where they must do something wrong to save a life, as in the terrorists on a plane example considered previously.

However, we often call things ethical dilemmas when they are not. In the case above, this is a dilemma of ethics versus economic benefit. We could also be in a situation where something was illegal but we felt it was ethical, in which case we would have a dilemma of ethics versus law. For example, church communities who have sheltered illegal immigrants whom they believed were being persecuted in their home countries. By calling something an ethical dilemma, we can hide and obscure an issue, and excuse ourselves for taking the non-ethical approach.

If we are honest we start to address whether we are selling our ethics for personal benefit, or following laws that we believe to be unethical. Getting to this level of honesty requires us to dive behind the label of ethical dilemma and really look at the nature of the challenge we face, which can be very uncomfortable. Look in the newspapers for issues that are held up as ethical dilemmas and try to identify the two issues at play – is it truly an ethical principle versus another ethical principle, or are the issues actually being obscured by language. Practising and noticing this will help to clarify your own thinking.

If we go back to the issue we started with of whether to speak up regarding the procedures, there is, if we assume that the procedures are ethical, a dilemma of an ethical principle versus a personal benefit (not an economic benefit this time, but more of a social benefit of being accepted and liked in the workplace). Being rigorous in our thinking, combined with centring to connect to what we care about, allows us to choose our ethical decisions more wisely.

It is easy for all of us to label something as an ethical dilemma, and then rationalize a way to do what benefits us personally in the short term. This results from flawed thinking and is often driven by emotions of which we are dimly aware. In leading others, whether we like it or not, we will be held to a high ethical standard, and indeed from my perspective leading others well and effectively for the long term requires a high standard of ethics to be effective. Understanding ethical frameworks and dilemmas, combined with centring, can allow us to face and deal with the accompanying social pressures that we experience in organizations.

Resisting social pressures and rationalizations

Solomon Asch conducted experiments where participants were asked to judge the length of various lines, but were in a group where others (who were actors) publicly stated the wrong answer.[11] Many people began to doubt their own thinking or went along with the group so as not to cause trouble. When we are dealing with ethical issues there will often be people giving rationalizations and obscuring the issue, combined with social pressures, which means that it is very easy to doubt our own thinking or feel pressured to conform.

Interestingly, Asch also discovered that when one of the actors gave the correct answer, yet all others agreed on the wrong answer, it was much easier for the participants in the research to trust their judgement and give the correct answer. This shows how one person taking leadership and bursting through the social pressures of the situation can give permission to others to do the same. Leadership is a very social act, and when we take leadership and speak out despite social pressures it gives permission for others to also take leadership.

But how does that first person do it? What allows them to be immune to social pressures, and have the presence of mind to be able to think things through and not doubt their own thinking?

Although we may judge from the outside that they don't appear to doubt their own thinking, this is unlikely to be true. They are likely to doubt their own thinking – this is only human, and perhaps not to do so would be a little arrogant – but they do not let their doubting get in the way of taking action and sharing their concerns.

They may also appear to be immune to social pressures, but this again is not quite accurate. They are aware of and experience these social pressures the same as everyone else; however, they are able to see them, experience them and still have choice about their behaviour.

The answer to the earlier question is contained within that question, in the phrase 'presence of mind'. They have a presence of mind to be able to notice and experience what is happening, and the social pressures they experience. What should be clear at this point is that this presence of mind is gained through being in the present moment. This is achieved through connecting to our physical bodies and the five senses, which are in the present moment, rather than our thoughts, which are all over the place. This is a quality of centring and connecting to our body.

In addition, when we are connected to our body we are also in touch with what we care about and what's important to us, which is vital in dealing with ethical issues. When we face making an ethical decision, the strategies for short-term advantage and gain are generally not the things that we truly value and hold as important for the long term, and when we are connected to ourselves in this way, we have no problems distinguishing between the two. We may find that in a few seconds we doubt what we feel, but if we look we will then realize our attention is in our head, constructing rationalizations, and that we are no longer centred. While we are centred we are clearer about what we care about, and re-centring ourselves repeatedly may be required in these situations.

Resisting social pressures and holding to our ethical principles requires a series of moves beyond just centring. Centring is the starting point for each move – the one that gets you in the game – but there is more required, and each move requires practice. The key leadership moves I will focus on here are:

- taking a stand;
- saying 'no'/declines;
- insists;
- quits.

These are moves that are required in leadership generally, and are not just related to ethics, but I will describe them here from the perspective of ethics.

Taking a stand

Taking (or making) a stand is similar to the process of living a declaration (after you have created one) that I described earlier; however, it is for a shorter period of time. Put yourself in the situation of being the person in an industrial company who takes a stand for following procedures, in the story at the start of this chapter, in order to prevent industrial accidents. What does it take from you as a person to take a stand for health and safety in that circumstance?

Ultimately it requires the ability to put ourselves 'at risk'. Now the body, and older parts of the brain, will experience the risk as a life-threatening one, rather than a social one, and learning to take a stand is about learning to be comfortable with discomfort. In doing this we are aware of our feelings of discomfort, but we are also connected to what is important to us, and we are making a choice to take a stand for that which is important.

This is very different from getting angry and ranting about something, which is where we are caught in a reaction and are off-loading our frustration. As a result, it is also experienced differently by those around us. They do not experience it as an outpouring of anger, but as our being deeply committed to what is important to us, even though they may or may not agree.

This is, however, really not an easy thing to do. Many of us like to think that when it comes down to it, if we were in a really important situation, we would suddenly have the ability to take a stand for what we care about. However, the reality is that many small situations pass us by daily where we could take a stand, yet we barely even notice them and can often rationalize them away. Sometimes we may realize later that there was a time or a place where we should have taken a stand for our own dignity, but at that moment we had not been aware enough to notice and it is only afterwards, on reflection, that we realize our dignity was taken away from us (we were undermined or put down in some way).

The reality of life is that if we don't do it at the small moments, we won't do it in the big, important ones. We like to believe that we would, but most people in those big important situations rise to the level of their practice – they respond in the big moments as they have practised responding in the many small moments. This is why people in sports spend so much time practising, and why people in the military spend so much time doing drills. You practise repeatedly, practising in the smaller moments so that you have the capacity to take action when it's really important.

When we find ourselves in these small moments, if we notice them we might say, 'Well it's not that big a deal,' or we can rationalize all of the reasons why speaking up is not a good idea. We can always find a way to rationalize our way out of it, and if you keep on practising rationalizing your way out of it, then you'll get better and better at doing this, and rationalizing will be an automatic, embodied practice. This is then what will show up at that important moment where it really is a big issue.

A friend and colleague who was working on the ability to take a stand developed a way of practising this for himself. He is based near London and regularly takes London black taxis. Now, if you've ever ridden in a black taxi in London, you'll know that the drivers will regularly engage you in conversation about issues that are in the popular news, and will often use this as an opportunity to tell you all of their opinions about how it should be handled. My colleague's strategy was to practise centring himself and disagreeing – politely and in a friendly way. By doing this he was practising holding his position in the face of usually quite determined arguments, and taking a stand. It didn't matter what his genuine position was on any of the issues discussed, he was just practising centring and taking a stand. Through this he was able to develop his capacity to take a stand around issues that were important to him.

Some questions for you to reflect on:

- What is it that you are 'putting up with'?

- What are you practising by doing this?

- What is it that you would really like to do (from a centred place of taking a stand for something you believe in, rather than taking a swing at someone you disagree with)?

- What will it take for you to take a stand on this issue? (Hint: practice should be part of this answer!)

- How can you find opportunities to practise taking a stand?

Saying 'no'/declines

I mentioned earlier that one of the most common things that people come to leadership development programmes looking for, is the ability to say 'no' more often. They will find themselves in situations where they take on too much work and aren't able to say 'no' to others in a way that is heard and respected.

One of the things we need if we are to deal with ethical challenges effectively is to be able to say 'no'. There are requests that are made that contravene our ethics, and that we need to decline. There may be times we need to stop something in order to ensure that safety is taken care of, in some way. The trouble is most people are pretty bad at doing this, and aren't able to distinguish between saying 'no' to the request and saying 'no' to the person.

So what happens to us when we say 'no'? Often people feel guilty – that they should be taking on more work, or that others will have to do this if they say 'no' and they know those others are really busy.

This is a form of putting other's needs before your own. Some people will fear that others will think they are being lazy if they say 'no'. Some feel that they won't be liked, or will offend the person concerned; and if the request comes from their boss, that powerful person will be angry and have some form of vengeful response. These are just some of the stories that people hold for why they find it difficult to say 'no'. Underlying these stories are emotions and sensations that drive them, and of which most of us are usually unaware.

It is only through building awareness of these sensations, and the ability to be centred and at choice while we experience them, that we can build the ability to say 'no' more easily. Then, just as with taking a stand, we need to practise. When I am working with people on this issue I encourage them to have a target for saying 'no' every day, and to find opportunities (again working on the small stuff) where they can practise this. I then encourage them to reflect on the stories, emotions and sensations that arise in the process of saying 'no' so that they can build their self-awareness.

Some questions for you to reflect on:

- What are you not saying 'no' to that you would like to say 'no' to?

- Why do you feel that you can't do so?

- What are the stories, sensations and emotions that are getting in the way?

- What can you do today, from a centred and grounded place, to start practising saying 'no' and becoming more comfortable in doing so?

Insists

A move that is needed more rarely, but that needs to be part of the armoury in dealing with ethical issues, is that of insisting. There are times when all of us need to insist on something. If we make a request for someone to do something safely and they keep on doing it in a way that is dangerous, then we may need to insist.

Insisting is not a move that needs to be made on a regular basis by most people; therefore, it is often one that is done poorly. When it is done, most insisting that I see is done from a place of being in a reaction and comes across as an angry response. This is not what I am intending. Nor is insisting something to be done lightly – someone not understanding your request does not equal a need to insist, but rather a need to clarify your request.

However, there are times when it does need to be done and it is a powerful move when it is done from a centred place. For many people the lack of practice that is available to them in making this move, combined with the perceived social risk, makes it a difficult move. It is perceived as, and it is, a socially risky move, and it should therefore be used carefully. However when an ethical principle is at play, this is a move that lets others know the importance of the principle in question. When safety is an issue and lives are at risk, this is the move that insists on principles being followed, despite the fact that it will be socially unpopular.

Because this is a more difficult move, it is likely that we will be tense when we try to do it. That tension will be experienced by the other person, and they will likely tense up in response. This has the possibility in ending with two people in conflict. Relaxing and centring ourselves will minimize our conditioned tendency response, and it is likely to encourage the other person to remain relaxed and centred also.

So when insisting, we need to speak to the other person with a high degree of presence if we are to be taken seriously. We need to be centred and carry with us a mood that is serious but not aggressive. This requires the skills that have been developed in taking a stand and declining, but brought to this present situation.

Some questions for you to reflect on:

- What are some issues about which you may need to insist?

- Are you sure that you need to insist – have you ensured that the request has been understood (remember that what is obvious to you is not necessarily obvious to someone else)?

- How do you feel about insisting?

- What are the stories, sensations and emotions that are getting in the way?

- What can you do today, from a centred and grounded place, to start practising insisting and becoming more comfortable in doing so (acknowledging that opportunities are limited)?

Quits

To quit is perhaps the most extreme action to take, but quitting a relationship or an employment is always an option. We are always able to make a choice, even when our ethical principles are not being abided by. It is possible to quit individual relationships when someone will not treat us with dignity, or behaves in ways that are against our ethics, and is unwilling to change. This is only done as a last resort and there will be a number of conversations that lead to it.

Likewise in our organization, if we see behaviour that will lead to, for example, a bank collapsing or an industrial accident where lives are lost, and we have tried other ways of addressing the issues, then a 'quit' may be the appropriate move.

This is not an angry storming out of the office telling everyone what I think of them, 'I quit' – that is a reaction. Rather it is a process where after trying to address the issues, we take responsibility for ourselves and our own ethical principles. For example, if we are repeatedly asked to do something we consider to be unethical, we can take responsibility for addressing this within the organization, but if this doesn't work we may need to leave.

Many people whom I meet are afraid of this possibility, because of fears about quitting relationships (being alone), the job market and other job options, but when you really settle yourself in the place of being able to leave, and knowing what your ethical standards are, then this can give a real sense of freedom.

I don't want to play down the fears people have about this option – they are real and the job markets can be tough. And we can use these fears as the basis for rationalizing plenty of reasons to stay. In reality, knowing that you can leave gives you more freedom to take the actions you need to for both your ethical principles and your leadership more generally. This awareness can often be the root of success for many people, as this leadership, which is committed to organizational success and ethics rather than to social acceptance, is often admired.

Insists and quits are more difficult moves to practise, given that we do not need to use them as often. However they are important moves, and the same principles apply with these moves as apply with the others – the importance of centring so that we're in choice rather than reaction, and so that we're connected to what we care about, which can guide our actions.

What about controls?

In this review of ethics in organizations, I have focused heavily on the leader's ability and capacity to notice and engage with social pressures and dynamics. This has left out the whole issue of systems, processes and controls to ensure ethical behaviour. Frankly this is because, whilst these are important, they are also the easy bit, and they will never be complete. A former colleague of mine was involved in investigating a banking scandal where many millions of pounds were lost. The following is a list of some of the controls and checks that were in place in that organization:

- internal audit;
- external audit;
- middle office (with people for each of the trading books involved);
- compliance officers;
- back office trade reconciliation;
- front office senior management;
- The Financial Services Authority (FSA);
- The Bank of England;
- European Central Bank regulations;
- top-of-the-line risk-management computer systems in the back, middle and front office.

Despite this impressive list of controls, a huge amount of money was lost! We must always remember that no matter how many controls and checks we have in place, it is the human response to these, driven by our organizational cultures and the social pressures, that really define whether or not anyone pays any attention to these controls. To assume that by solely investing in checks and controls, we have a system that will prevent banking or indeed other corporate scandals is naive to say the least.

Exercising ethical leadership

Any leadership implies risk. It requires us to step above the pressures of social conformity and take action, and the reality is that not everyone may like what we choose to do. When we do this, some may ask 'who do you think you are to be doing that?' Others may come to us with their problems, requests and challenges, seeing us as someone they can become dependent upon, and abdicating any responsibility for their own problems.

Ethical leadership carries these challenges and more. It requires us to be in touch with our values, and to say when we believe something to be wrong, without making the other person wrong. This is a challenging balance – no one likes to be accused of being unethical and to be made wrong for it, and the reaction to this happening is usually defensiveness. The reason is simple – we all have a view of ourselves as ethical people, and having that sense of our own identity challenged can be deeply troubling.

The challenge of addressing ethical situations in the workplace, as a leader, is to be able to cultivate recognition of our human errors – we are all human and we make mistakes. Social pressures, rationalization, self-doubt in our own thinking, lack of education in ethical reasoning and in understanding ethical frameworks and dilemmas, combined with a cultural disconnection from our felt sense of our values in our bodies, mean that we are open to making such mistakes more than we ever realize.

This is, I believe, the challenge of our time. Cartesian duality, which has dominated much of our cultural and business thinking, has disconnected us from our bodies, emotions and moods to the extent that in many organizations they are seen as unimportant and irrational. However, our emotions and moods, which are expressed in our bodies, drive our behaviours and tell us ultimately what we care about. By ignoring our bodies, and treating leaders and leadership as an exercise in rationality, we have created a system in which good well-meaning people create collective results of which none would be proud.

In disconnecting from our bodies we also disconnect from our biological heritage, and separate ourselves from the biosphere of which we are a part. Sometimes we speak of the environment as if it is something out there, but we need to remember that we are a part of this environment. A recent radio interview reminded me of this when the speaker commented that if all the bacteria in the world were wiped out we would die, as they sit at the bottom of a food chain and ecological system that we sit on top of, and that this would collapse with no bacteria. We cannot so easily remove ourselves from the environment, despite our attempts to do so.

If we are disconnected from our bodies and the felt experience of being alive, we can objectify the world and rationalize that it is ok. In removing ourselves we can pollute our air and water, destroy our food-producing land, make species extinct and melt the polar ice caps, and see all that as inconsequential or something that science can fix. We do not learn the lessons of past civilizations that died out through over-use of resources on a more local scale, and we seek to repeat the experience on a global scale.[12] If we connect to ourselves and the felt experience of being alive, we can feel our connection to an entire ecological system and feel the implications of our actions.

As integrated human beings, we must see ourselves in a community of beings, and connected to a biosphere of which we are a part. Any view of human beings that does not include this is incomplete. Any view of leadership that does not include this is likewise incomplete.

Creating an ethical code

One of the best leadership books I have read is a book on ethics. Many of the ideas in this chapter have their roots in that book and the thinking I have done since. The book challenged me to be clearer in my ethical thinking, and to look clearly at the ways in which I rationalized my behaviour so that I was 'almost ethical'. It confronts us to be more honest and clear in our ethical behaviour.

The book takes you through the process of developing an ethical code, thinking through all the complex ethical issues and coming to a set of principles that you can consciously articulate and live by. I recommend this book highly, and the development of an ethical code is one of the practices that I am giving in this book. The book is *Ethics for the Real World: Creating a personal code to guide decisions in work and life*, by Ronald Howard and Clinton Korver. I encourage you to buy and work through this book as a part of your leadership development.

Recommended reading

Ethics for the Real World: Creating a personal code to guide decisions in work and life, by Ronald A Howard and Clinton D Korver.

The Lucifer Effect: How good people turn evil, by Philip Zimbardo.

Collapse: How societies choose to fail or survive, by Jared Diamond.

Ethics: The heart of leadership, by Joanne B Ciulla.

Ethicability: How to decide what's right and find the courage to do it, by Roger Steare.

Working Ethics: How to be fair in a culturally complex world, by Richard Rowson.

Notes

1 *The Economist*, 29 October 2009, 'Nestlé: The unrepentant chocolatier' [online] http://www.economist.com/node/14744982 (accessed 8 October 2012).

2 Howard, RA and Korver, CD (2008) *Ethics for the Real World: Creating a personal code to guide decisions in work and life*, Harvard Business Press, Boston, p 57.

3 Tallis, R (2011) *Aping Mankind: Neuromania, Darwinitis and the misrepresentation of humanity*, Acumen, Durham, p 350.

4 http://youtu.be/uuvGhn31M.

5 Zimbardo, P (2007) *The Lucifer Effect: How good people turn evil*, Rider, London, p 172.

6 Ibid, p 445.

7 Richard, FD, Bond, CF and Stokes-Voota, JJ (2003) 'One hundred years of social psychology quantitatively described', *Review of General Psychology*, 7 (4), pp 331–63. Cited in: Zimbardo, P (2007) *The Lucifer Effect*, pp 322–23.

8 Damasio, A (2006) *Descartes' Error*, revised edn, Vintage, London.

9 Howard, RA and Korver, CD (2008) *Ethics for the Real World: Creating a personal code to guide decisions in work and life*, Boston, Harvard Business Press, pp 43–44.

10 Ibid.

11 A video clip of these experiments is available here: http://youtu.be/sno1TpCLj6A.

12 Jared Diamond's book *Collapse: How societies choose to fail or survive* gives an excellent overview of the collapse of historical societies and sets out the challenges faced by humanity to avoid the same problem on a global level.

Leadership for the 21st century

Have you ever sat in heavy traffic and thought to yourself that what they (whoever they are) need to do is to add another lane to the highway? I know I have. Sitting frustrated and potentially running late for a flight on the way to London's Heathrow Airport, I have often wondered about putting an extra lane on the M25 (London's ring road – at times London's largest car park!).

However, the interesting thing is that in 1968 the German mathematician Dietrich Braess conducted extensive traffic studies and showed that adding new lanes to a highway does not necessarily reduce rush-hour gridlock, but often makes it worse.[1] This is a classic example of what seems obvious actually being unhelpful.

You see traffic jams are incredibly complex things, and very difficult to understand; gridlock can travel back up on a road whilst cars move forward, for no apparent reason. To understand this phenomenon it doesn't make sense to try and understand the behaviour of the whole system in a top-down fashion, but rather as a series of independent entities, each selfishly making their own choices and following their own rules, which collectively give a set of outcomes.

Each independent driver will make a choice of road route depending on the flow of traffic in order to maximize their ability to get to their destination quickly. In the current state (without the extra lane) the system has equilibrium of sorts; however, adding a new lane to the highway will increase speeds on that route and disrupt the equilibrium. Now all drivers using all roads in the area will react to maximize their independent interests, and that will involve a greater number of drivers moving to using the highway, despite the fact that the combined effect may remove the advantage that is being sought. In addition it may also lead to an increased number of car journeys (rather than public transport, for example), as people will perceive journeys to be quicker as a result of the improved highway.

Over time a new equilibrium will develop, and from studies in traffic we know that this may not necessarily be better than the previous one. This is in addition to the fact that a new lane will allow drivers to speed up and to change lanes more often for their individual advantage, which once again may produce further traffic jams.

A top-down solution to the problem would be an ordered one, where everyone drove at a fairly constant speed, didn't change lanes, didn't get too close to each other, and drove on set roads that were defined for them on the basis of optimizing average traffic flow for the benefit of everyone. However, we human beings tend to resist such top-down solutions that dictate our actions, and hence we have traffic jams, and a system where increasing capacity doesn't result in quicker traffic flows.

Traffic flows are what is referred to as a complex system. In such systems interventions that make sense from a top-down rational perspective (such as adding lanes) may in fact make the situation worse, and this makes them very difficult for us to manage.

Organizations are much like traffic flows, and the larger and more global the organization is, the more like a complex traffic flow it becomes. In traffic there are rules (traffic laws) that some will follow and others will break, and there are individual rules (slowing down to let other drivers change lanes or enter onto a road, how close to get to the car in front, etc), and all the individuals are trying to achieve their own personal target of getting to their destination in the quickest time, and are taking action to achieve that.

In an organization each individual has a set of company rules (policies, codes of conduct, corporate values, etc) that they may or may not follow, as well as individual rules (local cultural traditions for that country, the individual's beliefs and motivations around achievements, whether we focus on tasks or relationships, ethics and values, etc), and each individual will be trying to achieve or exceed their personal targets in their role, in the most efficient way possible.

Just like with a traffic jam, this can often result in a series of actions that individuals take across a whole population throughout an organization, but when they don't understand their interdependencies with each other this can often deliver worse results for everyone. This is unintentional, as everyone is trying to do the best for themselves, their team and their organization through achieving their results. However, when a worse result occurs, the leadership is usually blamed for not setting direction clearly enough or some other perceived fault. And, just like with traffic jams, as human beings we would probably resist any attempt at top-down control, if such a thing were even possible.

As well as creating blame towards the organizational leadership, this scenario can create confusion, distrust and enmity within the organization. Say, for example, someone from Finance is instituting a new system to ensure transparency of reporting and to comply with global financial regulation, which is part of her personal targets and on which she will be measured. Meanwhile, someone from Sales is trying to get something done quickly for a customer, to ensure more business is won (again part of his personal targets) and gets around the system by using his personal relationship to achieve his results.

The Finance person may perceive her Sales colleague as being a rebel, perhaps untrustworthy, or perhaps a political animal using his personal relationships to bypass the system. The Sales person may perceive his Finance colleague as officious and bureaucratic, and ultimately as someone who is getting in the way of serving the customer, which is what the organization is there to do ultimately, isn't it? Each may appeal to their respective line managers and it may progress its way up in the organizational hierarchy to two people who have limited time and are disconnected from the issue, and who are then expected to sort it out.

Organizational politics is essentially the series of opinions that we have about how others go about independently achieving their objectives inside such a system, and from this it's easy to see how organizational silos and political wars emerge. Often on the back of such things there will be organizational restructures, but the structure of the organization did not cause these problems, and a restructure will not solve them!

This pattern of complexity is true of organizations, but it is also true of countries. One country, for its own advantage, reduces corporate taxes and regulations to attract inward investment, and others follow. Over time we have a process of competing to the bottom, where each country competes through lowering its taxes and regulations so that no country ends up gaining significant benefits from corporate investment.

It can also be seen in publicly owned companies. As one company goes for a short-term profit, it gains share price and investors move their money from competitors to that company. Subsequently, competitors can feel pressure from their shareholders and corporate boards to follow suit, even if following this strategy is not in the long-term interest of the organization.

Inside these systems no one individual person has the power to stop it, control it, or make it function better for all. That just isn't possible – no CEO can change the market forces, no country president or prime minister can change the behaviour of all countries, no driver can change the behaviour of all drivers, and no leader can change or enforce the behaviour of people in their organization (this doesn't stop some from trying!).

We now live in a world of large complex systems such as those I have been describing. From my perspective, the defining feature of the leadership that we require in organizations and in the world more broadly, in the 21st century, is leadership that is able to encompass this complexity. Notice that these are not complicated systems, but complex systems. A complicated system is one such as a Ferrari. It can be taken apart and put back together by experts, and it is very complicated. A complex system such as traffic management or global markets cannot be taken apart and put back together by experts – it is a complex system in which there is flux and uncertainty, and patterns emerge over time. A complicated system requires expertise; a complex system requires creativity and innovation.[2]

Working with complex systems

A couple of years ago, a colleague and I conducted a piece of research in which the CEOs, CFOs and chairs of FTSE 100 companies were interviewed on how they were responding to changes in the business world.[3] The kind of pressure I described above, to respond to the market pressures and the actions of competitors in order to ensure advantage for their companies, was described as a real concern by the CEOs we interviewed. This was accentuated by the pressure on decision making that came from being in a connected world where responses were expected instantaneously to every event.

A key element that emerged from this research was the requirement for companies to be able to generate a diversity of thinking throughout their organizations. The interviewees realized that their decisions, just like the decision to add an extra lane to the highway, had unintended consequences, and were often creating the future problems to which they would then need to respond. The challenge was that in the little time they had available to respond to any issue, they needed a diversity of points of view and ways of thinking to be able to deal effectively with these challenges. In a short time, with complex issues, you need different creative perspectives, so that you don't make a choice that just creates new problems.

They also noted that through globalization their businesses were now serving a global customer base, and that they were competing against local competitors who understood local needs more clearly and who were customizing goods and services in ways that they as global players were often too inflexible to be able to respond to adequately. This again required the ability to have an increased diversity of thinking so as to be able to respond to the needs of this increasingly global customer and competitor base.

This led them to the belief that they needed to develop a culture where people could genuinely think differently, where they could be creative and hold different points of view, and where those different points of view and that creativity could be heard, accessed and built upon into innovations within the organization – either product innovations in diverse markets, or innovations in how they handled the global challenges of running their organizations.

The CEOs saw diversity as being a key strand of their strategy going forward – they needed greater diversity in their organizations in order to be able to quickly and adequately respond to the challenges they faced. However, organizations have been trying for years to increase diversity in the population of their employees, and haven't really managed to deliver the change. The people we interviewed felt that diversity would not be achieved through hiring lots of diverse people who then leave when the organization tries to make them conform to its standard models and ways of thinking. Rather they felt that they needed to develop an organization where a diversity of thinking was a part of its culture and fabric. With this they would then be able to attract and keep a diversity of talent in the organization and ensure such diversity of thinking.

Now, at some level, this may seem to be an obviously good idea, but the reality is that organizations have spent many years working to develop alignment (just have a flick though a copy of *Harvard Business Review* and you will see a range of strategic models designed to produce alignment). There have been strategic alignment initiatives and exercises to create a unified culture, to ensure that we are all facing the same direction and focused on achieving the same results. Army-like images of conformity and uniformity spring to mind, and at some levels this has been a part of the unconscious metaphors that many business leaders have been using.

This is, at least to some degree, driven by our control needs; we all have a desire to be in control, whether or not we are 'control freaks'. However, as I mentioned in Chapter 7, we do need to get more comfortable with a lack of control and ambiguity, because the world is an ambiguous place and feelings of control tend to be elusive and illusory. That is not to say that some commonality, consistency and clarity is not useful or needed; just that the degree to which we seek this may be driven by our control needs rather than the organization's needs. To step into an organization where people genuinely think differently and innovation is embedded in the culture requires something different from the leaders, and indeed everyone throughout the organization. To explore how to create these types of organizations, I will start from developing an understanding of innovation and creativity.

Innovation and creativity

Many people seem to use the terms creativity and innovation interchangeably, and there are many myths about creativity that obscure the field.

Peter Denning and Robert Dunham, in their book *The Innovator's Way*, define innovation as 'The adoption of an idea or technology into practices that produce new outcomes'.[4] Notice that this does not refer to the generation of a new idea, but focuses rather on the adoption of that idea, and the results that it can produce. Yes, there does need to be a new idea, but that lies in the realm of creativity or invention; innovation is held to a higher standard where that idea produces a change.

Creativity, then, relates to generating ideas and inventions, which can then lead to innovation and changes in the world. A famous example of this is the time when both VHS and Betamax video tapes were released. Betamax was probably a better standard in terms of quality – it was a better invention. However, VHS was more successful due to the work that was done to sell and promote this standard – it was a better innovation, as it was adopted more widely.

So innovation is the business of bringing new ideas to the world or to an organization in such a way that they are adopted; they change the way in which people do things and the results they get. In the context of the complex systems described above, this is the process of getting ideas and different thinking heard, and ensuring that this thinking has an impact.

Creativity

It is worthwhile looking at the process of creativity itself, the process of generating different thinking. The accepted wisdom is that ideas arrive in some 'Eureka' moment (a flash of insight, a stroke of genius) where we arrive at some moment of creativity. Another piece of accepted wisdom is that often someone who is unencumbered by knowledge will be able to be more creative; they won't be too close to the problem and they will be able to challenge accepted ways of thinking in the ways that those who are experts won't. Additionally we tend to believe that some people are just more creative than others. Unfortunately it appears that all of these pieces of accepted wisdom aren't really true.

Stephen Johnson has studied where good ideas come from and one of his conclusions is that there is no 'Eureka' moment, but that this is a post-rationalization that people tell after the event.[5] He describes how Darwin, for example, wrote in his autobiography about his moment of coming up with the idea of Natural Selection as a moment of inspiration in October 1838, but he had actually written the idea out in his journals months before his supposed 'Eureka' moment.

Johnson shows how great ideas often, in fact, linger at the back of our minds over a long period of time, and that it is the process of socializing this knowledge – that is, articulating it to others – and combining with other ideas that generates breakthroughs. This is perhaps less romantic than the idea of the solitary genius working away in their study and coming up with a wonderful insight, but it does put the process more under our control. If we understand ideas this way, we don't have to wait for the flash of insight whenever it is ready to grace us, but rather we merely need to connect with others and discuss those nagging doubts/problems/thoughts and ideas that sit at the back of our minds.

The limiting effect of being an expert also does not appear to be true. Multiple studies of those who have produced great innovations (ie creative ideas that have also made it out and made an impact on the world) across music, arts, science, poetry, dance and psychology, show that they conform to the rule of 10 years (or 10,000 hours of practice) discussed in Chapter 2.[6] Harvard Professor Howard Gardner's book *Creating Minds* looked at the lives of seven creative giants in the 20th century – Albert Einstein, TS Eliot, Sigmund Freud, Gandhi, Martha Graham, Pablo Picasso and Igor Stravinsky – to develop an 'anatomy of creativity'.[7] In concluding the book Gardner wrote that he had, 'been struck throughout this study by the operation of the 10-year rule.'

Gardner's work shows that great new ideas require a level of mastery inside your field that takes around 10 years to develop. And the idea that only some people can be creative seems to be flawed also; as Geoff Colvin writes in his book *Talent is Overrated*:

> The heavy burden of evidence is that creativity is much more available to us than we tend to think. The most significant constraint, as with all kinds of exceptional performance, is most likely to be our willingness to do the difficult work required.[8]

This returns creativity from the domain of something brought in by some 'creative other person' who is not blinded by knowing too much, and once again puts this back under our control. This may feel a little uncomfortable, as we have taken something that was dependent on moments of inspiration by others and returned it to something that we need to do through hard work. It's perhaps more comfortable when we give responsibility for new ideas to others, than when we seat that responsibility at our own doors.

Ideas, or at least good ideas, come from people with a high level of mastery in their domains, developed through deliberate practice. Naive questions can indeed be helpful in sparking these ideas, but the naive question is rarely a good idea in and of itself. It is this level of mastery that can generate simplicity from complexity; simplicity that transcends complexity as expressed below:

> I wouldn't give a fig for the simplicity on this side of complexity;
> I would give my right arm for the simplicity on the far side of complexity.
>
> Attributed to Oliver Wendell Holmes Jr
> (1841–1935), American jurist

Indeed, Denning and Dunham state that one of the characteristics of those who have developed mastery is that they, 'offer interpretations that simplify complex situations and enable others to take useful action'.[9] So it seems that if we are to deal with the kind of complexity we face in our organizations today, we need a high degree of mastery.

We also, it seems, require high levels of presence to be able to transcend complexity in this way. In their book *Presence*, on how we can change the kinds of complex challenging problems we face in business and society today, Peter Senge, Otto Scharmer, Joseph Jaworski and Betty Sue Flowers state:

> We've come to believe that the core capacity needed for accessing the field of the future is presence. We first thought of presence as being fully conscious and aware in the present moment. Then we began to appreciate presence as deep listening, of being open beyond one's pre-conceptions and historical ways of making sense.[10]

The 'field of the future' is their description of solutions to complex problems, and in this quote they emphasize the importance of presence in developing these solutions. This is exactly the same as the emphasis I have had in this book for leadership. It is clear from Chapter 2, that bringing full presence to practice is what generates deliberate practice and deeper learning. It is clear that presence is something we look for in leaders, and is required for us to be able to move beyond our somatic marker responses to generate new choices. It also turns out that such presence is essential for generating new ideas. Denning and Dunham recommend mindfulness meditation, in their book on innovation, as a practice to improve our ability to sense and generate new ideas, drawing on the same fundamental requirement for presence to generate new solutions.

Presence connects us to our embodied experience and the new ideas that emerge as gut feelings and hunches that we feel physically. The lingering ideas that Stephen Johnson described above are more likely to be felt as a bodily sensation than experienced as a thought in our heads. The idea is not yet formed in our heads, but we feel something – a gut feeling perhaps, or something that is gnawing at us. It can be very easy to dismiss these feelings and sensations and as a result miss something that is emerging.

It is worth reminding ourselves of Antonio Damasio's research quoted in Chapter 4, where research participants were playing a card game with a complex pattern of winning and losing across four decks of cards. Of course, over time participants discovered the pattern, but what Damasio realized was that participant's behaviour changed before they knew why. They could not state why they had changed, but they had. Damasio was also able to identify a signal from the participants' bodies that guided their learning. Participants' skin conductance (the electrical conductivity of the skin, which increases with the amount of sweat on the skin) began to spike when they contemplated the more risky decks. Their body was responding to that risk with a somatic response – more sweating – and this response guided them to the safer decks.[11] Often our ideas and awareness of emergent complex patterns begins at the level of the body.

So it seems that the generation of new possibilities is an embodied experience, educated through developing mastery, in which we physically tune in to complex and emergent patterns of which our conscious mind has yet to become aware. We can get better at tuning into this more quickly and accessing this embodied wisdom, with practice.

Innovation

> Innovation cannot be managed. You have to satisfy necessary conditions for innovation to occur. To start with you have to listen to people.
>
> Eric Schmidt, Executive Chairman, Google

Innovation, then, becomes the implementation of these new ideas into practice. The implementation of new ideas throughout a wider organization is very challenging. It is essentially a process of organizational change. John Kotter, a writer and expert on organizational change, has found that 70 per cent of organizational changes fail to produce the results that are expected.[12] We therefore don't seem to be very good at organizational change. However, the fact that the changes we implement at times aren't 'simplicity at the far side of complexity' suggests that some of the failure may be due to our ideas having unintended consequences, because we didn't understand the emergent properties of the system we were intending to change.

If we intend to change an organization, we do need to understand what it is first of all. And this is not as simple a task as it may first appear. An organization is not a noun – it is not a thing – it is a process of organizing – a verb. This is a subtle and important point; we have taken a verb and created a noun, but there is no such thing as an organization really – it is a collection of (ever-changing) people, organized through a series of processes that can also change to achieve some end goal, which once again can change. When we speak of an organization as a 'thing', we start to treat an organization in a static way and give it permanence and set of characteristics, and often hold it to account for the collective behaviour of people within it. For example, I often hear people complain about their organizations and how it 'treats them' as if the organization was an entity that interacted with them.

In understanding organizations, as they are not real 'things' in any definable permanent form (like a tree for example), we have a tendency to see them through metaphors.[13] The most obvious metaphor for organizations is the machine metaphor, which I hear in language regularly. Talking of cogs in a wheel, seeing the people in an organization as a series of interlocking parts each with their own clearly defined role, and trying to make them work together efficiently. This fits well with the Cartesian dualist view of the world outlined in Chapter 3, where efficiency and rationality are elevated in importance and each individual becomes a cog in the wheel. It's also slightly dehumanizing and depressing, from my perspective.

I feel a more helpful way of seeing organizations is as a series of collective practices. So far in this book I have spoken about practices at the individual level, and how what we practise shapes and develops us. Equally, organizations have a set of practices that arguably shape and develop each organization. Some of these are detailed and documented as procedures and processes, while others relate to how people get things done despite the procedures and processes; some are formal, such as frequencies of and norms for meetings; others are informal, such as the gossip network in staff kitchens or restaurants. Whatever the organization, these practices exist, and they provide the character or personality of that organization, and are a significant part of the organizational culture.

Some organizations are very political and gossipy, while others are ruthless about results. Some are soft and caring, while others are bureaucratic nightmares. If you try to think about your organization as a type of person (or a breed of dog, if that works for you) what would the character attributes of your organization be? What are the practices that the organization embodies that produce that character?

Trying to change an organization so that new ideas are adopted and innovation occurs is, therefore, a process of designing and implementing new practices. For example, one organization I worked with was attempting to move from a command-and-control style of management to one that was empowered and more entrepreneurial. This was to support a strategic shift in the business, from one in which they provided basic operational services for their customers to one in which they brought significant expertise and provided solutions for their clients' problems. They recognized that bringing expertise and solving problems required a different orientation from people throughout the business – one where they took initiative and were more entrepreneurial – and they recognized that their command-and-control management style would not support this shift.

In one meeting I attended an executive director came to talk to the global senior managers' group, and spent half an hour basically shouting at them and lecturing them on how they needed to be more empowering with their people, and how they needed to stop telling them what to do all the time. The irony was amusing, but it showed how this very intelligent executive clearly understood what was required for the business to move forward, but had not yet changed his practices. Organizational change only came when they were able to change their practices, not their ideas, for example when they learnt that telling others to empower people was counterproductive and started to have more two-way conversations about how they could do so.

In this way of looking at organizations, a leader's role is not to control and make decisions, but to initiate, generate and embody practices that move the organization forward. In doing so leaders, like the executive director above, need to be very aware of their own practices, and which of those practices serve their aims and which do not, as well as the practices of the entire organization.

This is a subtle addition to the role of leadership from that discussed up to this point. So far I have focused on the leader developing a set of practices that will develop them in their leadership. However, in organizations, leaders need to also develop the entire organization if they are to deliver on their declarations. At the individual level leaders need to ask the question,' who do I need to be to deliver on what I care about?' and then design practices to develop themselves into that person. At the organizational level, it's about the character the organization (or department or team, at lower levels in the hierarchy) needs to have to deliver on that declaration, and what practices are required to develop and support that entity. Leadership is, therefore, at two levels – the individual level and the organizational level – and involves developing practices at both levels.

For example, what is your organization's practice for feedback and holding others to account? I have a colleague who has done significant work with failing organizations and has identified these two conversations as being universally missing in those organizations: conversations of feedback and accountability. They are difficult conversations, and will activate our somatic markers for conflict and rejection, but they are essential to the co-ordination of work within organizations. Developing an organizational practice of clear conversations for assessments and holding others to account changes the way people work together.

Another example would be your organization's practice for dealing with mistakes and blame. I remember coaching someone in an organization who stated, 'There's a blame culture in this organization, and it's all their fault,' referring to the senior leadership. She stubbornly refused to see the irony in her statement for as long as she could, but in many ways it was a beautiful illustration of how she was embodying the organization's practices for blame. What are your organization's practices for this, and do they serve the organization in moving forward?

Part of the role of leadership therefore becomes one of shaking up old practices and instituting new ones. At times this will need to be done publicly and significantly for people to see that new practices are being used. Old practices need to be challenged and openly discussed – if everyone has spent years practising one way of behaving, moving to new practices will be a challenge for all, including those in senior management, who need to be open to such challenge also.

This in itself, however, is not enough to produce an organization where creativity and innovation thrive, where people genuinely think differently. That requires an organization where there are people taking leadership throughout. Where there are people making declarations across the organization and taking actions to deliver on those declarations. This provides new directions within the organization and a diversity of thinking; ultimately this allows organizations to be able to respond to complex emergent events. This means that organizational leadership must inspire leadership throughout the organization. This is reminiscent of the idea of leaderful organizations discussed in Chapter 1.[14]

Often the idea of all this unleashed diversity of ideas and directions can produce nervousness for the senior management – how does the organization stay aligned and have any sense of unity as one organization. How does it ensure consistency across the organization? The unity and alignment in this way of thinking come not from the ideas and concepts, but rather from the consistency of practices across the organization, as discussed above.

It does, however, raise a significant challenge. This requires people throughout an organization to develop mastery, to take on new practices and be leaders – is that realistic?

We are motivated to be leaders

There's an interesting phenomenon in our current world where people who are doing technically demanding and well-paid jobs work in their spare time for free to create things that are given away. Open-source software is just such an example. Linux and Apache software under-lie many corporate and web servers around the world, and are produced by people working in just such a way. Wikipedia has useful, often very knowledgeable and scholarly, articles on an extremely wide range of topics produced in just such a way. From traditional rational economic theory this is madness: why would anyone use their hard-earned capital, their knowledge and experience, and not get it paid for it? But it happens.

Daniel Pink, who has done significant research into motivation, identifies three aspects that lie at the root of what really motivates us: autonomy, mastery and purpose. Understanding these helps to explain the phenomenon of people working for nothing.[15]

Autonomy is about allowing people to follow their own ideas. It's not about saying 'we want new ideas, so let's put a reward system in place to generate them' (actually his research shows this doesn't work), it's about assuming people have ideas and want to work on them, and about the importance of getting out of their way. This is what I describe above – unleashing the leadership of each individual and allowing innovation and creativity to live throughout an organization.

Mastery is about allowing people to have the satisfaction of getting better at things. This is why people play musical instruments and practise in their free time, for no reward. People are intrinsically motivated by practising and improvement, and so an organization that is consciously creating practices and working to improve is likely to be a more motivating place to work.

Purpose is about having a sense of connection to something beyond just making money and growth for growth's sake. Daniel Pink points out that when organizations detach the profit motives from purpose, bad things happen. This relates both to bad things ethically, but also to poor and uninteresting products and services that inspire no one. Steve Jobs spoke about creating insanely great products, and of making a dent in the universe.[16] This vision inspired not only his staff, but a community of product users around the world. Leaders need to be speaking declarations that provide this sense of purpose for their organizations, and that allow others to join with them.

The simple truth that Pink's work reveals is that if we trust people, trust that they can be leaders, that they can be creative, and we can give them some autonomy, we get better results. The old ideas of carrots and stick, driven by monetary rewards, he shows to be useless in driving motivation and performance. For simplistic tasks his research shows that carrots and sticks can work, but for tasks that involve any sort of cognitive work (and dealing with the complex emergent problems we face in organizations today does require this) then more financial reward actually reduces performance.

To truly engage people in organizations in dealing with the kinds of complex problems we face in the 21st century, and in fact to lead them, we must get them to take leadership and give them the autonomy to do so. Inspiring leadership in others must therefore be the work of any organization's leadership.

Innovation = leadership

Peter Denning and Robert Dunham in their book on innovation state:

> In many ways leadership and innovation overlap and are expressions of the same thing – changing the future for a community.[17]

I agree – as we have explored here, delivering innovation is about leading change in organizations or communities. However, if we understand the complex nature of the challenges that we face in today's world, we can see that this means leadership must be shared, rather than something that sits with a few select individuals. We require leaders throughout our organizations, each developing and bringing to life their own declarations, and each developing mastery in the craft of their particular work. And if those in the senior leadership positions of these organizations are masterful in their leadership, they will see the development of leadership throughout the organization as their responsibility.

This brings us back to an old and wise quotation on masterful leadership, from Lao-tzu, the founder of Daoism:

> When the Master governs, the people
> Are hardly aware that he exists.
> Next best is the leader who is loved.
> Next, one who is feared.
> The worst is one who is despised.
> If you don't trust the people,
> You make them untrustworthy.
> The Master doesn't talk, he [she] acts.
> When his [her] work is done,
> The people say, 'Amazing:
> We did it, all by ourselves![18]

> Lao-tzu, Chapter 17

Recommended reading

The Innovator's Way: Essential practices for successful innovation, by Peter Denning and Robert Dunham.

Presence: Human purpose and the field of the future, by Peter Senge, Otto Scharmer, Joseph Jaworski and Betty Sue Flowers.

Drive: The surprising truth about what motivates us, by Daniel Pink.

Images of Organisation, by Gareth Morgan.

Where Good Ideas Come From: The seven patterns of innovation, by Steven Johnson.

Notes

1 A good discussion of this effect is available in 'Predicting the unpredictable' by Eric Bonabeau, an article in *Harvard Business Review*, March 2002.

2 A discussion of the difference between simple, complicated, complex and chaotic contexts is given in 'A leader's framework for decision making', an article in *Harvard Business Review*, November 2007.

3 This research report is entitled 'Thriving in a Diverse Business World' and is available here: http://www.roffeypark.com/download-data-collection/?download=Thriving in a diverse business world.

4 Denning, PJ and Dunham, R (2010) *The Innovator's Way: Essential practices for successful innovation*, MIT Press, Cambridge, MA.

5 See: *Where Good Ideas Come From: The seven patterns of innovation*, by Steven Johnson (2011), or his TED Talk, available online: http://www.ted.com/talks/steven_johnson_where_good_ideas_come_from.html.

6 *Talent is Overrated: What really separates world-class performers from everybody else*, by Geoff Colvin (2008). See Chapter 9: 'Performing great at innovation'.

7 Gardener, H (1994) *Creating Minds: An anatomy of creativity seen through the lives of Freud, Einstein, Picasso, Stravinsky, Eliot, Graham and Gandhi*, Basic Books, New York.

8 *Talent is Overrated: What really separates world-class performers from everybody else*, by Geoff Colvin, 2008. See Chapter 9: 'Performing great at innovation', p 165.

9 Denning, PJ and Dunham, R (2010) *The Innovator's Way: Essential practices for successful innovation*, MIT Press, Cambridge, MA, p 367.

10 Senge, P, Scharmer, CO, Jaworski, J and Flowers, BS (2004) *Presence: Human purpose and the field of the future*, Society for Organizational Learning Cambridge, Massachusetts, p 11.

11 Damasio, A (2006) *Descartes' Error*, revised edn, Vintage, London.

12 Kotter, John (1995) 'Leading change: why transformation efforts fail', *Harvard Business Review*, March–April. See also his book entitled *Leading Change*.

13 An excellent exploration of the metaphors we use to understand organizations is available in Morgan G (1997) *Images of Organization,* Sage, London.

14 See: *The Leaderful Fieldbook: Strategies and activities for developing leadership in everyone* by Joseph Raelin for a wider discussion of leaderful organizations.

15 Pink, DH (2009) *Drive: The surprising truth about what motivates us*, Penguin, New York. See also his RSA Animate talk, available at: http://www.thersa.org/events/video/animate/rsa-animate-drive.

16 *Steve Jobs: The exclusive biography* by Walter Isaacson is definitely worth a read to understand Jobs' purpose in creating his products.

17 Denning, PJ and Dunham, R (2010) *The Innovator's Way: Essential practices for successful innovation*, MIT Press, Cambridge, MA, p 252.

18 This translation I have taken from: Lee, Yeuh-Ting, Han, Ai-Guo, Byron, TK and Fan, Hong-Xia (2008) 'Daoist leadership: theory and application', in *Leadership and Management in China: Philosophies, theories, and practices*, ed Chen, Chao-Chuan and Lee, Yueh-Ting, Cambridge University Press, Cambridge.

11 Conclusions

I was discussing the ideas behind this book recently with some MSc students in organizational development (all mature students who are practitioners of organizational development in organizations). Something that came up during our conversation was a concern that the standard that I set for leadership here is very high. I ask that someone is clear on what they are committed to achieving through their leadership (or at the very least having some sense of this), something that they felt was absent in many of the managers and leaders in their organizations. I also ask these leaders to engage with a deeper journey of self cultivation and to engage in practising in a committed way – am I not just crazy to expect managers in organizations to do this?

On the first point I argued that if I am to follow someone, I want to know what they are committed to achieving. If I am a leader without some sense of commitment to achieving/creating/building/doing or changing something, then what am I leading people towards, and am I actually leading them? Or, as I see regularly in my travels in organizations, am I just in a position of leadership because moving up the hierarchy is a good thing to do, but I don't have a genuine sense of what I want to achieve through being in this position?

This is, I believe, one of the most fundamental challenges of our current world – we have people in positions of leadership who aren't clear for what purpose they are leading. The people whom they are supposed to be leading know this, at some level, and live in a world of cynicism and suspicion about their leader – I have seen this time and again in organizations and it is poisonous and destructive.

Someone in this conversation asked me if I was putting a moral position about leadership by saying that leaders need to know what they are committed to achieving through their leadership, and I have thought about this for some time. I think the answer is no; I think I am just not clear how someone can genuinely be leading without a clear sense of purpose to their leadership. For me this sense of purpose and commitment is constitutive of leadership. Leadership, as I define it here, is about setting direction and providing meaning, and not doing this means that there is no leadership.

The collection of concerns above – about purpose, about practising and self-development that these MSc students shared with me – reflects, I believe, the fact that they and we have low standards and expectations of our leaders.

If we look at Daniel Pink's research cited in Chapter 10, then we see that people are fundamentally motivated by purpose, by developing mastery through practice, and by autonomy, and this is definitely my experience. When I engage with people in this work, they are often hungry and motivated for it, but they often lack good models and examples of such leadership that cause them to aspire to be better leaders. My hope is that the people who read this book, who engage fully with embodied leadership, and perhaps attend programmes based on this work, will provide such a model or image of leadership so as to raise all of our standards for the kind of leadership we expect from others in organizations, and from ourselves.

We live in a world with massive inequality and substantial challenges. As I write this the Euro-zone looks extremely precarious; Japan and China are in a stand-off over islands in the China Sea; the US presidential elections are upcoming and politics there is looking ever more polarized, to the extent that the business of government is becoming impossible; changes in weather patterns have sent food prices rising and, despite the fact that there is more than enough food in the world to feed everyone, a combination of wastage and an economic system human beings have created keeps millions starving; the Middle East still has long-term challenges and conflicts; and there are ongoing worries about religious extremism and terrorism. And I could go on.

Inside this set of global and world challenges we each go about our daily business, keeping things going and dealing with problems at the small-scale level where they are more easily comprehensible and where we feel we can deal with them. Some of us go further and take stands on the issues that are important to us in our communities and our organizations. A few go even further still and commit themselves to action on the big global issues that face us.

A different future involves all of us. Plato in *The Republic* spoke of a 'spiritedness' required of the citizenry – this was something that was their responsibility, in return for the rights of citizenship. Culturally we have lost this sense of spiritedness – a deep commitment to making the future a better place – and we have begun to focus solely on our rights.

It is the same for our organizations – these in many respects represent the modern communities in which we spend most of our time. Is there a spiritedness in your organization for making the future of that organization better?

My argument here is not intended to be so much a moral one, as a pragmatic one:

- We need a spirited commitment to the future of our organizations, communities and our species if we are to address the problems we face.
- This requires leadership that embodies such a commitment.
- This requires us to know what we care about and to develop ourselves so that we can deliver on these commitments.
- Research shows us that this is profoundly motivating for us as human beings, and produces a long-term sense of satisfaction and happiness (as opposed to short-term hedonism).

My hope is that this book will both inspire you and show you how to progress along this path.

Taking up this challenge

Throughout this book I have suggested a series of practices that will serve you in developing your leadership. All of these practices need to be done with conscious intent – what I mean by this, is that if you do them mindlessly and do not pay attention you will gain nothing. These need to be done with an attention and focus that means you fulfil the criteria for deliberate practice outlined in Chapter 2.

Each of the practices is outlined in the list below. Some will give more immediate payoffs than others, but each will give you a substantial return on the time you invest if you persist with it. Like practising a new golf swing, doing it once and then moving on will make very little difference, but doing it a hundred times will. If you would like to truly take this seriously, and therefore develop your mastery in your leadership, it will require that you start setting time aside on a daily basis to practise. I know that you didn't start this book with loads of time free in your day and looking for things to practise, and many of the practices do not require you to add more time to your day – rather they involve doing what you already do, in a more conscious way. However, it will take some time from you and that may require you to start by getting clear on what you need to stop doing.

Whenever I coach someone who has just been promoted, I often ask them to create a 'stop-doing' list. This is a list of all the things that they need to stop doing now that they have been promoted. It's easy for us to keep doing the things we were good at and enjoyed in our previous role and just carry them into this one. It's easy for us to accumulate things even in a current role, without a promotion, that we should really delegate.

Create your own stop-doing list and use the time created to give you space for these practices. If you do nothing else from this book but create and implement a stop-doing list, you will be a more effective manager in your work. However, bringing in these practices has the potential to move you towards being a masterful leader.

Practice 1: Deliberate reading

Set yourself a practice of reading for 20 minutes every day, and remember, this is a mindful approach to practices. Bring your full attention and concentration to this – it's not the same as reading a novel in bed for pleasure. Do this when you're alert and can concentrate. Keep a notebook and make notes on what you are learning; seek opportunities to apply and use the knowledge you have gathered that day. If you read it, make a note of it, and then use it that same day, it is more likely to stay with you for the long term.

I have included a range of books at the end of each chapter that you can use for inspiration. Also there are journals, magazines and things that are specifically related to your industry or organization. Take the time and do this properly and you will notice a difference in your knowledge and understanding of leadership, your organization and your industry, and so will those around you!

In all the books highlighted here I have mentioned three that I would like to mention again here specifically: *The Leadership Dojo, The Anatomy of Change* and *Holding the Center: Sanctuary in a time of confusion*, all by Richard Strozzi-Heckler, who is my teacher in this work. These will build on your knowledge and thinking in working with embodied leadership and will help you progress in your leadership development.

Practice 2: Moods

Notice your mood (eg regret, guilt, shame, pity, compassion, sadness, nostalgia, gratitude, apology, anger, anxiety, dread, courage, resignation, resentment, boldness, frustration) at the start and end of each day, and take a note of it – you can use a notebook, your phone or whatever device you choose. Just begin by noticing what it is and where you experience it in your body. As you do this, notice how your moods shape your orientation to the world and your actions and thinking. Just this simple act of noticing will increase your self-awareness, and should enable you to have more choice in your actions and words in various situations.

Moods are infectious in organizations so noticing, taking responsibility for and managing your moods is a key task of leadership.

Practice 3: Reading others' emotions

'Information is power', so the saying goes, and whilst there are flaws with this idea, it is certainly true that more information and knowledge will be useful to you. Developing the ability to read other people and their emotions is a very useful piece of knowledge, provided you use it with good intent. If you find yourself excited by the idea of being able to read other people and manipulate them to your ends, then you shouldn't use this tool. If, however, you feel that being able to read the emotions of others could help you build stronger and deeper relationships as a leader, then this will be extremely valuable.

Paul Ekman's Micro-Expression Training Tool is available on his website (**https://face.paulekman.com/**). I recommend completing this on a quarterly basis as one of your practices. Once you have signed up you can go back in and re-take the training as many times as you like, although they do recommend not taking the post-test more than once per quarter. Doing this as a practice will enhance your ability to effectively read others and build stronger relationships with them.

Practice 4: Centring

Set yourself a reminder to do this on a regular basis. Perhaps if you have a watch that beeps every hour you can use that, or use the phone ringing, or the ping of your computer notifying you that an e-mail has arrived; something that gives you the chance to practise this on a regular basis. Go through the process in a structured way, allowing yourself to get familiar with where you hold tension. Develop the capacity to be truly comfortable and relaxed in your own skin.

Practice 5: Your declaration

Spend time working on your declaration. It doesn't have to be perfect and it doesn't have to be permanent, but what do you want to achieve through your leadership. Reflect on what is important to you and get to some level of clarity on your declaration. Then every time you centre yourself, repeat your declaration to yourself – use it to provide a focus and clarity to your leadership. When you know what you are committed to achieve, you will know what is important and what is unimportant and you will be more effective in managing your time, you will know what you need to accept and what you need to decline. Remember that if everything is important, nothing is important.

There is a story often told of three stone cutters. A man walks by three stone cutters and asks each one what they are doing, although they are all doing exactly the same thing, and each is a master of his craft. The first replies that he is cutting some stone, the second that he is building a wall, and the last that he is building a cathedral. He will not live to see the cathedral completed, but his children and grandchildren will use it.

What is your 'cathedral story'? A story that motivates you and lifts your head above the day to day and connects you with a higher sense of purpose. Keep looking through what you care about, and the declarations and commitments you make, for the deeper story that provides purpose and meaning to your leadership and your life.

Practice 6: Massage or body work

For most of us, we have spent a lifetime practising a particular shape to our bodies (our personality and our way of being), and the muscles may be so used to being contracted around this that we have trouble relaxing and letting go for any length of time. Massage and body work can help in this process and can speed up the process of reshaping yourself. Remember to pay attention to the touch of the person who is working on you – bring your attention to the point they are working on and set an intention to relax more in that place. Use this almost as a practice of mindfulness, bringing your attention away from drifting off into thoughts, and back to the reality of the present moment. This way you will develop a greater awareness of where and how your hold tension, but also you will relax more deeply and be able to reshape yourself more quickly.

Practice 7: Conditioned tendency

Get to know your conditioned tendency. Spend time getting familiar with your reactions when you are knocked off-centre and into your stress response, at the levels of physical sensations, emotions, and thoughts and narratives. Understand these are all representations of the same embodied reaction, but that we experience it at these three different levels. Become aware of the situations in which your conditioned tendency is triggered, and begin to use centring as a way to manage your stress levels.

Practice in increasing your awareness of your conditioned tendency will allow you to centre more quickly in response. As you do this you will manage your stress levels very differently, which will allow you to be more present when you are at home and this will improve your work–life balance. In addition, with increased awareness of your conditioned tendency and as you practise reaching out to understand others, you will develop your ability to be more effective in conflict situations. This will mark you out significantly from those around you, as in organizations most people are fairly poor at dealing with conflict.

Practice 8: Assessments

Do you know someone who's very good at giving assessments? They somehow manage to say things in a way that is heard by the other person, and your felt sense is that their intention seems aligned with what they are saying? If you do, you'll also know that this builds trust. If someone gives you honest feedback, in a way in which they are congruent, and they have done the work required to extract that part of the assessment that is more about them than you, then you don't need to worry about what they might think about you any more, because you'll know. You may also notice that because they are able to give good assessments in the human domain people will ask them for their assessments across a range of issues – the trust they build with their assessments extends across to other domains.

The truth is that, like everything else, this is a skill that is cultivated. We need to bring our assessments to consciousness, extract the part of the assessments that is more about us than the other person, be able to see what that person does to produce the assessment and then speak it to them in a way they can hear. There is no other way to get good at this than to practise. Go through the processes listed in this book and keep practising – with time you will get to the place where people will see you as someone who gives good feedback and in whom they have a deeper level of trust.

Practice 9: Mindfulness meditation

Twenty minutes per day will provide significant results for your health and well-being, but importantly for this book, it will dramatically accelerate your process of development as a leader, support your centring practice and develop your capability to manage your conditioned tendency more effectively. It is an extremely powerful practice and worth every moment of your investment. Remember not to get disheartened if your attention is all over the place – just stay with the process of bringing your attention back to your breath.

Practice 10: Develop an ethical code

Ethics is fundamental to your leadership. Spend time working with the ideas presented here and follow up on the books recommended. Develop clarity on your ethical principles and what is important to you, and stay connected to those through centring. Use this as a guide in your life and be conscious of the compromises that are offered to you. Remember that small ethical compromises sit at the root of many industrial accidents and corporate scandals, and be alert to the social pressures to conform and go along with things that aren't quite ethical.

Practice 11: Taking a stand

Find opportunities to practise taking a stand, saying 'no' and insisting. Practise these in small situations where the consequences are not major, so that when you need to, as a leader, these moves are available to you. Remember the example of my colleague who practised with London black-taxi drivers – where are the opportunities for you to create practices so that you can get better at taking a stand so that this move is available to you whenever you might need it? Centre as you do this – remember that the more you centre and relax, the more you will be able to do this in a way in which the other person feels their dignity is respected.

Eleven practices that I encourage you to take on through this work. Don't try and take them all on at once, build your way up to this – some will take more time at the start than they will after a month. Build it up, and as you do so each practice will get easier and require less time.

The reading, Paul Ekman's online micro-expressions training tool, mindfulness meditation and massage practices are the only ones for which you need to set time aside out of your day, so that will require you fitting in 40 minutes to your current day, plus an hour every few weeks, and some time once a quarter. However, the reading time is probably something you should be doing anyway and is a valid way to spend time at work. Remember to do this in a mindful way – not trying to cram it in over lunch. The massage is some precious time just for you, so protect it and try not to let it be overtaken with meetings and last-minute panics.

The other practices involve a combination of some initial work, followed by an ongoing practice that can happen during your day. You're queuing for something – use it as an opportunity to practise centring. You cross the street and someone blares their horn at you and you notice adrenalin and your conditioned tendency response – use it as an opportunity to observe your response and practise centring.

There are places and opportunities for us to practise during our days, every day, in which we don't need to take time out or put more in our diary. All we need to do is to stay mindful of what we are practising in the ongoing process of everyday life. At the start this might be hard – you may find that at the end of the day you remember about your intention to do this, but that the entire day has slipped away without you actually doing it. Don't worry if this is the case – use this as an opportunity to reflect on the day and what happened – what were the times in which you were triggered? What did that look and feel like? When should you have centred? Spending time reviewing these experiences will help you to be able to catch them in future. Use a journal or notebook to capture these thoughts and continue to reflect as you engage in the process of practising.

In Chapter 2, I spoke about how for mastery we need to practise for 10,000 hours. This comes from looking at world-class sportspeople, musicians, drivers and many other experts. This is how to get to being world class in anything, including leadership.

If you practise two hours per day for 10 years, then you collect around 7,000 hours of practice, and given that you will not come to leadership with a blank slate, for many of you this will enable to you achieve 10,000 hours.

Now I acknowledge that this may feel like a lot to take on, but as I detailed above many of these times of practice can be just in the process of everyday life – you don't need to find two empty hours per day! In addition 10,000 hours is how musicians get to be world-class soloists, and sportspeople get to the top of their games. The reality of leadership is that there are few leaders in our world today operating at the equivalent of world-class musicians. When we think of truly world-class leaders we think of Gandhi, Martin Luther King, Nelson Mandela and Aung San Suu Kyi; we rarely think of the CEOs of investment banks or automotive manufacturers. There is a paucity of good leadership in the corporate world, so taking on these practices and working with them will allow you to shine in really quite a short time.

In Shakespeare's *King Henry IV Part 1*, at the end of Act 1, Scene 2, the young Prince Hal closes the scene with a speech to himself. He states:

> And like bright metal on a sullen ground, my reformation, glittering o'er my fault, shall show more goodly and attract more eyes than that which hath no foil to set it off.

The young Prince has been enjoying the shadow side of life, and is planning his reformation, which will be all the more shining because of the dark shadowy background. Truly great leadership in organizations stands out in the same way, and so I hope will you 'show more goodly and attract more eyes, than that which hath no foil to set it off' against the background of mediocre leadership to which we are accustomed in many of our organizations.

Practise, practise, practise...

You are always practising something. As you read this book you are practising; in your everyday life a lot of what you do is well practised. Through this book it is my aim to bring your attention to what you practise, why you practise it and how you can develop a set of practices that will support you in achieving what is important to you.

My Aikido teacher tells me that when he steps out onto the Aikido mat, he begins by practising the first move he ever learnt in Aikido.

This is not common sense in our culture, where the orientation is that when we have learnt something we move on and learn something else. However, in the continued practice of something we 'already know', new possibilities open up and we deepen our understanding.

I continue to work with and practise assessments – it is a part of my working life as a consultant, facilitator and coach to provide assessments to others every day. I could do this mindlessly, but I choose to work on doing this consciously and practising more, and it is through this that my ability develops. This is a potentially never-ending process – just as in driving we can learn to drive, or we can continue to push our levels of mastery to be a Formula 1 driver.

Continue with this process and be curious about, with practice, how good you can become. The world needs more leaders who have high levels of mastery and who are world class. We know how to develop Formula 1 drivers; we are only beginning to understand how to develop world-class leaders. In the past we have had these leaders come along, but we have never studied how to produce them consistently. Now we are starting to uncover how to do this, which makes this a very exciting time.

Push yourself and continue to practise, for your own leadership, for what you care about, to make the world a better place and to provide models for future leaders.

Embodied leadership development programmes

During this book I have referenced an embodied leadership development programme that was attended by Jane and John. Whilst you will be able to develop yourself as a leader through the ideas presented here, spending time with a teacher of this work and in a community of learners will speed up your progress.

The embodied leadership programmes that I have been involved with come from the Strozzi Institute, based in the United States. I mentioned at a number of points in this book my teacher Richard Strozzi-Heckler. He in turn has his teachers, and this locates embodied leadership in a lineage of teachers who have passed on this work. It is that lineage that I have been representing through this book.

There are open embodied leadership programmes (where individuals attend from a range of organizations) that take place in the United States, Europe and in Asia, as well as in-company programmes run for specific organizations. The Level 1 and Level 2 open programmes together make up nine days, and ideally should be done within the space of a year alongside some one-to-one coaching between the two programmes. Doing this means that you will have immersed yourself in practising the embodied principles for nine days, which will significantly move you forward in your path to developing mastery. It will accelerate the process of your development more quickly than if you were to spend just two hours a day. It will also assist you in the process of developing your practices.

Alongside this, or indeed alternatively, you could choose to engage a somatic coach to work with you, to help bring you through the practices and hold you to account for doing them on an ongoing basis.

I recognize that not everyone will be able to take the time or have the resources to attend such programmes, which is why in this book I have aimed to give you a programme that you can work though in a self-managed way.

For more information on embodied leadership programmes and certified Somatic Coaches you can go to my website: **www. uncommonleaders.com**, or to the website of the Strozzi Institute: **www.strozziinstitute.com**.

Certifying as a somatic coach

Some people reading this book may be consultants or coaches who are interested in certifying as somatic coaches. This process begins with the same series of courses as mentioned above, and continues with programmes focused on your ability to coach in this way. The starting point is around developing your own somatic awareness and understanding, and continuing with your ability to bring this to others. There are two levels of coaching certification available, somatic coach and master somatic coach.

More information on the somatic coaching certifications is available on the website of the Strozzi Institute: **www.strozziinstitute.com**.

Further resources for consultants and coaches

If you are a practitioner of leadership development or coaching, and you want to further your knowledge in this field, then in addition to the reading listed at the end of each chapter, the following may be helpful. They are in no particular order, and they take embodiment from very different perspectives, some from coaching, some from psychotherapy, some from trauma, some from leadership, and even one (Presence) from an acting perspective. Together they form a library of approaches, thought, ideas and perspectives on working with the embodied mind.

In Search of the Warrior Spirit, by Richard Strozzi-Heckler.

Being Human at Work, by Richard Strozzi-Heckler.

Cutting Through Spiritual Materialism, by Chogyam Trungpa Rinpoche.

Shambhala: The sacred path of the warrior, by Chogyam Trungpa Rinpoche.

Emotional Anatomy, by Stanley Keleman.

Listening to Bodies, by Suzanne Zeman.

Coaching: Evoking excellence in others, by James Flaherty.

Coaching to the Human Soul, Vols 1, 2 (and 3 is on the way), by Alan Sieler.

Somatic Reality, by Stanley Keleman.

The Future of the Body, by Michael Murphy.

The Spell of the Sensuous, by David Abram.

The Intuitive Body: Discovering the wisdom of conscious embodiment and Aikido, by Wendy Palmer.

Trauma and the Body: A sensorimotor approach to psychotherapy, by Pat Ogden, Kekuni Minton and Clare Pain.

Waking the Tiger: Healing trauma, by Peter Levine.

Presence: How to use positive energy for success in every situation, by Patsy Rodenburg.

The Presence Process: A healing journey into present moment awareness, by Michael Brown.

The Way of Artistry and Grace, by Colin Reeve.

About a Body: Working with the embodied mind in psychotherapy, edited by Jenny Corrigall, Helen Payne and Heward Wilkinson.

Somatics: Reawakening the mind's control of movement, flexibility, and health, by Thomas Hanna.

Retooling on the Run: Real change for leaders with no time, by Stuart Heller and David Sheppard Surrenda.

See also **http://www.being-in-movement.com/catalog** for a series of e-books by Paul Linden, available for download.

To stay in touch with embodied leadership work, and Pete Hamill's writing, see:

www.uncommonleaders.com for the website of Pete Hamill's consultancy;

www.petehamill.co.uk for Pete Hamill's blog;

www.embodiedleadership.net for more information on this book, and further articles on the subject.

You can also follow Pete Hamill on Twitter: @hamill_pete.

INDEX

(*italics* indicate a figure in the text)

Printed in the USA
CPSIA information can be obtained
at www.ICGtesting.com
LVHW021451191123
764346LV00003B/123

9 780749 465643